WATSON AND HOLMES

Created by
Brandon Perlow & Paul Mendoza

Writer
Karl Bollers

Artists
Rick Leonardi - Chapter One thru Four
Larry Stroman - Epilogue

Color Artists
Paul Mendoza & GuruEFX - Chapter One thru Three
Archie Van Buren - Chapter Four and Epilogue
Jay David Ramos - Epilogue (pgs. 106-113)

Letters and Production
Taylor Esposito (with Dave Lanphear) - Chapter One
Nicole McDonnell (with Dave Lanphear) - Chapter Two thru Four
Wilson Ramos Jr. - Chapter Four and Epilogue

Assistant Editor
Zack Rosenberg

Senior Editor
Justin F. Gabrie

Publisher
Brandon Perlow

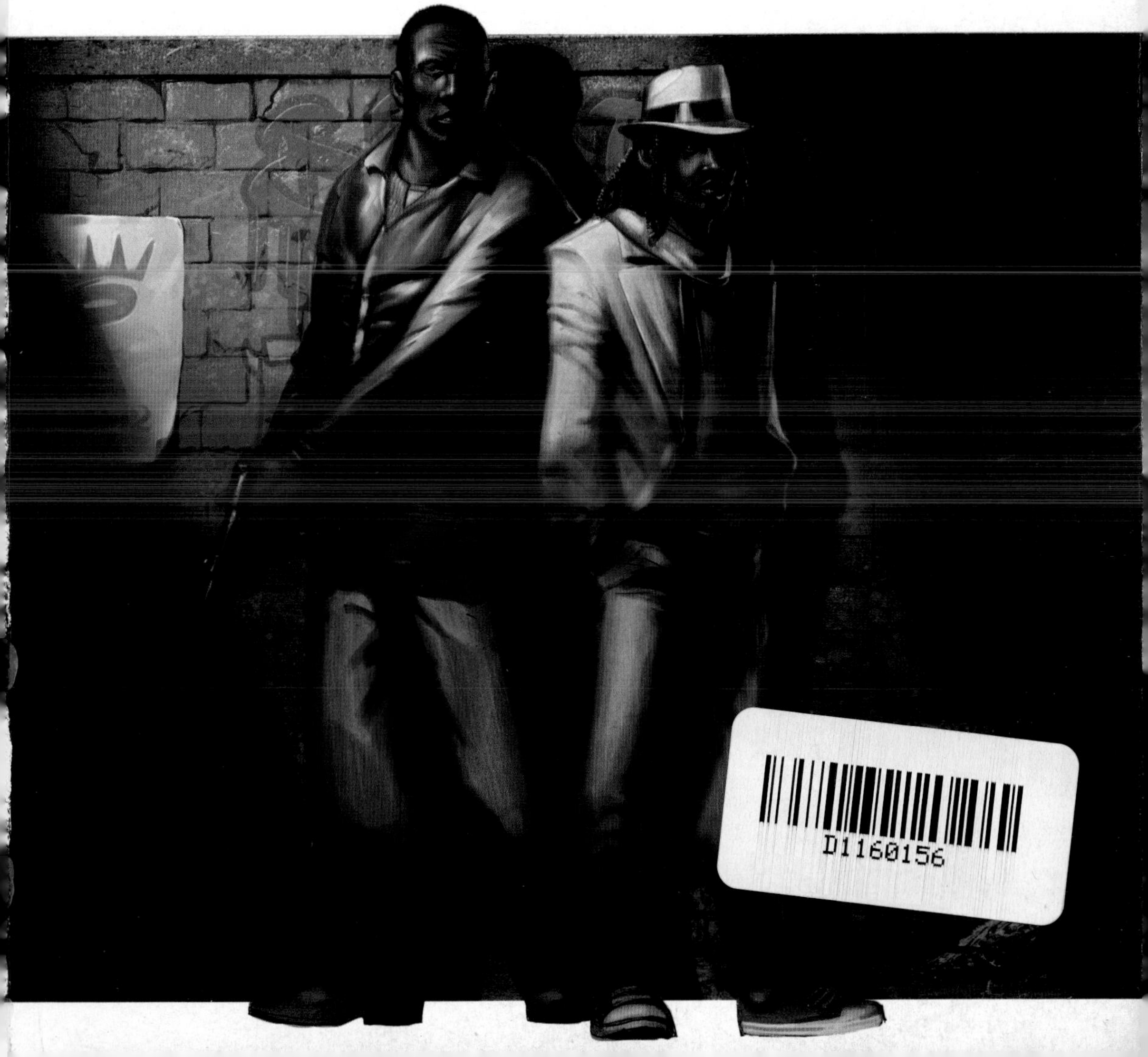

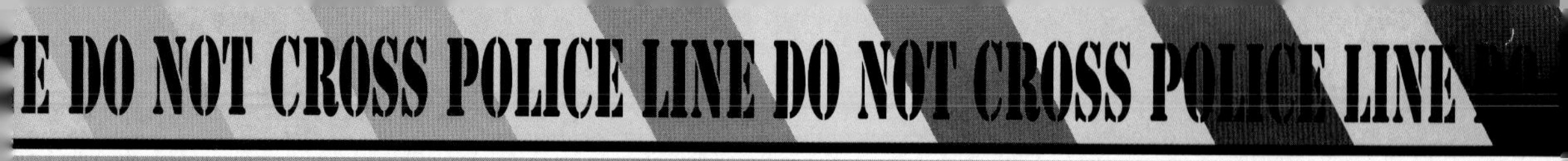
DO NOT CROSS POLICE LINE DO NOT CROSS POLICE LINE

Founder and President
Brandon Perlow

Director of Publishing
Justin F. Gabrie

Marketing and Promotions Manager
Zack Rosenberg

Film & TV Representation
Santosh Oommen

Book Design
Corey Breen
Wilson Ramos Jr.

Logo Design
Paul Mendoza

Trade Production
Wilson Ramos, Jr.

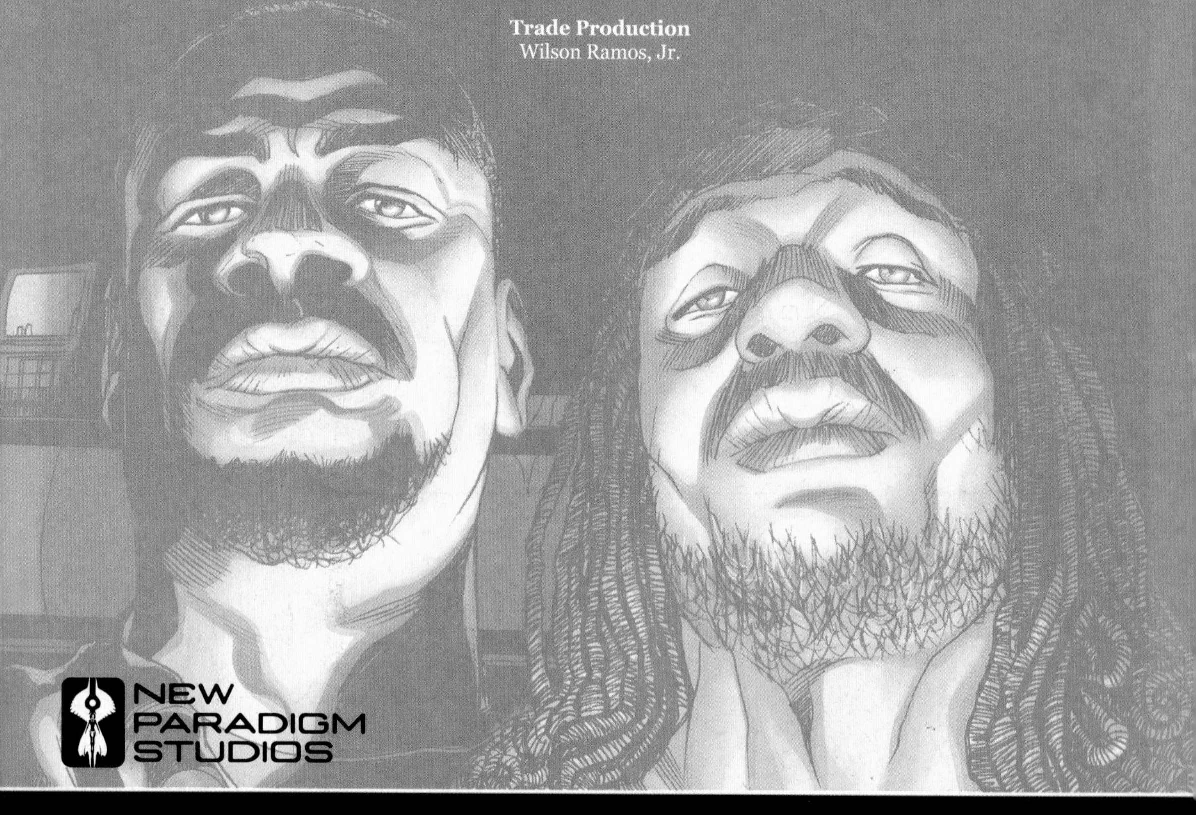

NEW PARADIGM STUDIOS

This volume collects issues #1-5 of the New Paradigm Studios ongoing comic series Watson And Holmes.

Published by
New Paradigm Studios
newparadigmstudios.com

First Edition: December 2013
ISBN: 1-939516-01-3

International Rights / Foreign Licensing - Grand Design Communications: (c) 917-747-5077 (e) granddesignagent@gmail.com

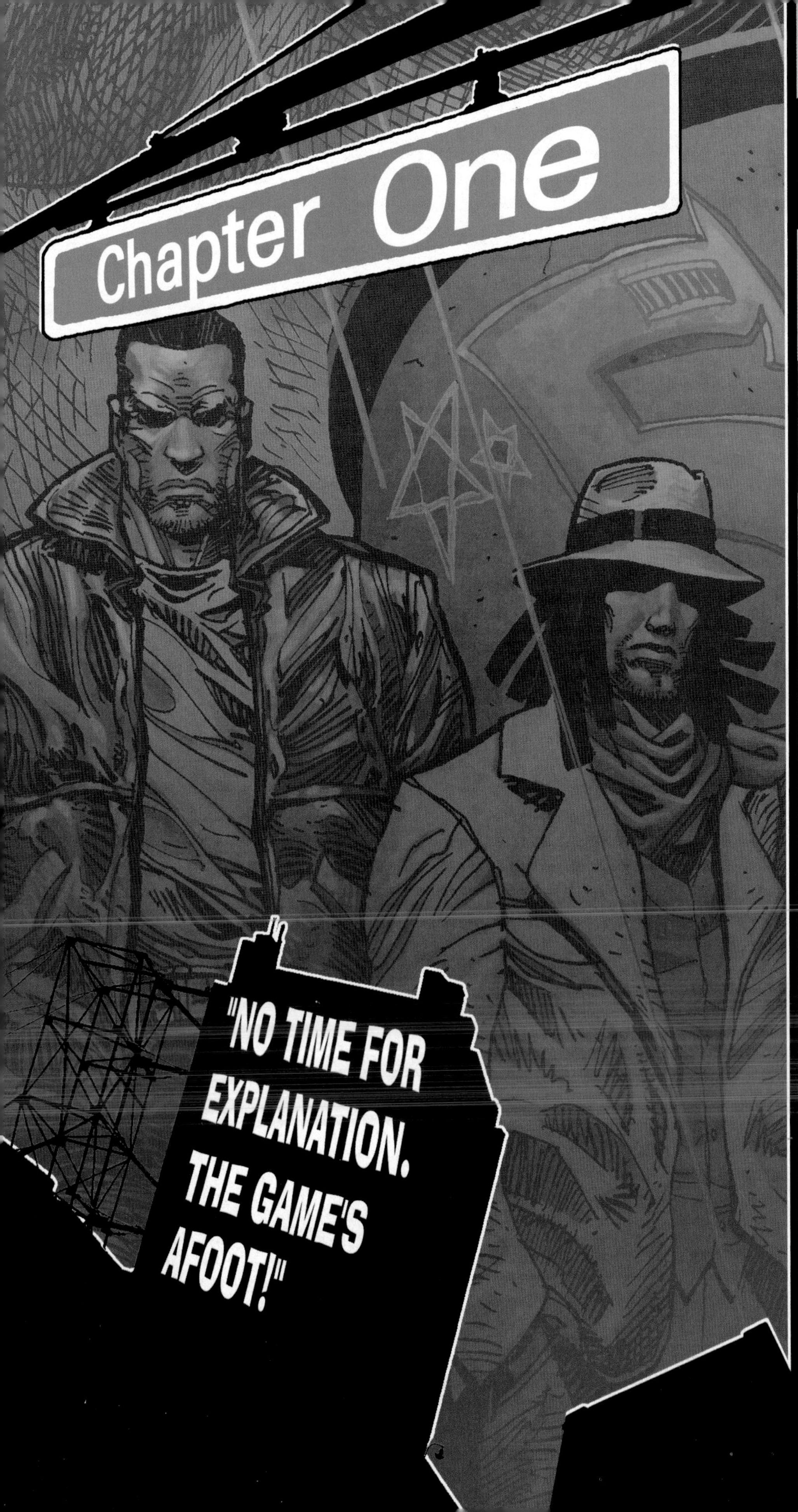
Chapter One
"NO TIME FOR EXPLANATION. THE GAME'S AFOOT!"

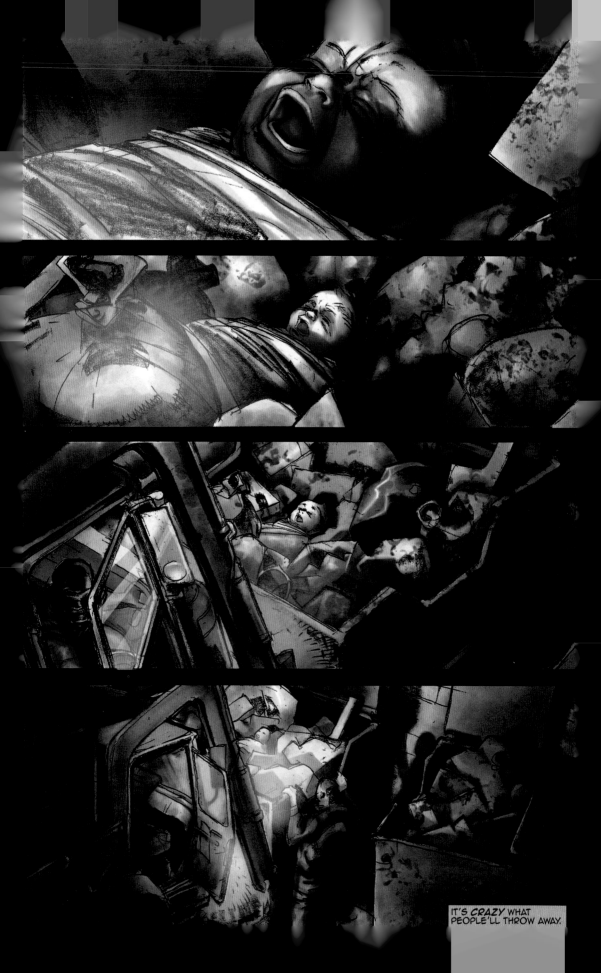

IT'S *CRAZY* WHAT
PEOPLE'LL THROW AWAY.

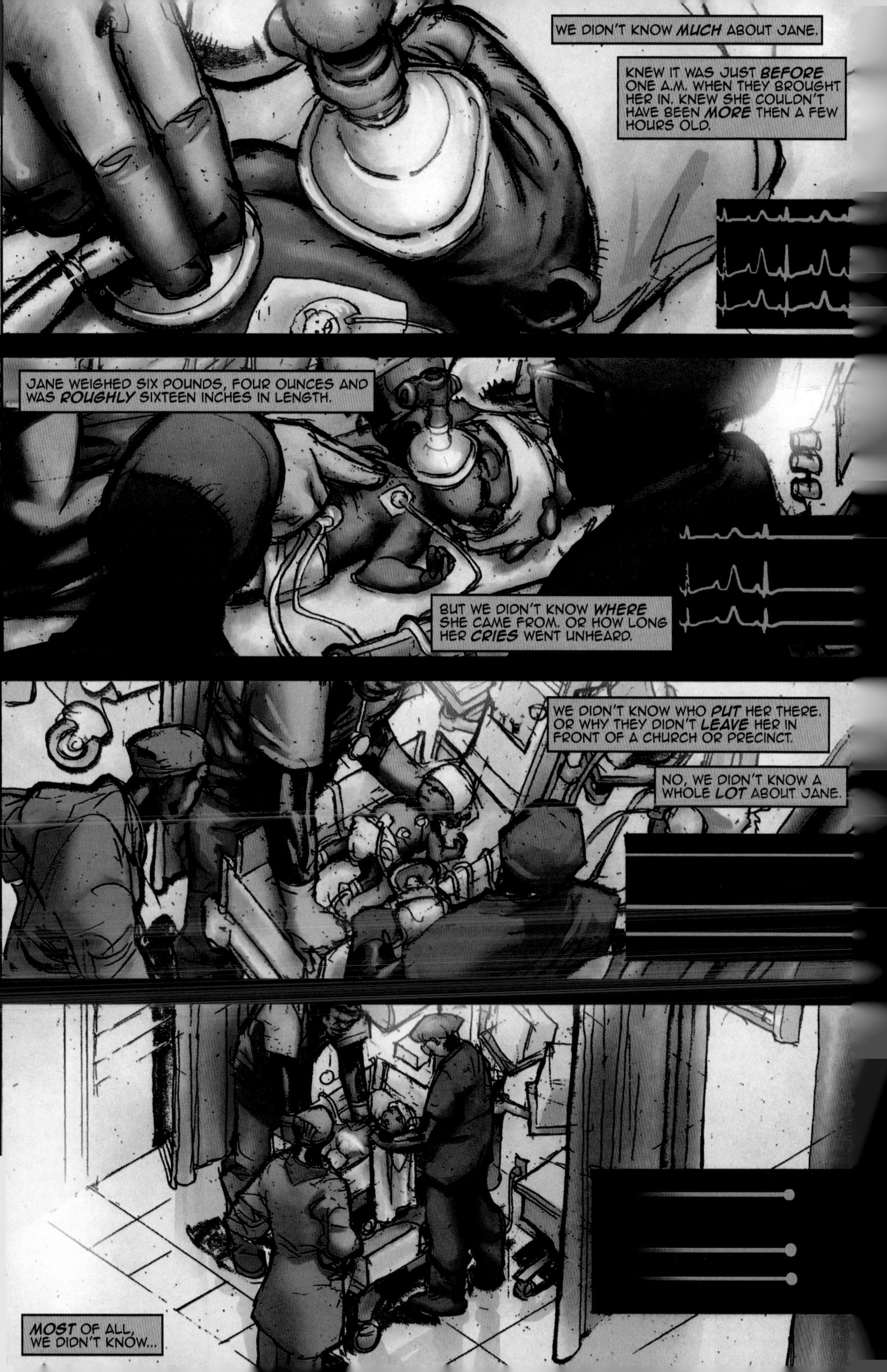
WE DIDN'T KNOW MUCH ABOUT JANE.
KNEW IT WAS JUST BEFORE ONE A.M. WHEN THEY BROUGHT HER IN. KNEW SHE COULDN'T HAVE BEEN MORE THEN A FEW HOURS OLD.
JANE WEIGHED SIX POUNDS, FOUR OUNCES AND WAS ROUGHLY SIXTEEN INCHES IN LENGTH.
BUT WE DIDN'T KNOW WHERE SHE CAME FROM. OR HOW LONG HER CRIES WENT UNHEARD.
WE DIDN'T KNOW WHO PUT HER THERE. OR WHY THEY DIDN'T LEAVE HER IN FRONT OF A CHURCH OR PRECINCT.
NO, WE DIDN'T KNOW A WHOLE LOT ABOUT JANE.
MOST OF ALL, WE DIDN'T KNOW...

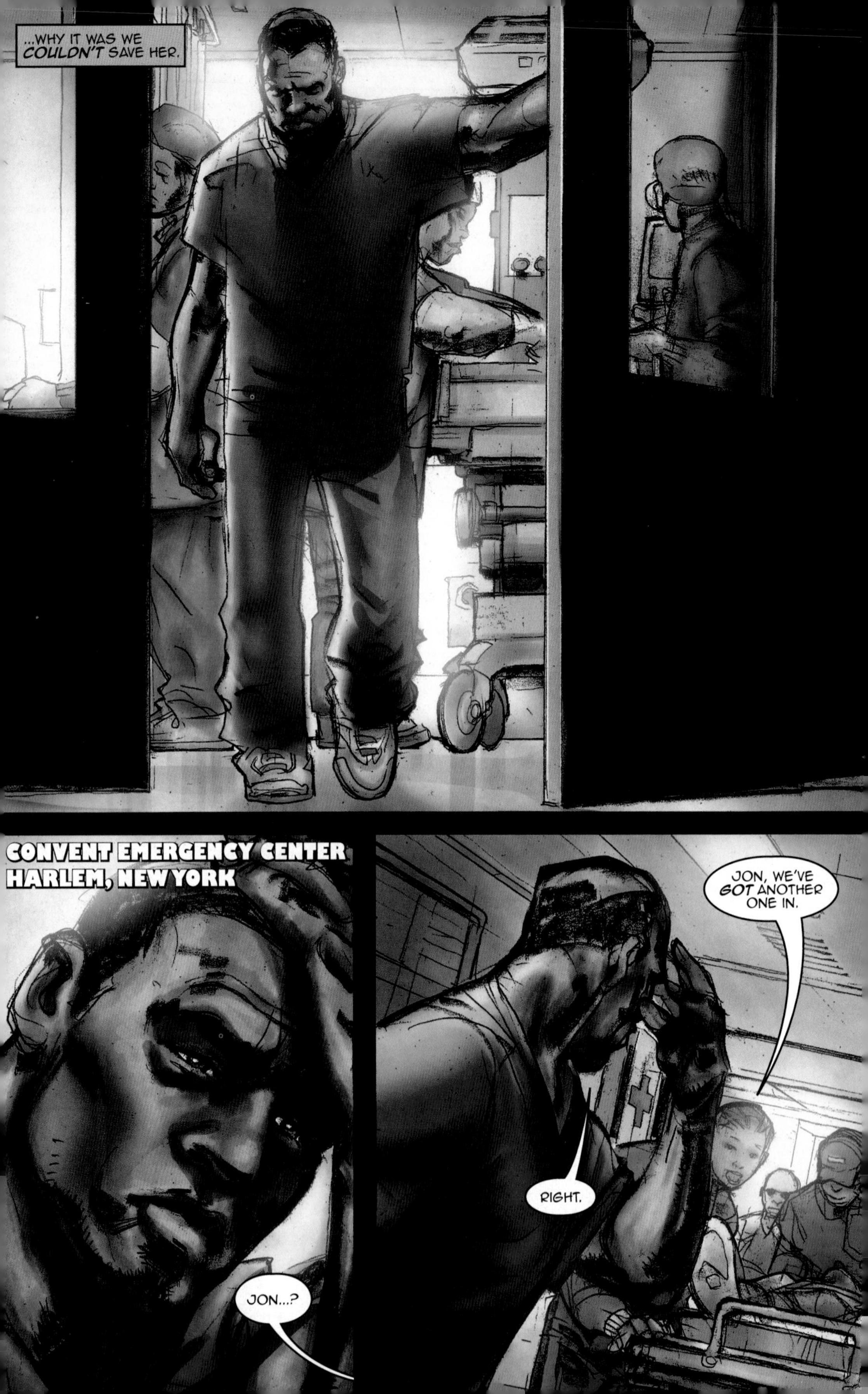
...WHY IT WAS WE COULDN'T SAVE HER.
CONVENT EMERGENCY CENTER
HARLEM, NEW YORK
JON...?
JON, WE'VE GOT ANOTHER ONE IN.
RIGHT.

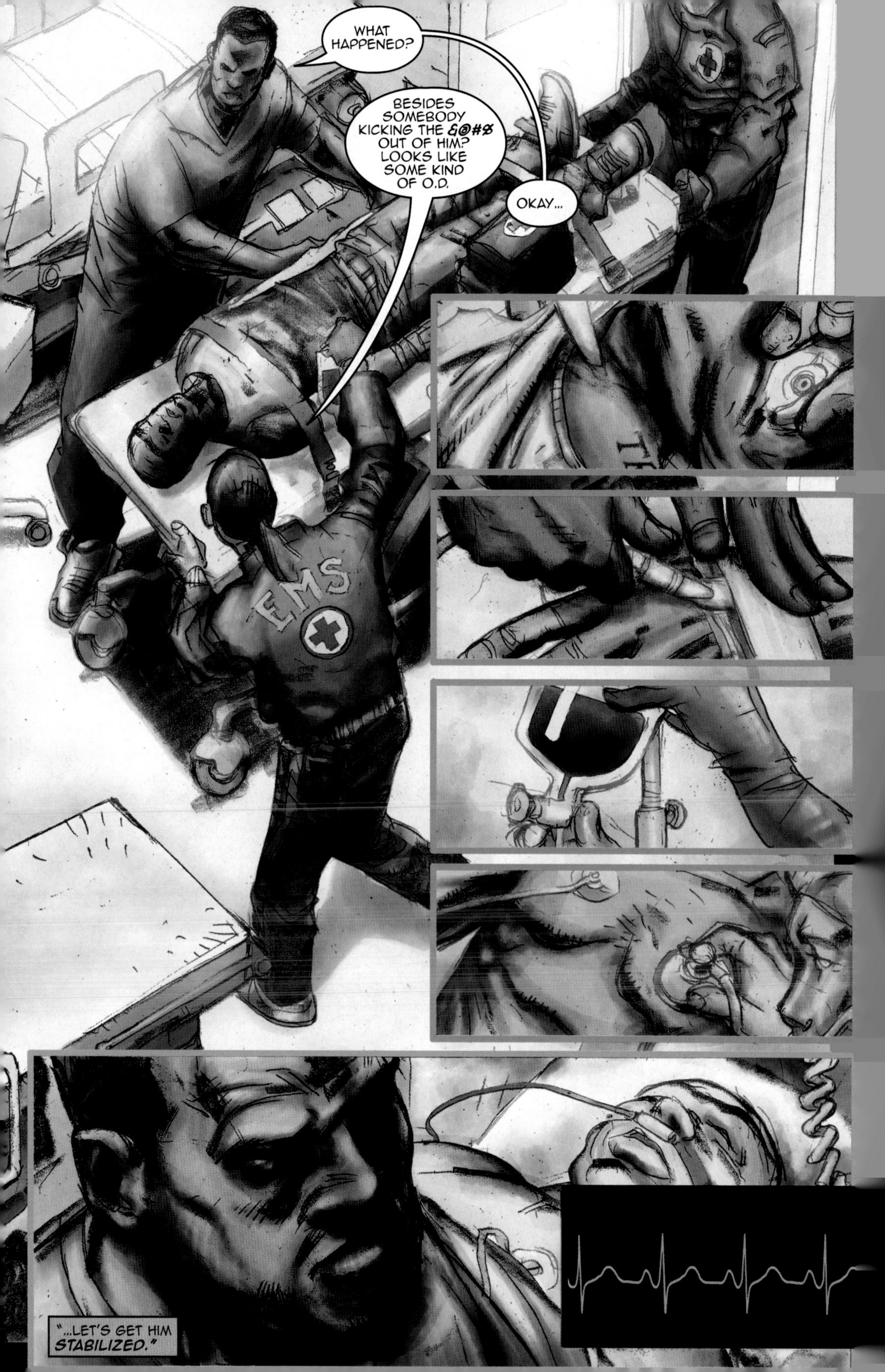
WHAT HAPPENED?
BESIDES SOMEBODY KICKING THE &@#$ OUT OF HIM? LOOKS LIKE SOME KIND OF O.D.
OKAY...
"...LET'S GET HIM *STABILIZED.*"

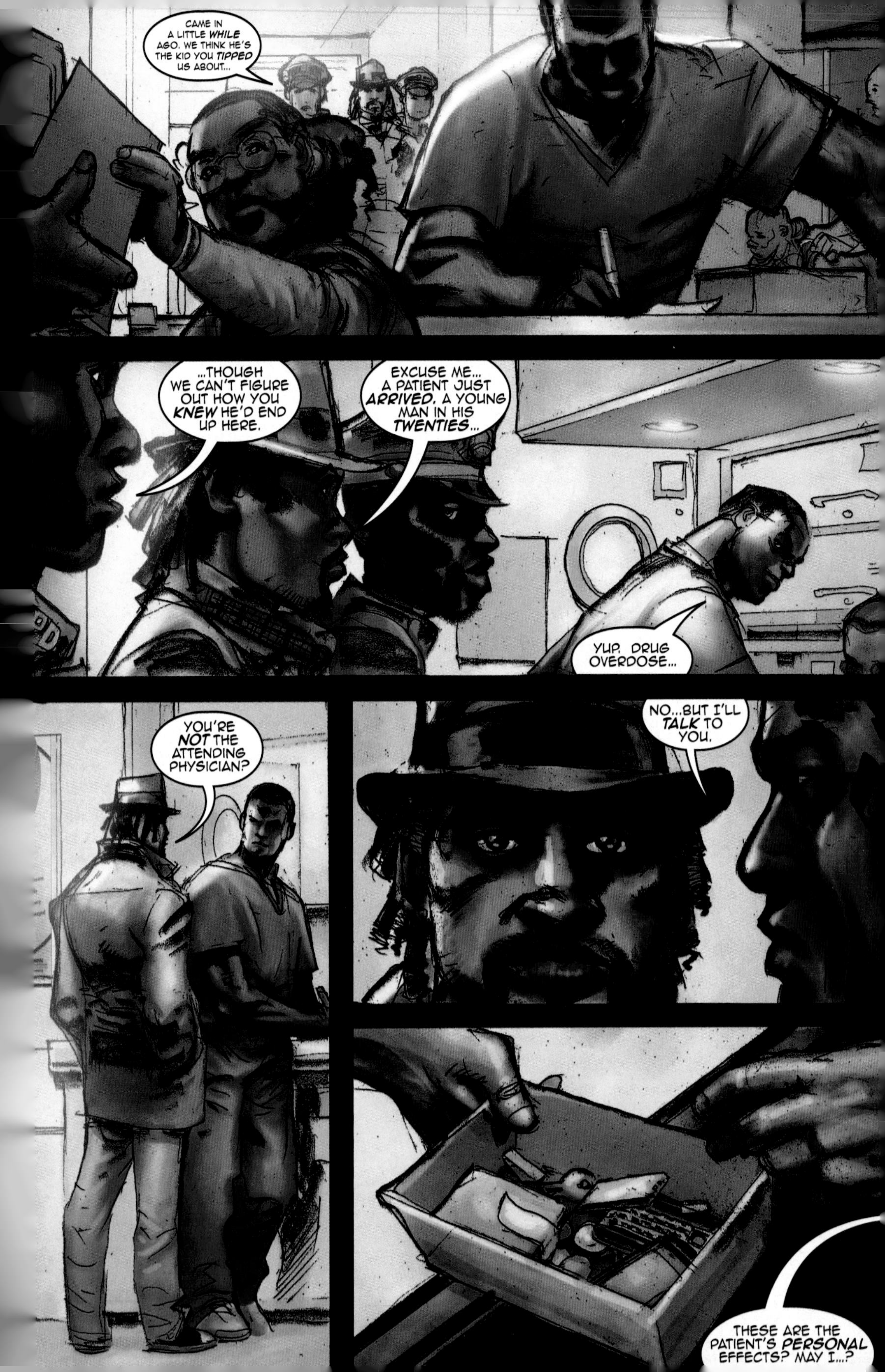
CAME IN A LITTLE WHILE AGO. WE THINK HE'S THE KID YOU TIPPED US ABOUT...
...THOUGH WE CAN'T FIGURE OUT HOW YOU KNEW HE'D END UP HERE.
EXCUSE ME... A PATIENT JUST ARRIVED, A YOUNG MAN IN HIS TWENTIES...
YUP, DRUG OVERDOSE...
YOU'RE NOT THE ATTENDING PHYSICIAN?
NO...BUT I'LL TALK TO YOU.
THESE ARE THE PATIENT'S PERSONAL EFFECTS? MAY I...?

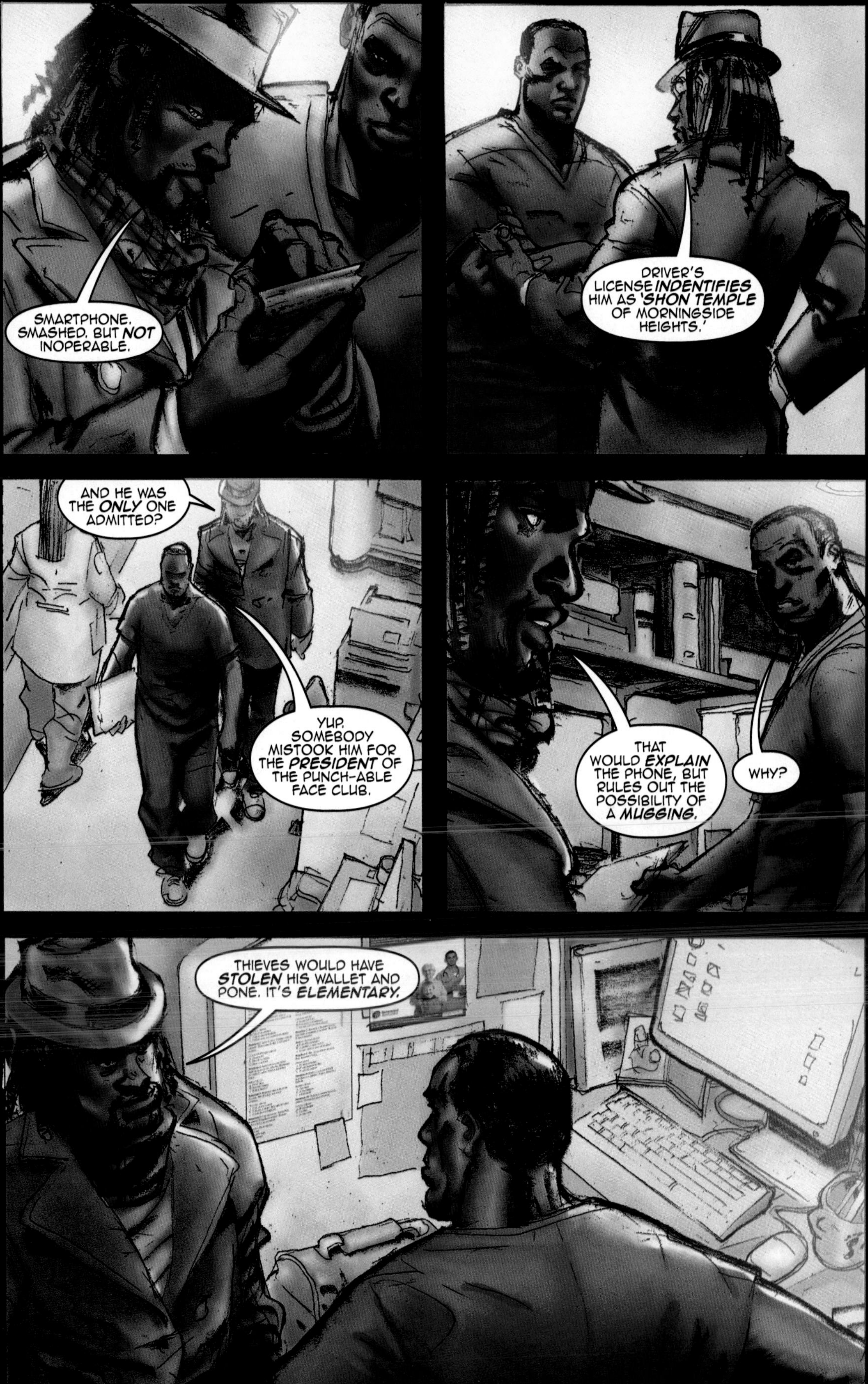
SMARTPHONE. SMASHED. BUT NOT INOPERABLE.
DRIVER'S LICENSE INDENTIFIES HIM AS 'SHON TEMPLE OF MORNINGSIDE HEIGHTS.'
AND HE WAS THE ONLY ONE ADMITTED?
YUP. SOMEBODY MISTOOK HIM FOR THE PRESIDENT OF THE PUNCH-ABLE FACE CLUB.
THAT WOULD EXPLAIN THE PHONE, BUT RULES OUT THE POSSIBILITY OF A MUGGING.
WHY?
THIEVES WOULD HAVE STOLEN HIS WALLET AND PONE. IT'S ELEMENTARY.

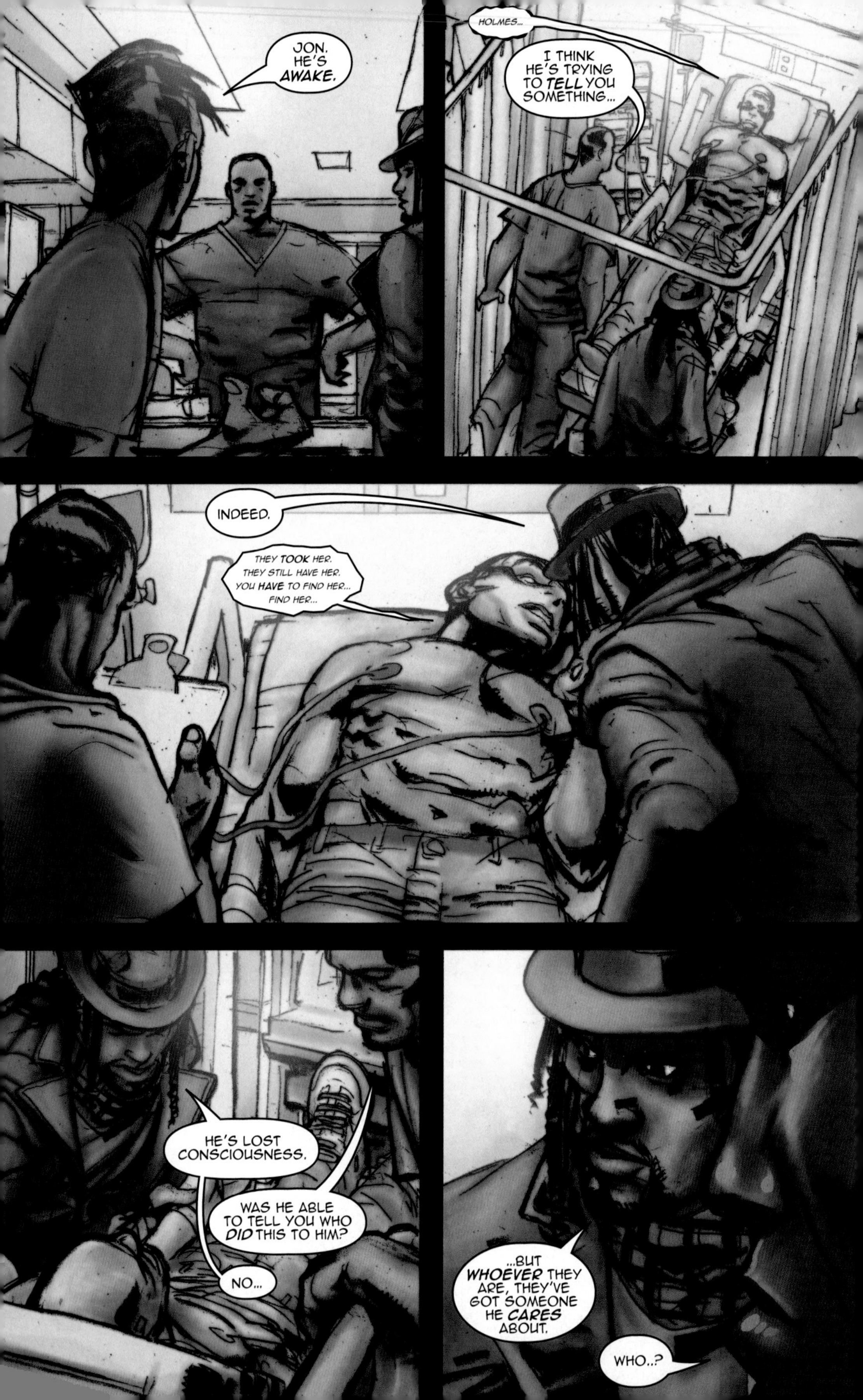
JON. HE'S AWAKE.
HOLMES...
I THINK HE'S TRYING TO TELL YOU SOMETHING...
INDEED.
THEY TOOK HER. THEY STILL HAVE HER. YOU HAVE TO FIND HER... FIND HER...
HE'S LOST CONSCIOUSNESS.
WAS HE ABLE TO TELL YOU WHO DID THIS TO HIM?
NO...
...BUT WHOEVER THEY ARE, THEY'VE GOT SOMEONE HE CARES ABOUT.
WHO..?

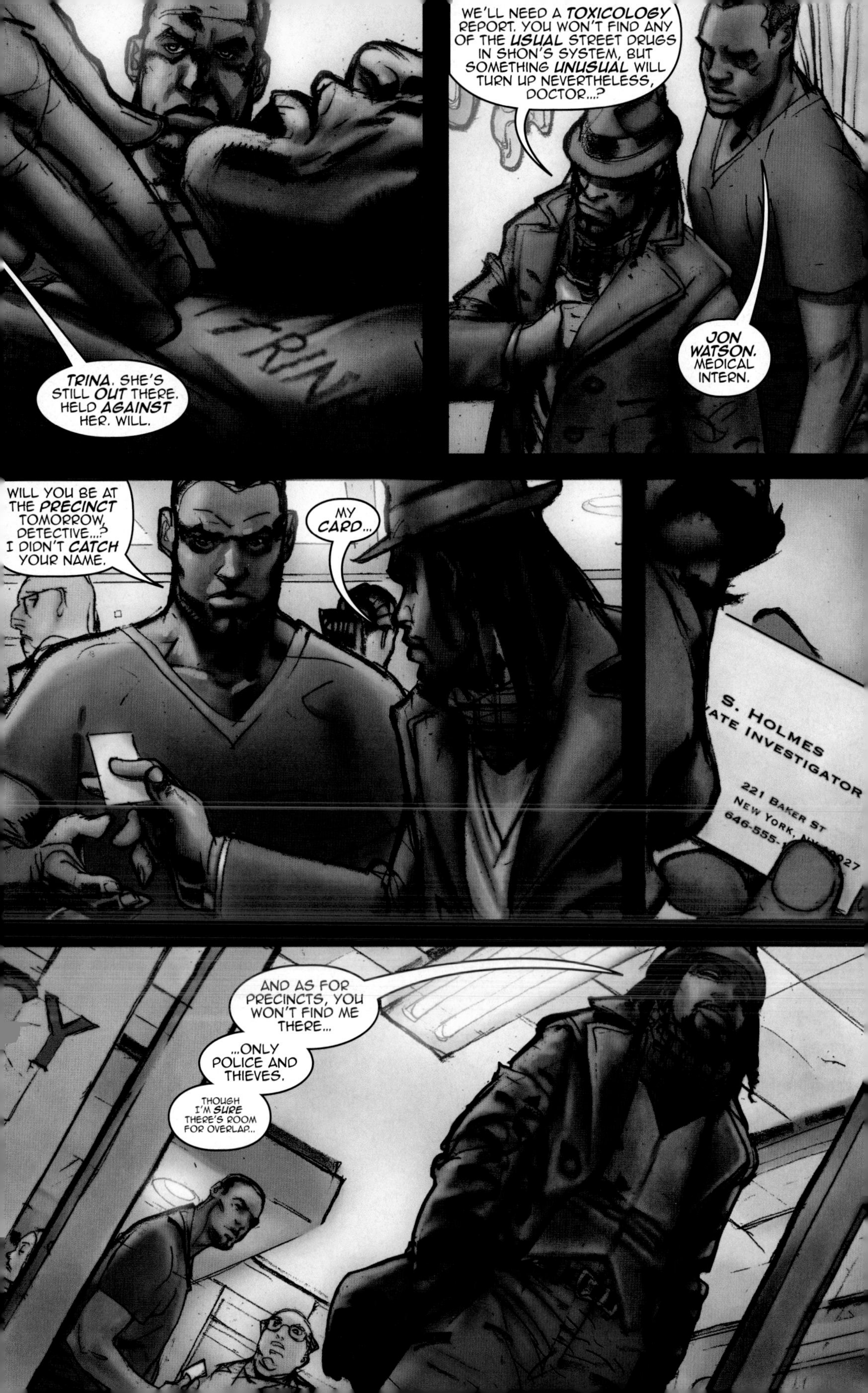

TRINA. SHE'S STILL OUT THERE. HELD AGAINST HER. WILL.
WE'LL NEED A TOXICOLOGY REPORT. YOU WON'T FIND ANY OF THE USUAL STREET DRUGS IN SHON'S SYSTEM, BUT SOMETHING UNUSUAL WILL TURN UP NEVERTHELESS, DOCTOR...?
JON WATSON. MEDICAL INTERN.
WILL YOU BE AT THE PRECINCT TOMORROW, DETECTIVE...? I DIDN'T CATCH YOUR NAME.
MY CARD...
S. HOLMES
VATE INVESTIGATOR
221 BAKER ST
NEW YORK, NY
646-555-
027
AND AS FOR PRECINCTS, YOU WON'T FIND ME THERE...
...ONLY POLICE AND THIEVES.
THOUGH I'M SURE THERE'S ROOM FOR OVERLAP...

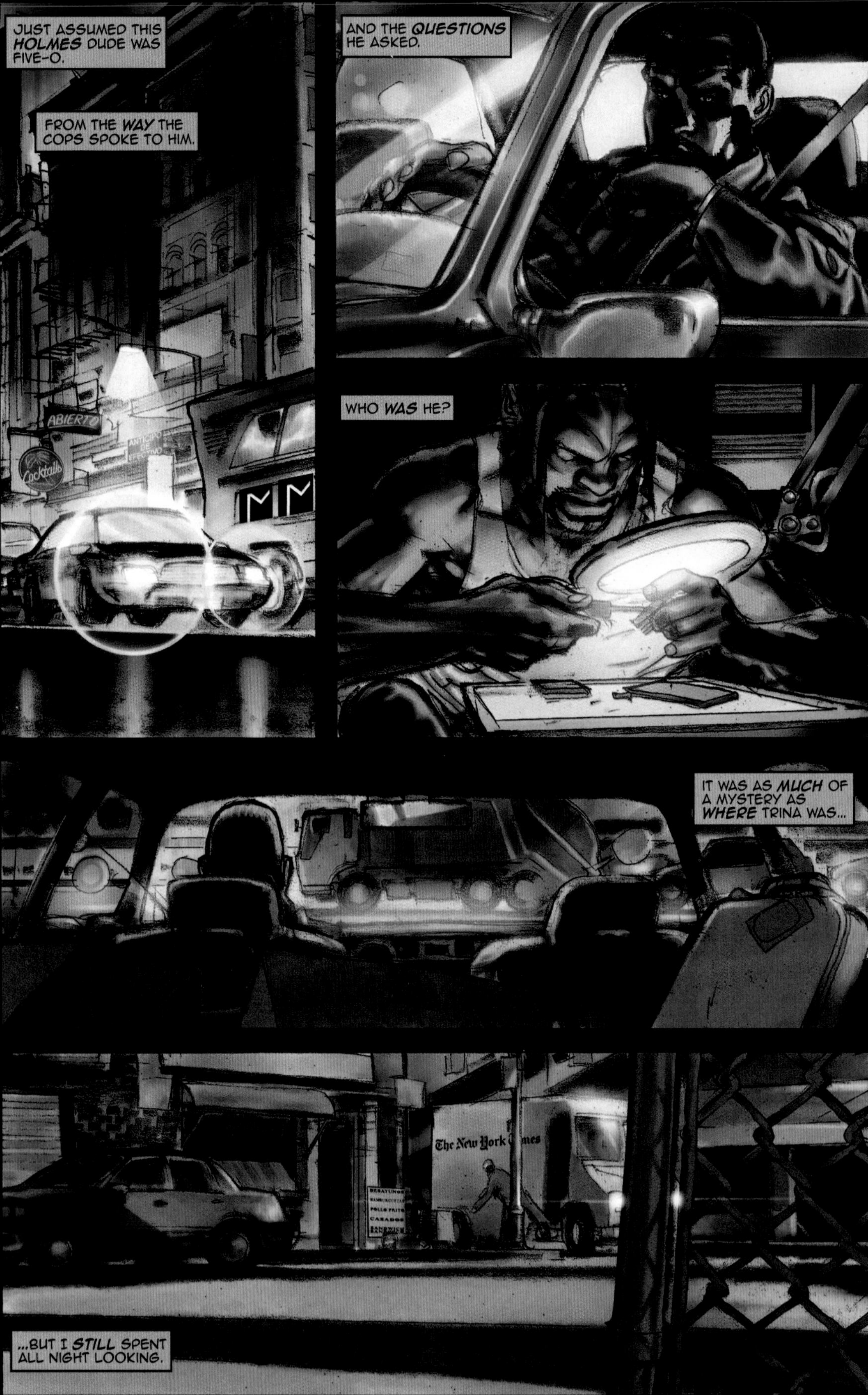
JUST ASSUMED THIS HOLMES DUDE WAS FIVE-O.
FROM THE WAY THE COPS SPOKE TO HIM.
ABIERTO
Cocktails
AND THE QUESTIONS HE ASKED.
WHO WAS HE?
IT WAS AS MUCH OF A MYSTERY AS WHERE TRINA WAS...
...BUT I STILL SPENT ALL NIGHT LOOKING.

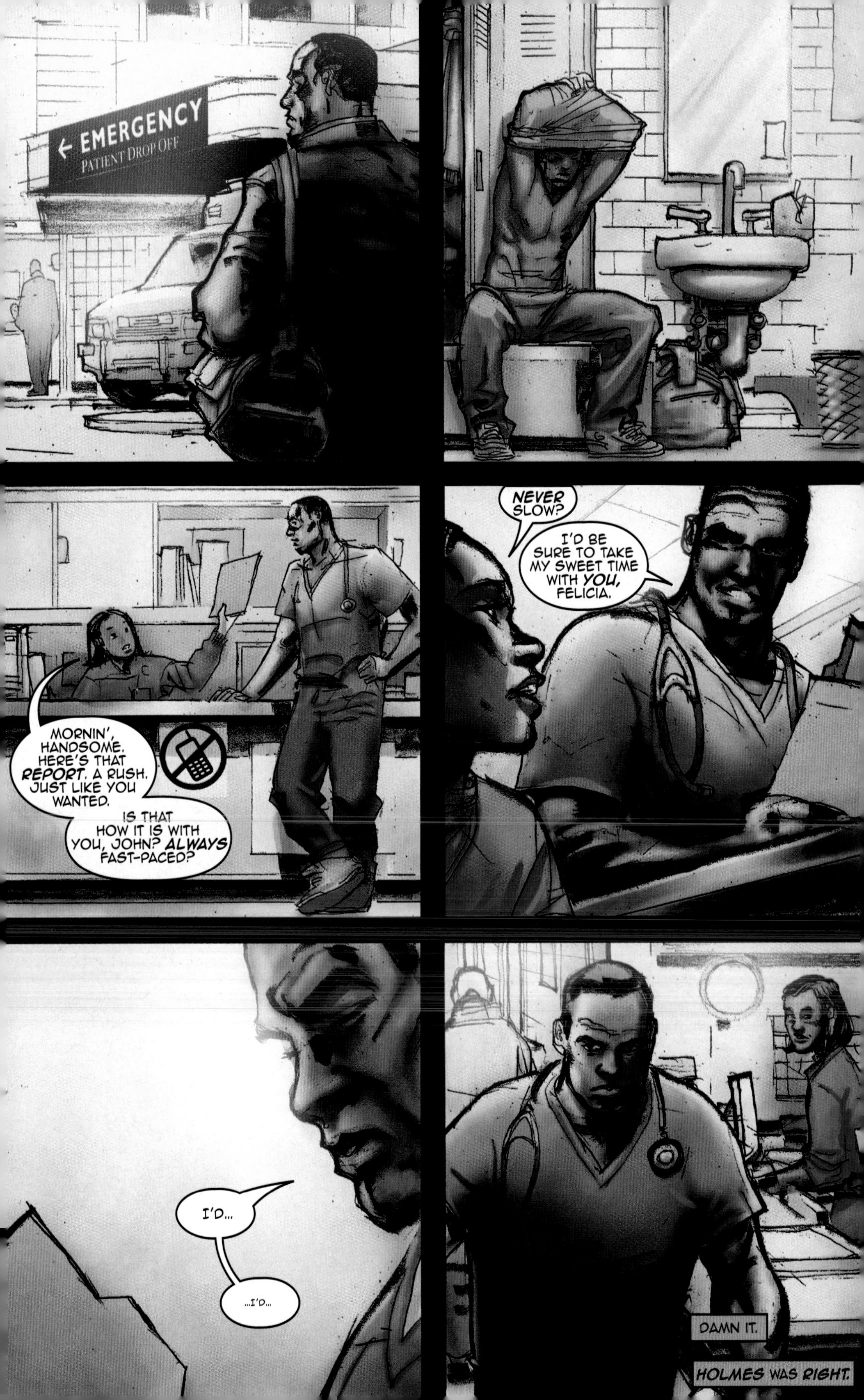
← EMERGENCY
PATIENT DROP OFF
MORNIN', HANDSOME. HERE'S THAT REPORT. A RUSH. JUST LIKE YOU WANTED.
IS THAT HOW IT IS WITH YOU, JOHN? ALWAYS FAST-PACED?
NEVER SLOW?
I'D BE SURE TO TAKE MY SWEET TIME WITH YOU, FELICIA.
I'D...
...I'D...
DAMN IT.
HOLMES WAS RIGHT.

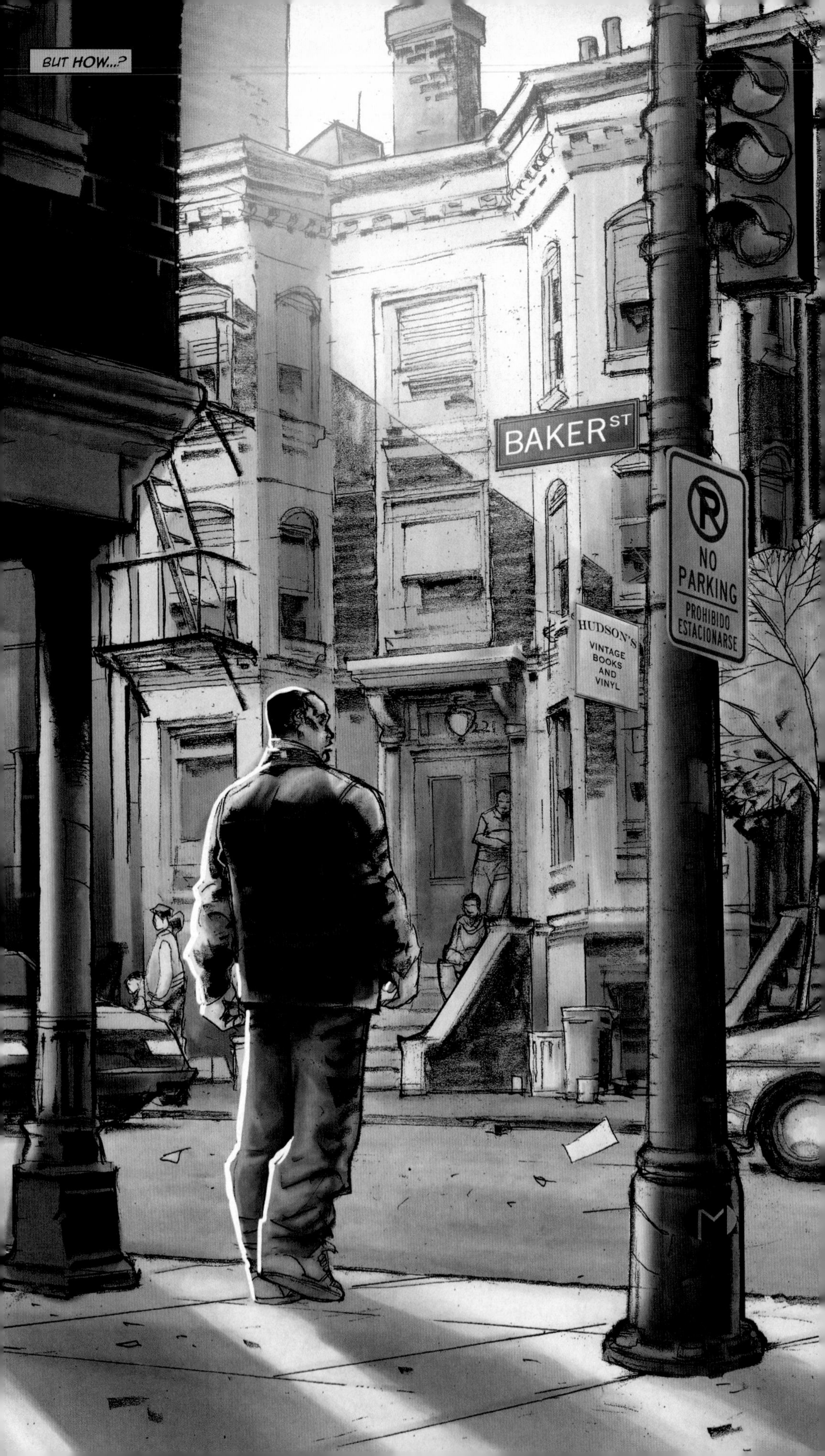
BUT HOW...?
BAKER ST
HUDSON'S
VINTAGE
BOOKS
AND
VINYL
NO
PARKING
PROHIBIDO
ESTACIONARSE

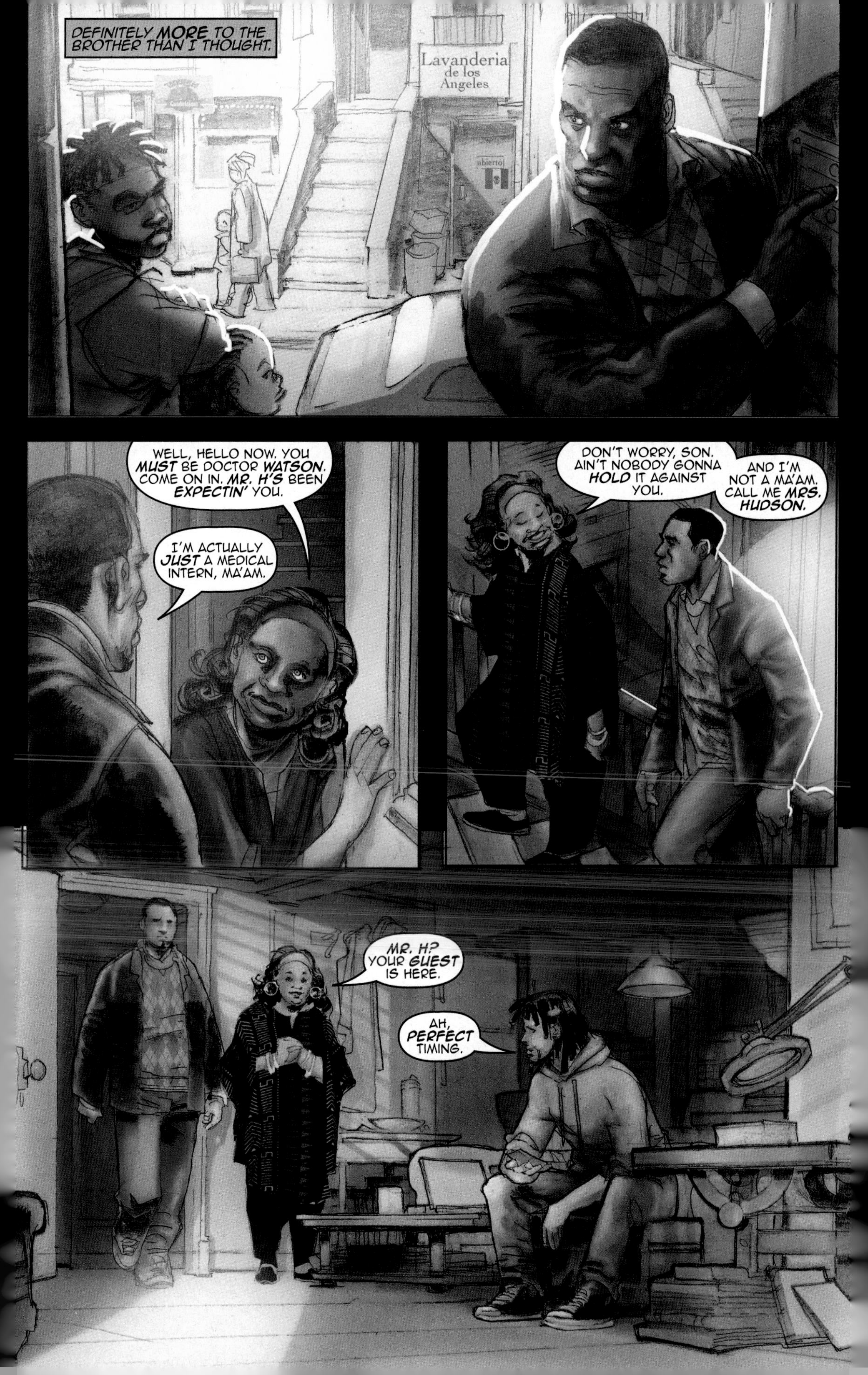
DEFINITELY MORE TO THE BROTHER THAN I THOUGHT.
Lavanderia de los Angeles
abierto
WELL, HELLO NOW. YOU MUST BE DOCTOR WATSON. COME ON IN. MR. H'S BEEN EXPECTIN' YOU.
I'M ACTUALLY JUST A MEDICAL INTERN, MA'AM.
DON'T WORRY, SON. AIN'T NOBODY GONNA HOLD IT AGAINST YOU.
AND I'M NOT A MA'AM. CALL ME MRS. HUDSON.
MR. H? YOUR GUEST IS HERE.
AH, PERFECT TIMING.

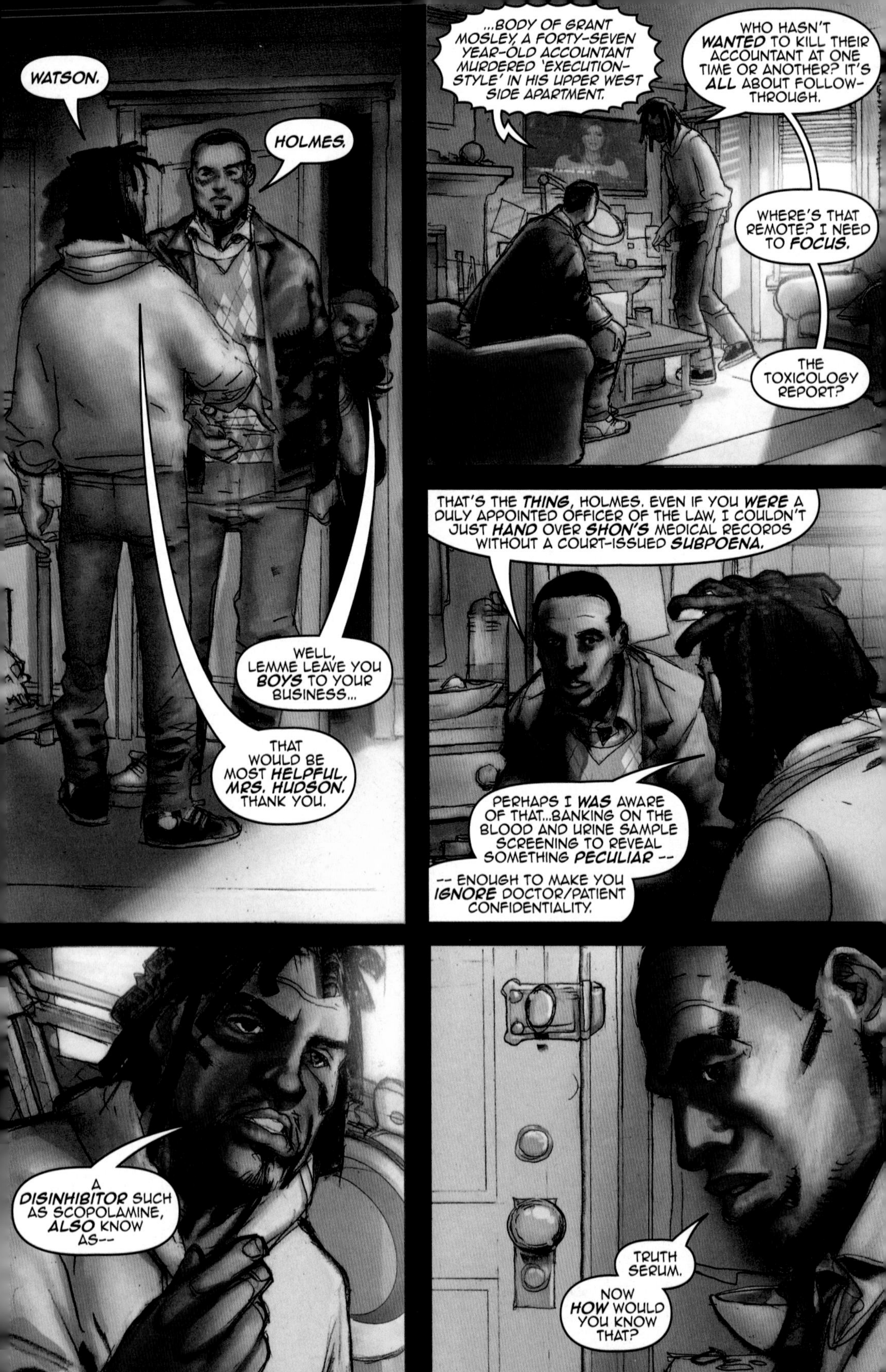
WATSON.
HOLMES.
WELL, LEMME LEAVE YOU BOYS TO YOUR BUSINESS...
THAT WOULD BE MOST HELPFUL, MRS. HUDSON. THANK YOU.
...BODY OF GRANT MOSLEY, A FORTY-SEVEN YEAR-OLD ACCOUNTANT MURDERED 'EXECUTION-STYLE' IN HIS UPPER WEST SIDE APARTMENT.
WHO HASN'T WANTED TO KILL THEIR ACCOUNTANT AT ONE TIME OR ANOTHER? IT'S ALL ABOUT FOLLOW-THROUGH.
WHERE'S THAT REMOTE? I NEED TO FOCUS.
THE TOXICOLOGY REPORT?
THAT'S THE THING, HOLMES. EVEN IF YOU WERE A DULY APPOINTED OFFICER OF THE LAW, I COULDN'T JUST HAND OVER SHON'S MEDICAL RECORDS WITHOUT A COURT-ISSUED SUBPOENA.
PERHAPS I WAS AWARE OF THAT...BANKING ON THE BLOOD AND URINE SAMPLE SCREENING TO REVEAL SOMETHING PECULIAR --
-- ENOUGH TO MAKE YOU IGNORE DOCTOR/PATIENT CONFIDENTIALITY.
A DISINHIBITOR SUCH AS SCOPOLAMINE, ALSO KNOW AS--
TRUTH SERUM.
NOW HOW WOULD YOU KNOW THAT?

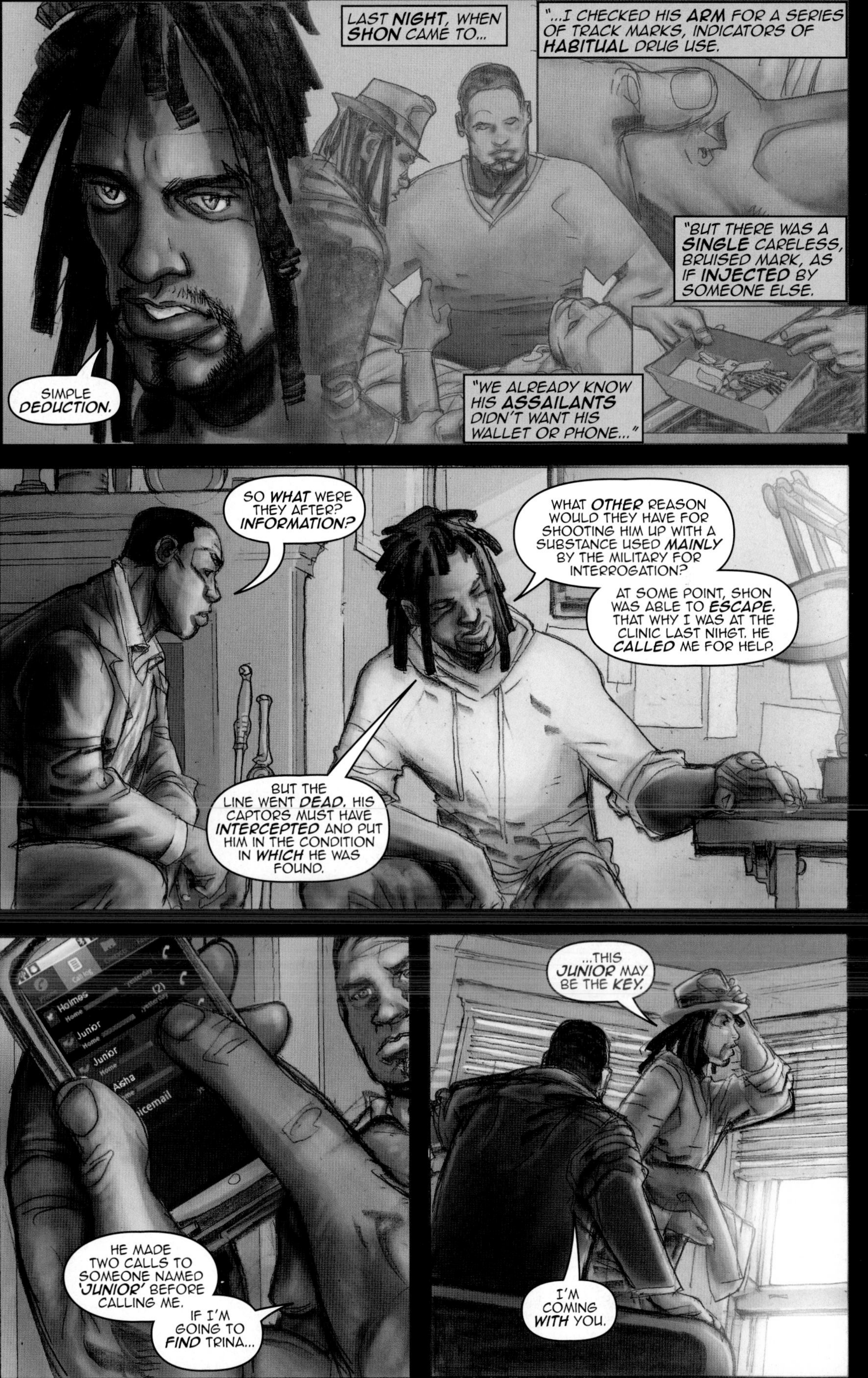
LAST NIGHT, WHEN SHON CAME TO...
"...I CHECKED HIS ARM FOR A SERIES OF TRACK MARKS, INDICATORS OF HABITUAL DRUG USE.
"BUT THERE WAS A SINGLE CARELESS, BRUISED MARK, AS IF INJECTED BY SOMEONE ELSE.
"WE ALREADY KNOW HIS ASSAILANTS DIDN'T WANT HIS WALLET OR PHONE..."
SIMPLE DEDUCTION.
SO WHAT WERE THEY AFTER? INFORMATION?
WHAT OTHER REASON WOULD THEY HAVE FOR SHOOTING HIM UP WITH A SUBSTANCE USED MAINLY BY THE MILITARY FOR INTERROGATION?
AT SOME POINT, SHON WAS ABLE TO ESCAPE. THAT WHY I WAS AT THE CLINIC LAST NIHGT. HE CALLED ME FOR HELP.
BUT THE LINE WENT DEAD. HIS CAPTORS MUST HAVE INTERCEPTED AND PUT HIM IN THE CONDITION IN WHICH HE WAS FOUND.
Call log
Holmes
Home
yesterday
Junior
Home
(2)
Junior
Home
Aisha
HE MADE TWO CALLS TO SOMEONE NAMED 'JUNIOR' BEFORE CALLING ME.
IF I'M GOING TO FIND TRINA...
...THIS JUNIOR MAY BE THE KEY.
I'M COMING WITH YOU.

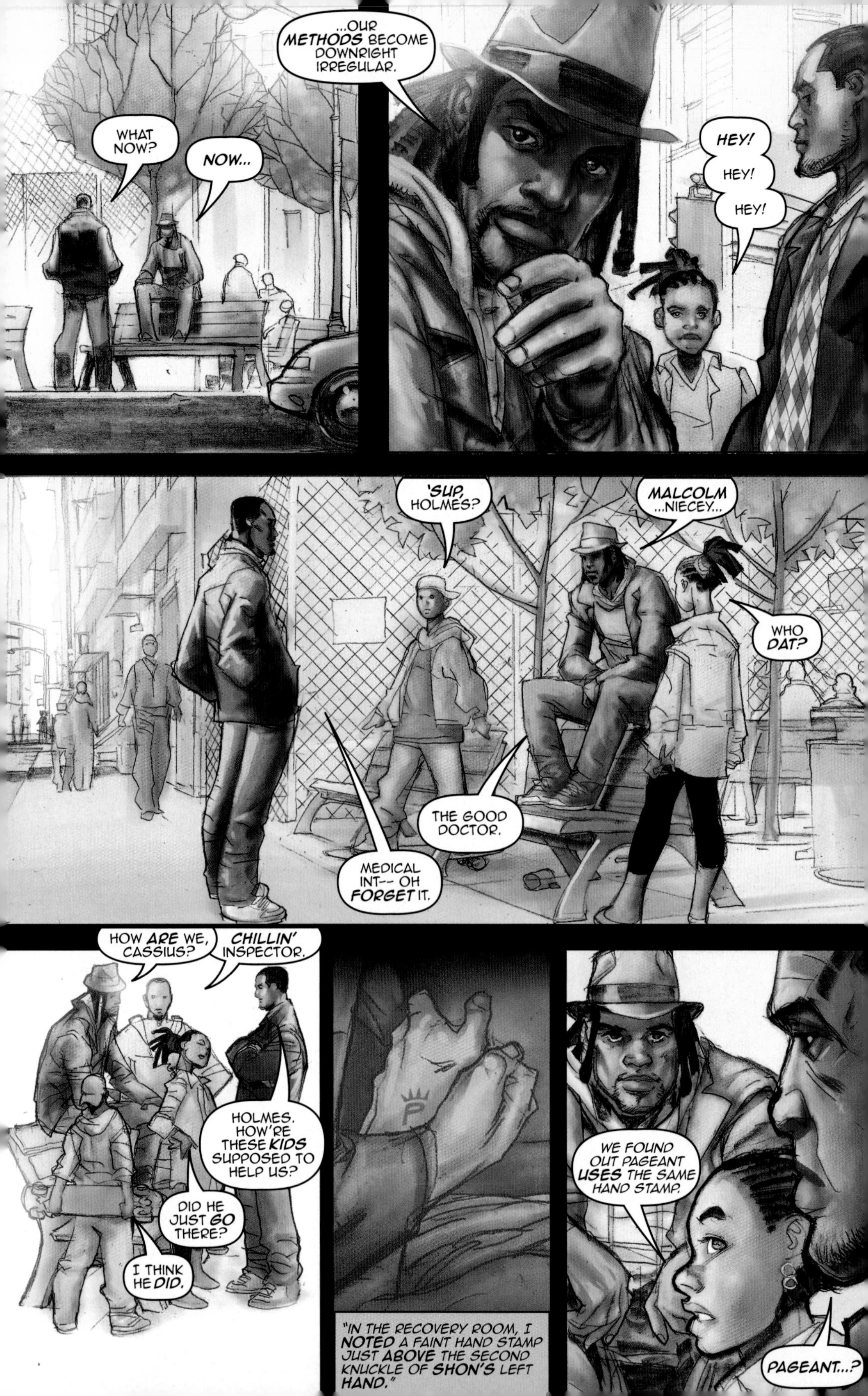

WHAT NOW?
NOW...
...OUR METHODS BECOME DOWNRIGHT IRREGULAR.
HEY!
HEY!
HEY!
'SUP, HOLMES?
MALCOLM ...NIECEY...
WHO DAT?
THE GOOD DOCTOR.
MEDICAL INT-- OH FORGET IT.
HOW ARE WE, CASSIUS?
CHILLIN' INSPECTOR.
HOLMES. HOW'RE THESE KIDS SUPPOSED TO HELP US?
DID HE JUST GO THERE?
I THINK HE DID.
"IN THE RECOVERY ROOM, I NOTED A FAINT HAND STAMP JUST ABOVE THE SECOND KNUCKLE OF SHON'S LEFT HAND."
WE FOUND OUT PAGEANT USES THE SAME HAND STAMP.
PAGEANT...?

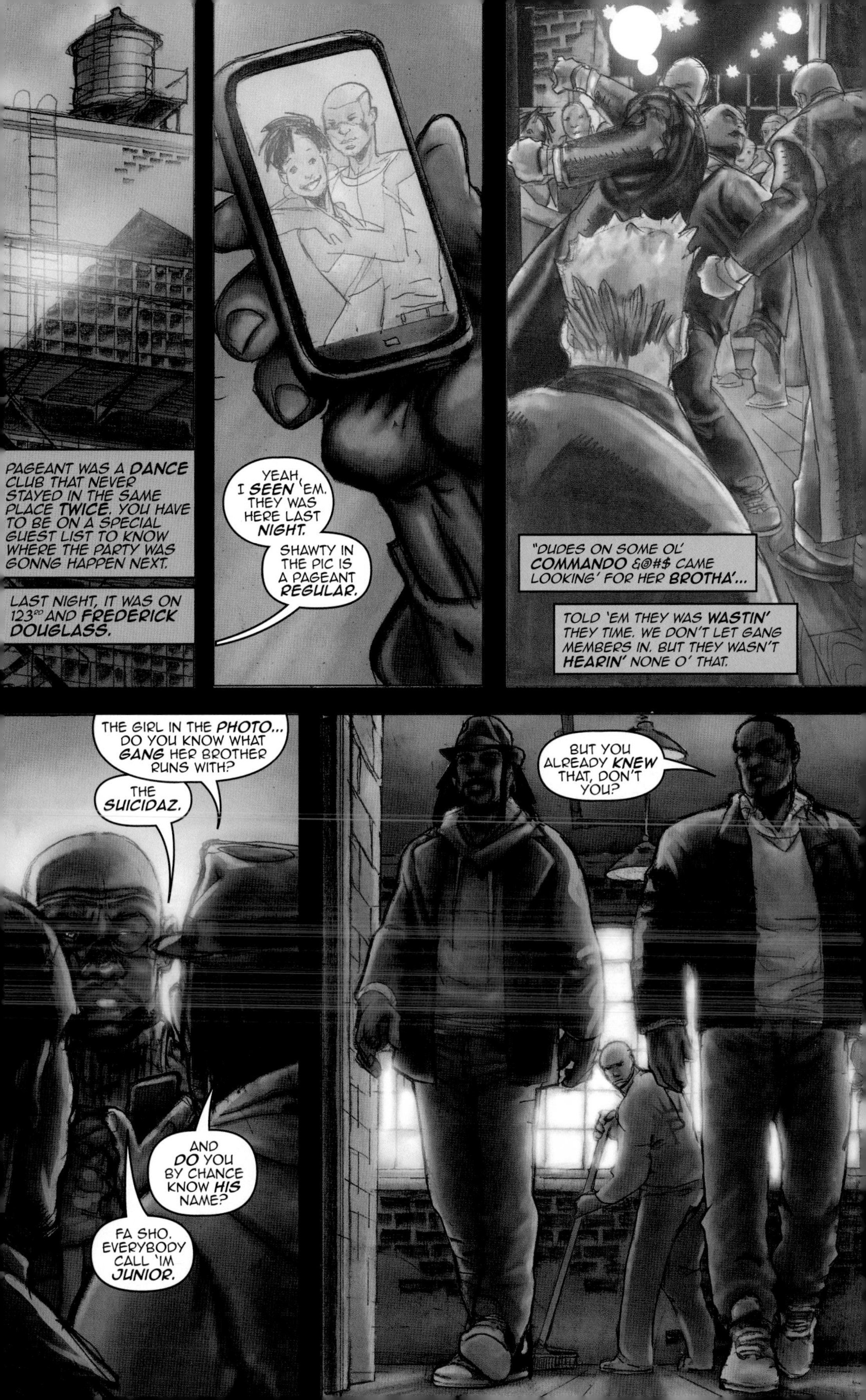
PAGEANT WAS A DANCE CLUB THAT NEVER STAYED IN THE SAME PLACE TWICE. YOU HAVE TO BE ON A SPECIAL GUEST LIST TO KNOW WHERE THE PARTY WAS GONNG HAPPEN NEXT.
LAST NIGHT, IT WAS ON 123RD AND FREDERICK DOUGLASS.
YEAH, I SEEN 'EM. THEY WAS HERE LAST NIGHT.
SHAWTY IN THE PIC IS A PAGEANT REGULAR.
"DUDES ON SOME OL' COMMANDO &@#$ CAME LOOKING' FOR HER BROTHA'...
TOLD 'EM THEY WAS WASTIN' THEY TIME. WE DON'T LET GANG MEMBERS IN. BUT THEY WASN'T HEARIN' NONE O' THAT.
THE GIRL IN THE PHOTO... DO YOU KNOW WHAT GANG HER BROTHER RUNS WITH?
THE SUICIDAZ.
AND DO YOU BY CHANCE KNOW HIS NAME?
FA SHO. EVERYBODY CALL 'IM JUNIOR.
BUT YOU ALREADY KNEW THAT, DON'T YOU?

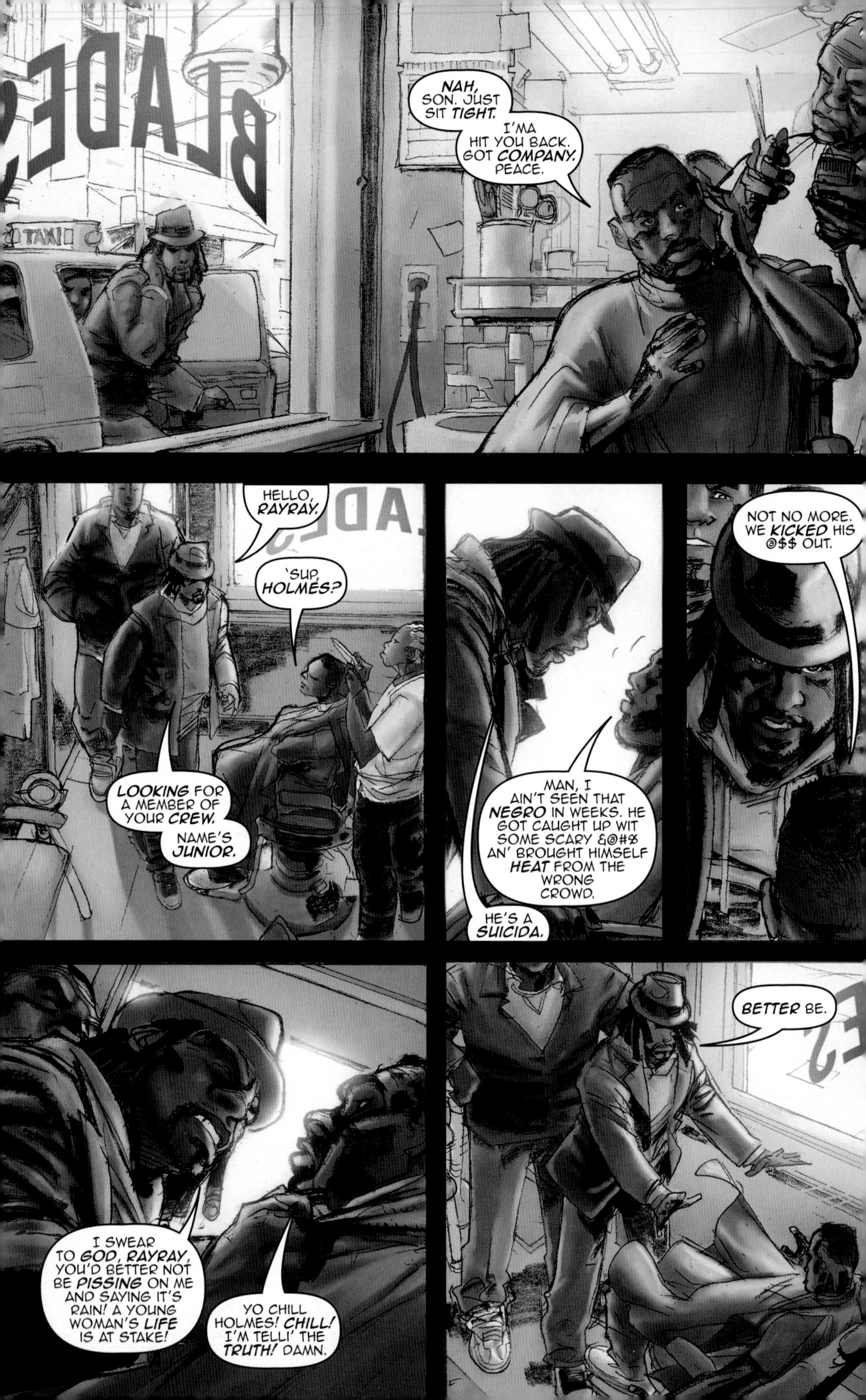
BLADES
TAXI
NAH, SON. JUST SIT TIGHT.
I'MA HIT YOU BACK. GOT COMPANY. PEACE.
HELLO, RAYRAY.
'SUP, HOLMES?
LOOKING FOR A MEMBER OF YOUR CREW.
NAME'S JUNIOR.
MAN, I AIN'T SEEN THAT NEGRO IN WEEKS. HE GOT CAUGHT UP WIT SOME SCARY &@#% AN' BROUGHT HIMSELF HEAT FROM THE WRONG CROWD.
HE'S A SUICIDA.
NOT NO MORE. WE KICKED HIS @$$ OUT.
I SWEAR TO GOD, RAYRAY, YOU'D BETTER NOT BE PISSING ON ME AND SAYING IT'S RAIN! A YOUNG WOMAN'S LIFE IS AT STAKE!
YO CHILL HOLMES! CHILL! I'M TELLI' THE TRUTH! DAMN.
BETTER BE.

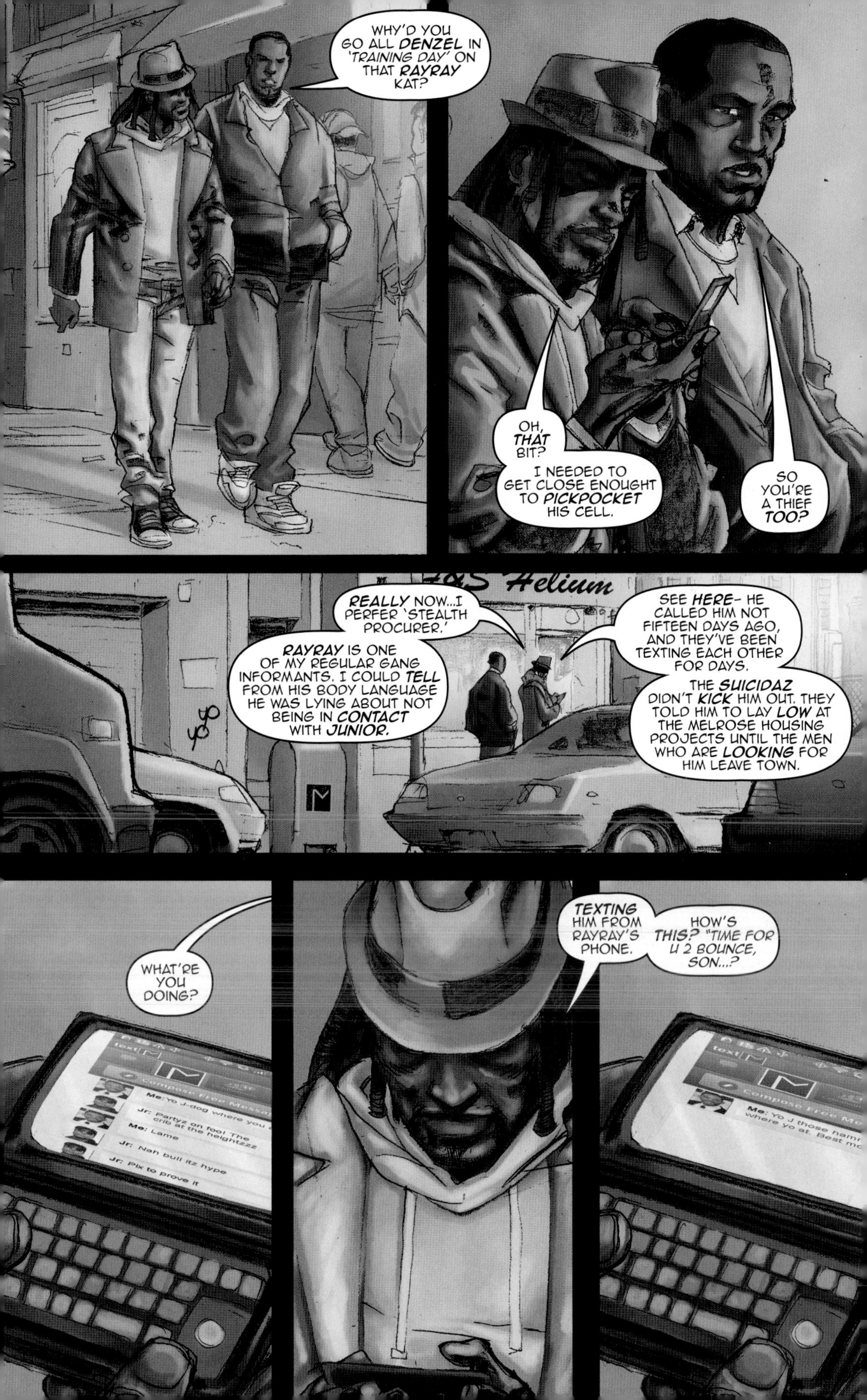
WHY'D YOU GO ALL DENZEL IN 'TRAINING DAY' ON THAT RAYRAY KAT?
OH, THAT BIT? I NEEDED TO GET CLOSE ENOUGHT TO PICKPOCKET HIS CELL.
SO YOU'RE A THIEF TOO?
Helium
REALLY NOW...I PERFER 'STEALTH PROCURER.'
RAYRAY IS ONE OF MY REGULAR GANG INFORMANTS. I COULD TELL FROM HIS BODY LANGUAGE HE WAS LYING ABOUT NOT BEING IN CONTACT WITH JUNIOR.
SEE HERE- HE CALLED HIM NOT FIFTEEN DAYS AGO, AND THEY'VE BEEN TEXTING EACH OTHER FOR DAYS.
THE SUICIDAZ DIDN'T KICK HIM OUT. THEY TOLD HIM TO LAY LOW AT THE MELROSE HOUSING PROJECTS UNTIL THE MEN WHO ARE LOOKING FOR HIM LEAVE TOWN.
WHAT'RE YOU DOING?
Me: Lame
Jr: Nah bull itz hype
Jr: Pix to prove it
TEXTING HIM FROM RAYRAY'S PHONE.
HOW'S THIS? "TIME FOR U 2 BOUNCE, SON...?

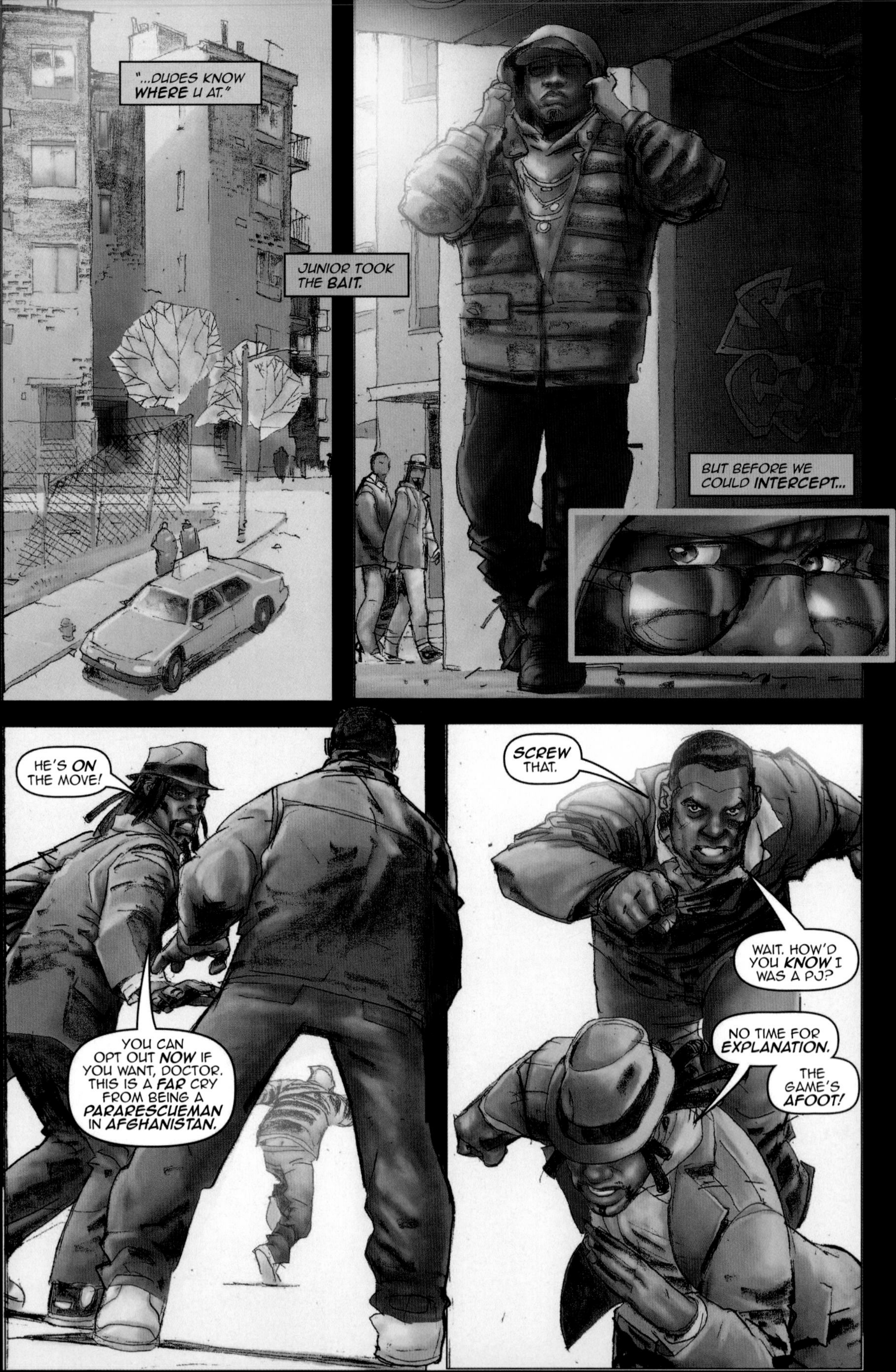
"...DUDES KNOW WHERE U AT."
JUNIOR TOOK THE BAIT.
BUT BEFORE WE COULD INTERCEPT...
HE'S ON THE MOVE!
YOU CAN OPT OUT NOW IF YOU WANT, DOCTOR. THIS IS A FAR CRY FROM BEING A PARARESCUEMAN IN AFGHANISTAN.
SCREW THAT.
WAIT. HOW'D YOU KNOW I WAS A PJ?
NO TIME FOR EXPLANATION.
THE GAME'S AFOOT!

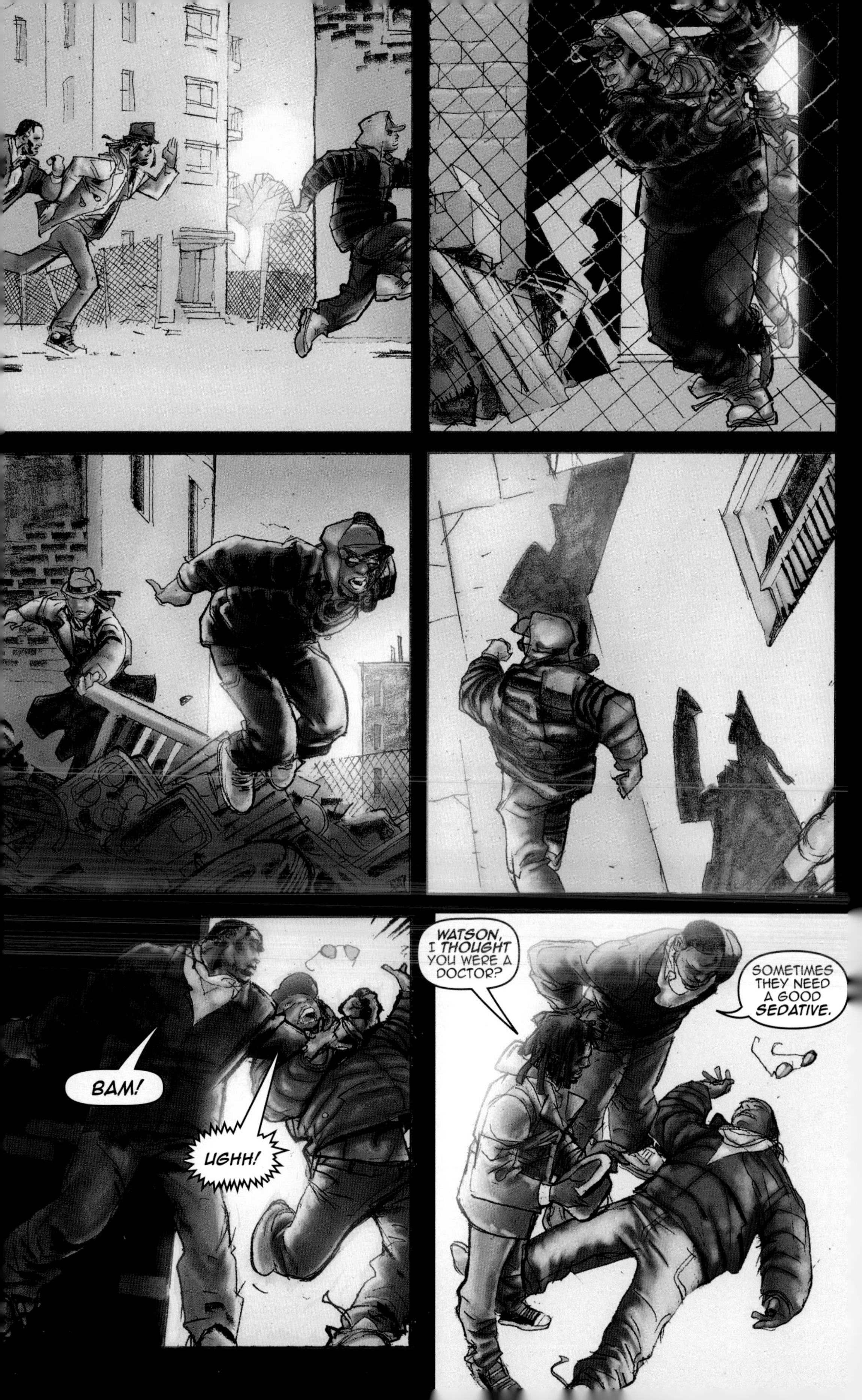
BAM!
UGHH!
WATSON, I THOUGHT YOU WERE A DOCTOR?
SOMETIMES THEY NEED A GOOD SEDATIVE.

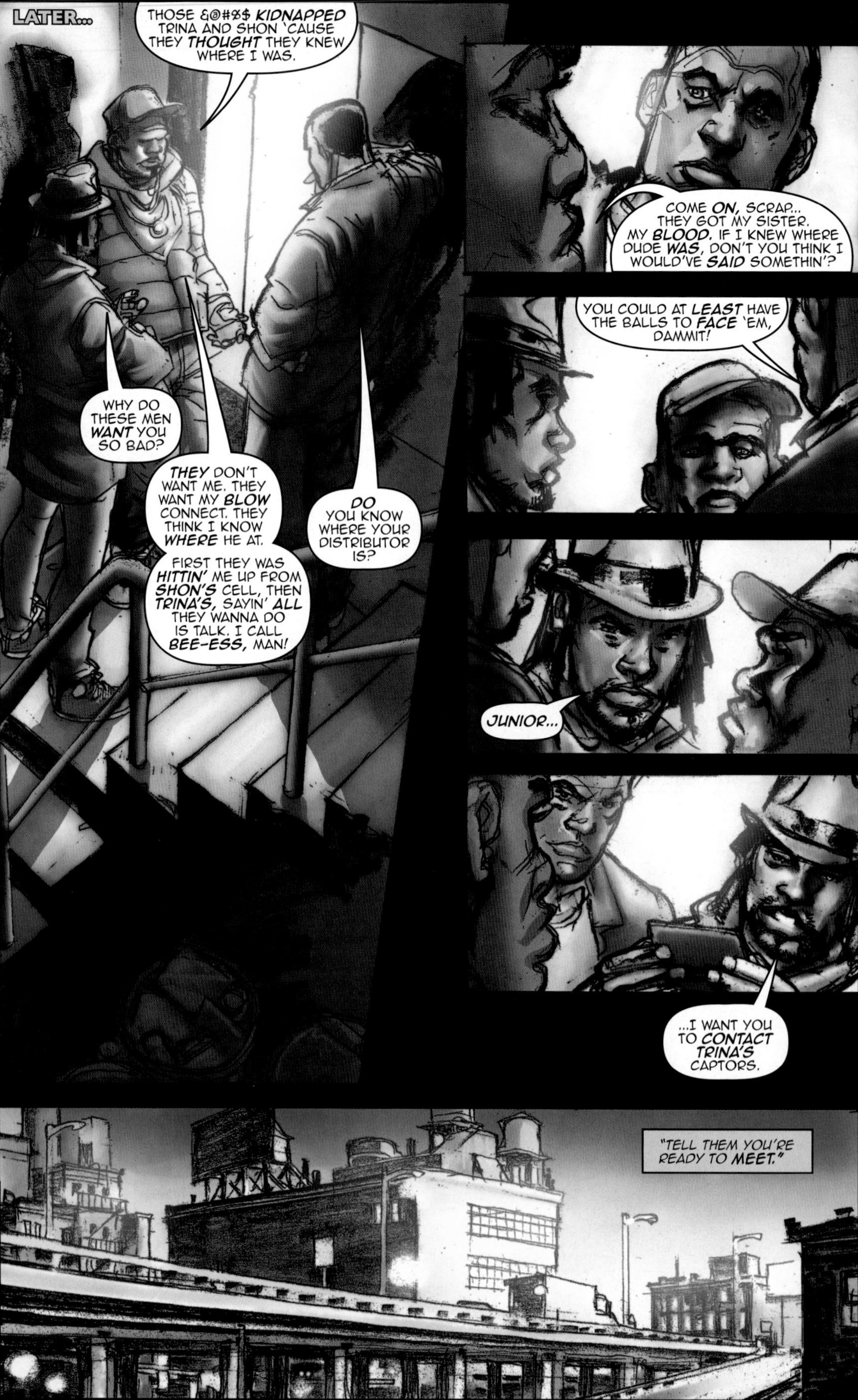
LATER...
THOSE &@#%$ KIDNAPPED TRINA AND SHON 'CAUSE THEY THOUGHT THEY KNEW WHERE I WAS.
WHY DO THESE MEN WANT YOU SO BAD?
THEY DON'T WANT ME. THEY WANT MY BLOW CONNECT. THEY THINK I KNOW WHERE HE AT.
FIRST THEY WAS HITTIN' ME UP FROM SHON'S CELL, THEN TRINA'S, SAYIN' ALL THEY WANNA DO IS TALK. I CALL BEE-ESS, MAN!
DO YOU KNOW WHERE YOUR DISTRIBUTOR IS?
COME ON, SCRAP... THEY GOT MY SISTER. MY BLOOD. IF I KNEW WHERE DUDE WAS, DON'T YOU THINK I WOULD'VE SAID SOMETHIN'?
YOU COULD AT LEAST HAVE THE BALLS TO FACE 'EM, DAMMIT!
JUNIOR...
...I WANT YOU TO CONTACT TRINA'S CAPTORS.
"TELL THEM YOU'RE READY TO MEET."

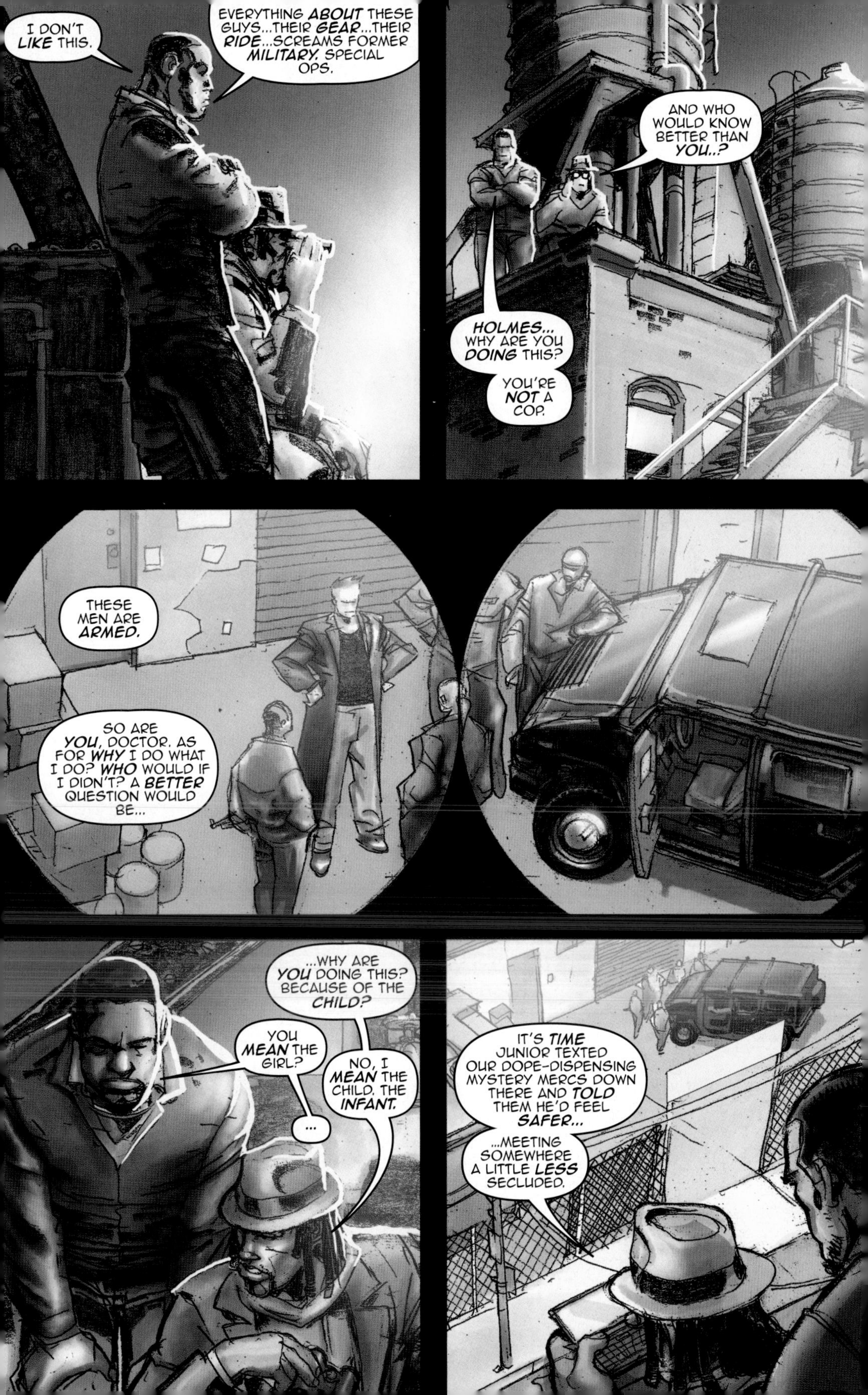
I DON'T LIKE THIS.
EVERYTHING ABOUT THESE GUYS...THEIR GEAR...THEIR RIDE...SCREAMS FORMER MILITARY. SPECIAL OPS.
AND WHO WOULD KNOW BETTER THAN YOU..?
HOLMES... WHY ARE YOU DOING THIS?
YOU'RE NOT A COP.
THESE MEN ARE ARMED.
SO ARE YOU, DOCTOR. AS FOR WHY I DO WHAT I DO? WHO WOULD IF I DIDN'T? A BETTER QUESTION WOULD BE...
...WHY ARE YOU DOING THIS? BECAUSE OF THE CHILD?
YOU MEAN THE GIRL?
NO, I MEAN THE CHILD. THE INFANT.
...
IT'S TIME JUNIOR TEXTED OUR DOPE-DISPENSING MYSTERY MERCS DOWN THERE AND TOLD THEM HE'D FEEL SAFER...
...MEETING SOMEWHERE A LITTLE LESS SECLUDED.

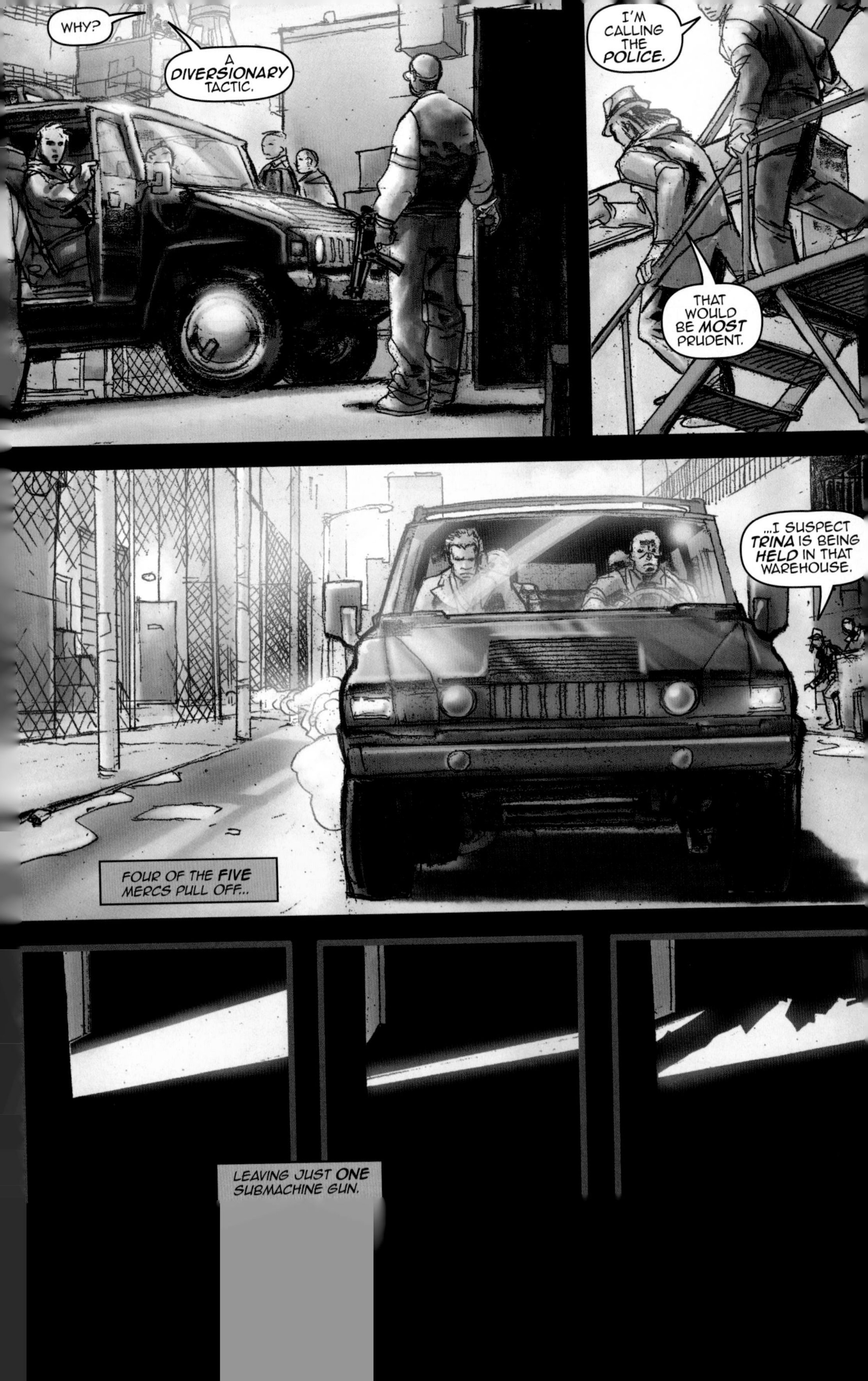
WHY?
A DIVERSIONARY TACTIC.
I'M CALLING THE POLICE.
THAT WOULD BE MOST PRUDENT.
...I SUSPECT TRINA IS BEING HELD IN THAT WAREHOUSE.
FOUR OF THE FIVE MERCS PULL OFF...
LEAVING JUST ONE SUBMACHINE GUN.

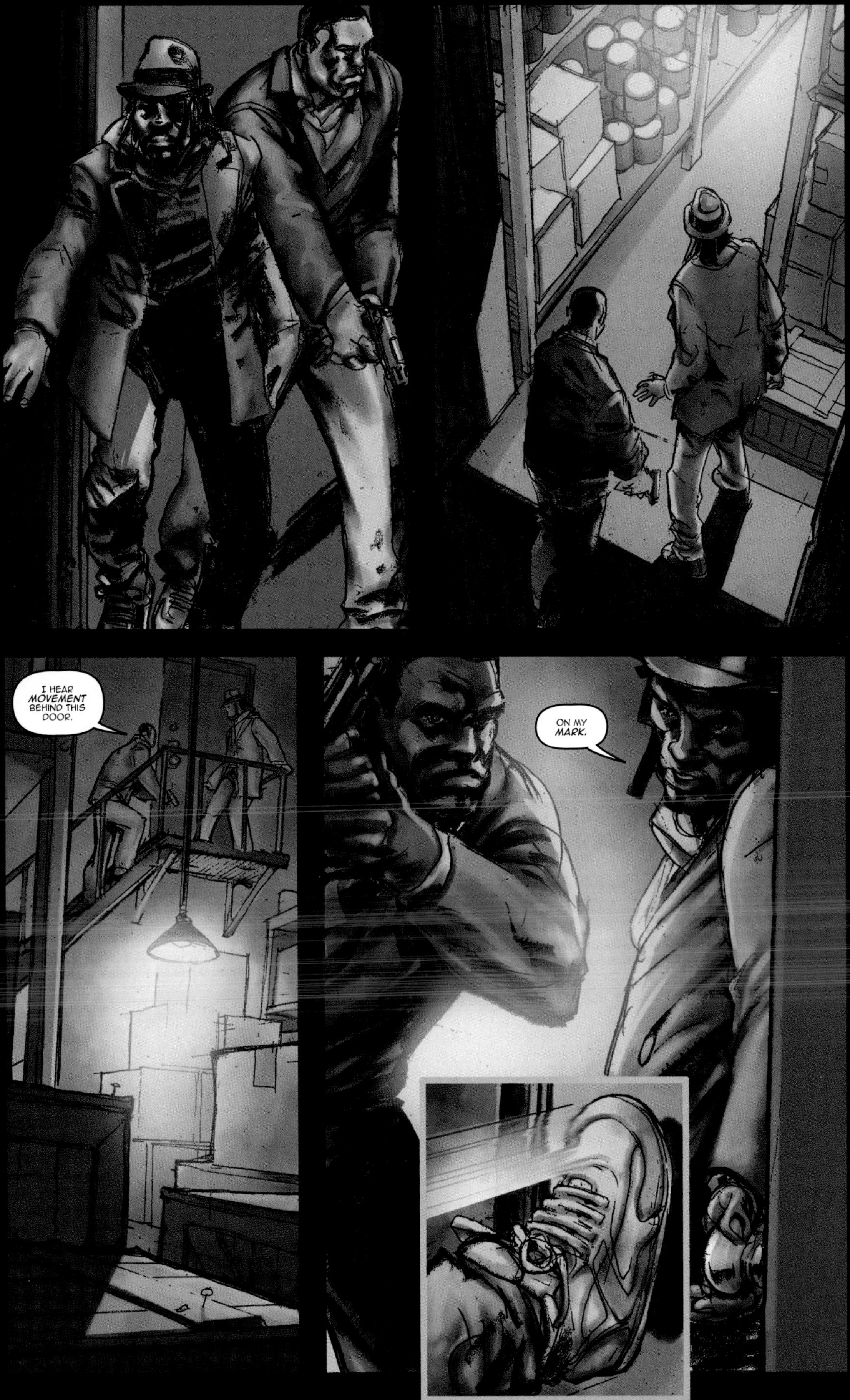
I HEAR MOVEMENT BEHIND THIS DOOR.
ON MY MARK.

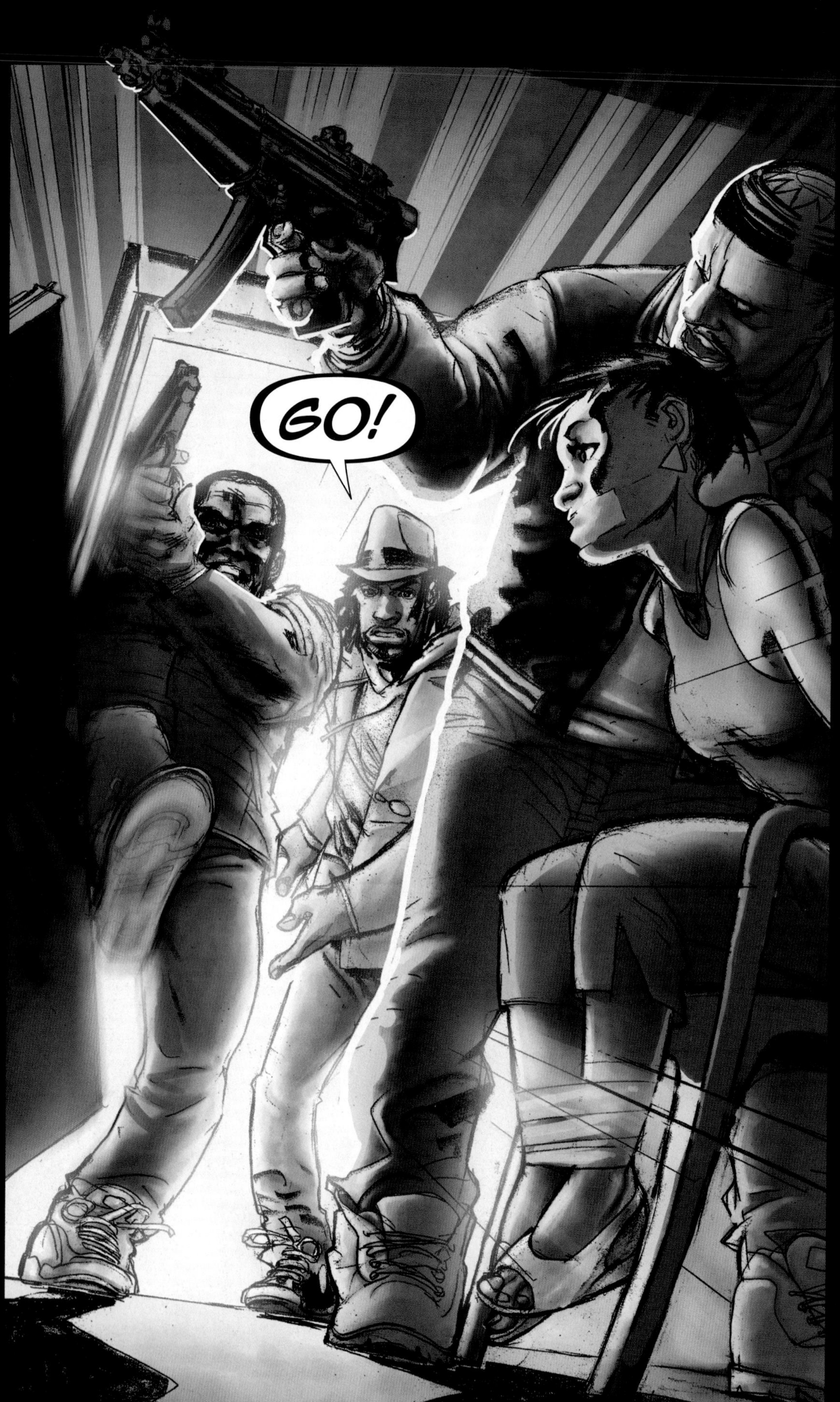
GO!

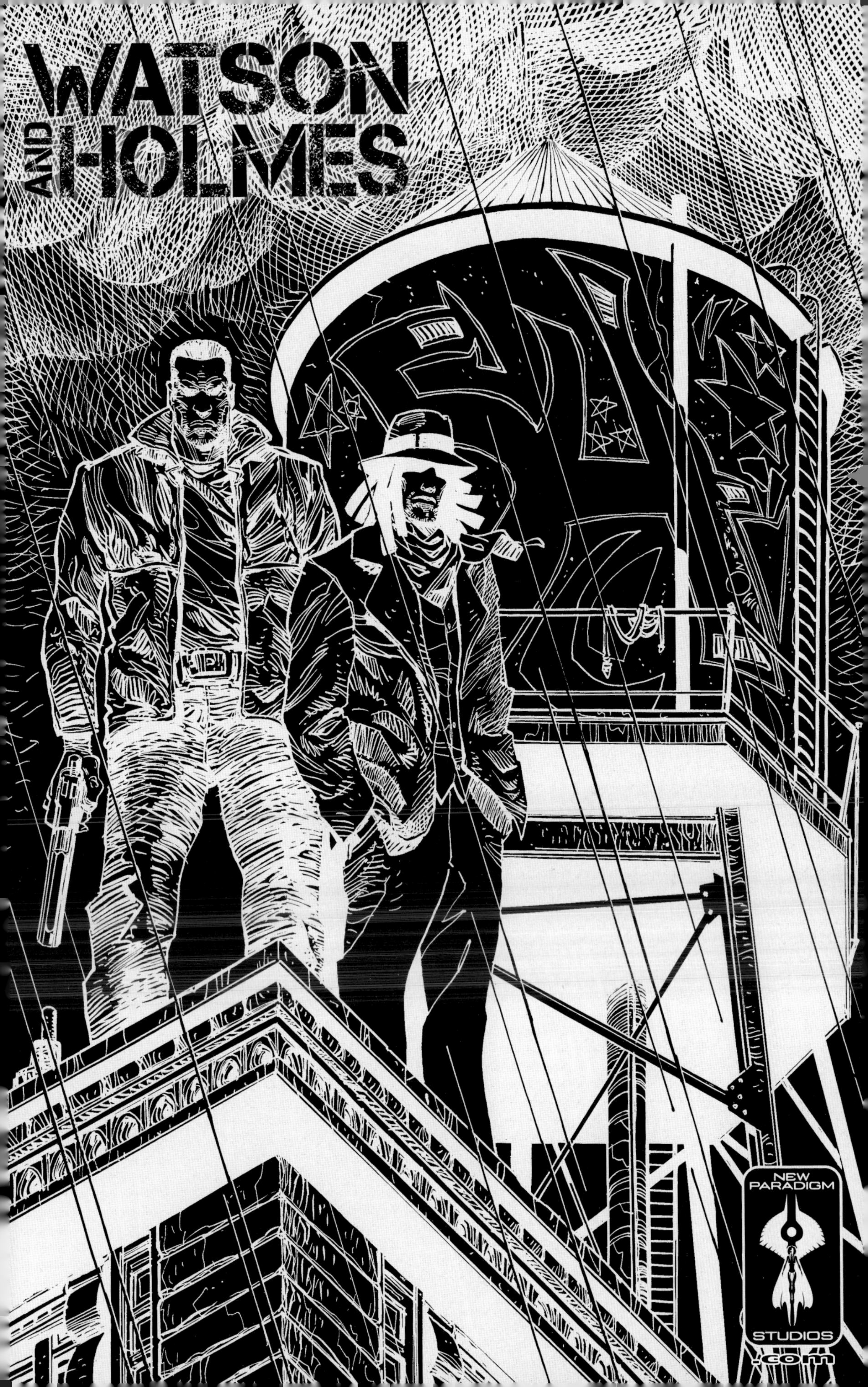
WATSON
AND
HOLMES
NEW PARADIGM
STUDIOS
.com

Chapter Two

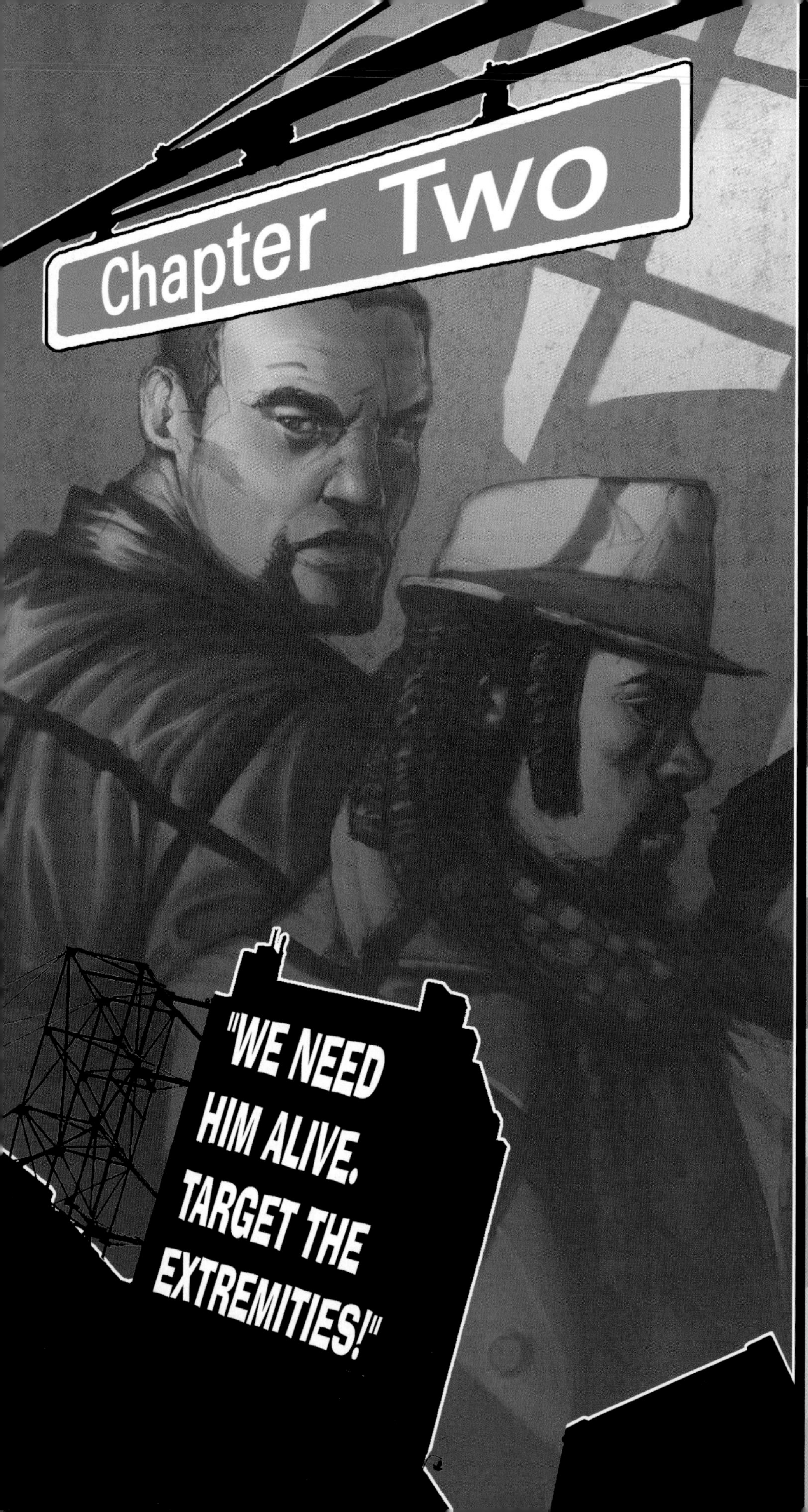
"WE NEED HIM ALIVE. TARGET THE EXTREMITIES!"

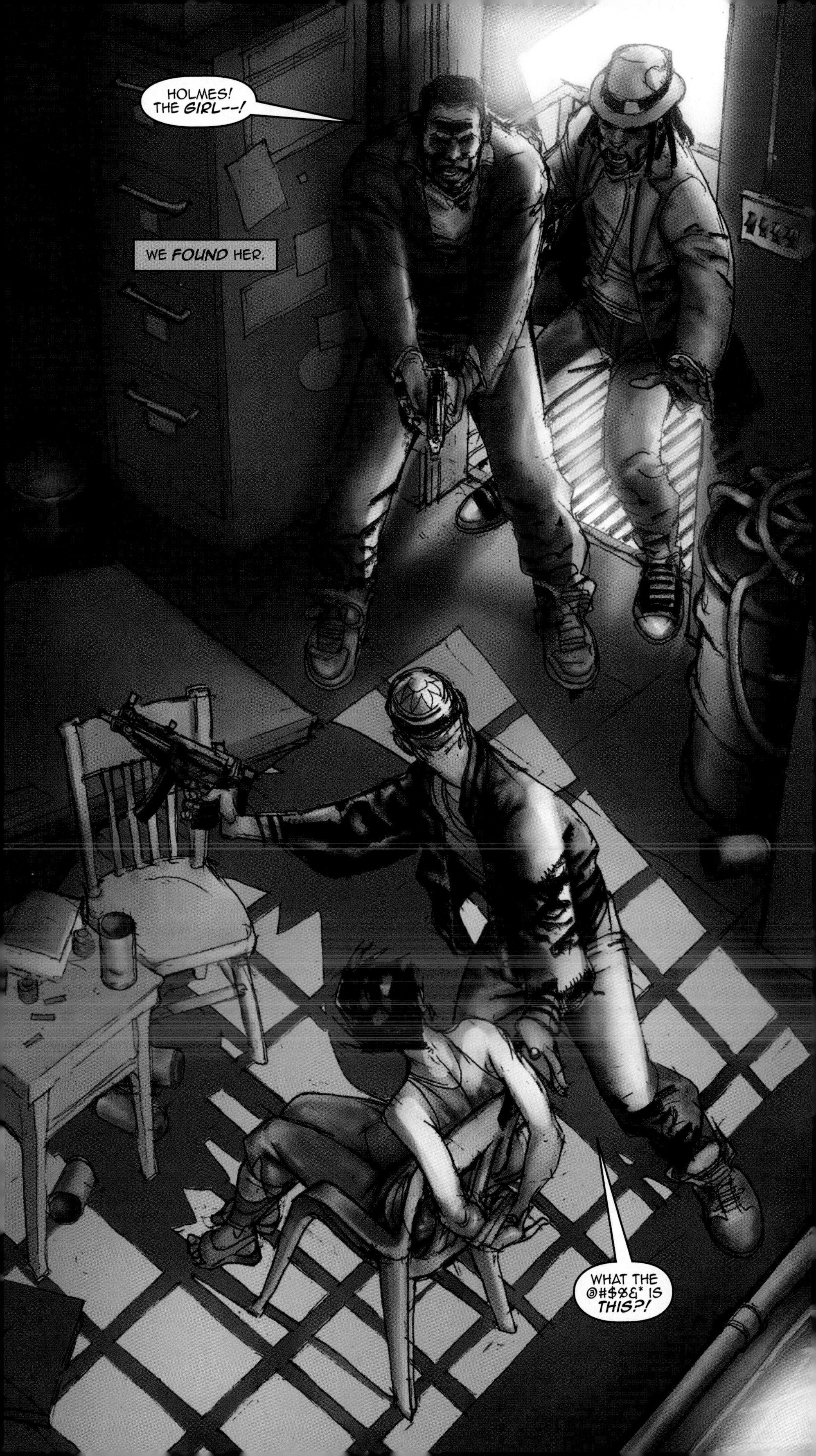
HOLMES! THE GIRL--!
WE FOUND HER.
WHAT THE @#$%&* IS THIS?!

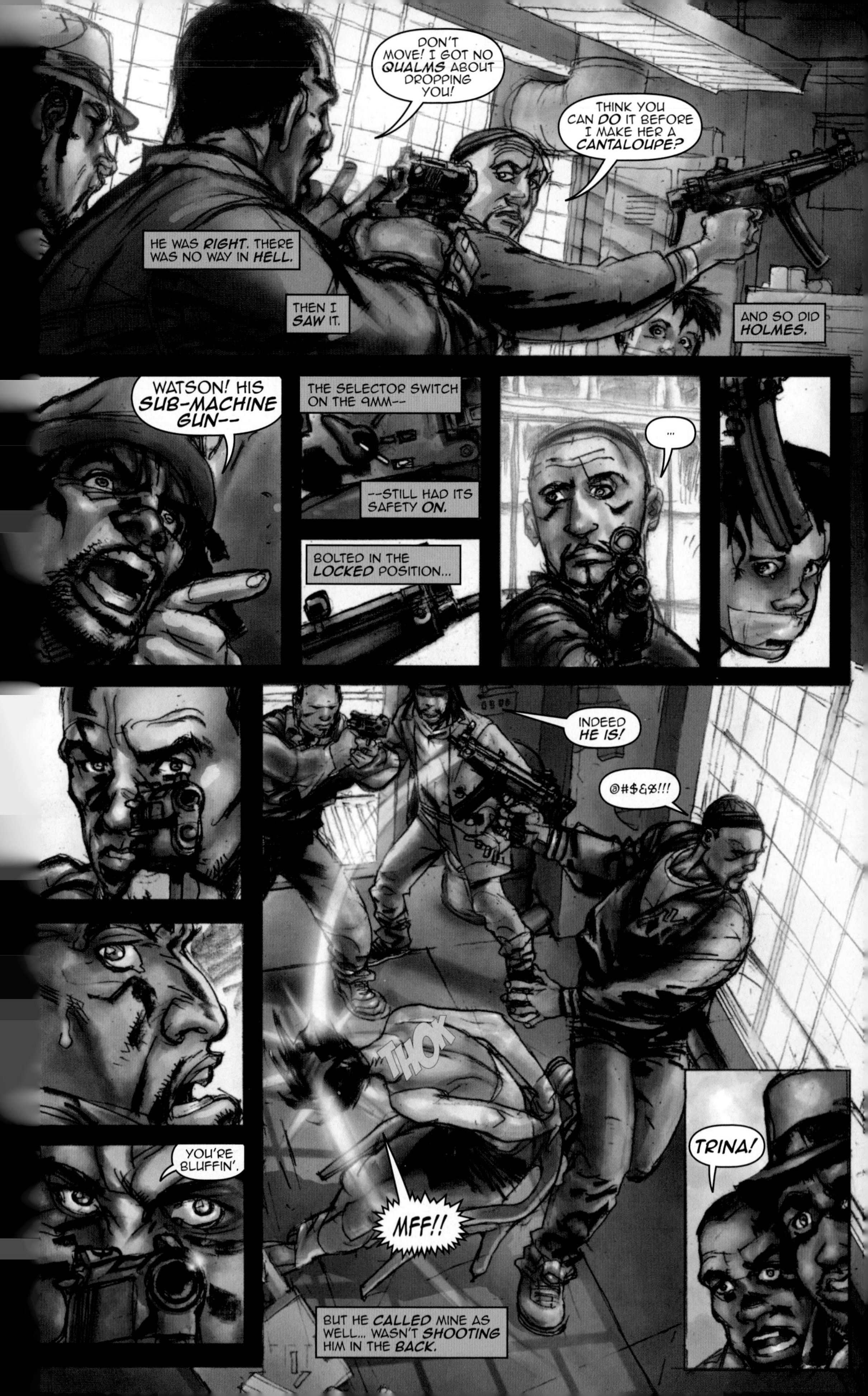
DON'T MOVE! I GOT NO QUALMS ABOUT DROPPING YOU!
THINK YOU CAN DO IT BEFORE I MAKE HER A CANTALOUPE?
HE WAS RIGHT. THERE WAS NO WAY IN HELL.
THEN I SAW IT.
AND SO DID HOLMES.
WATSON! HIS SUB-MACHINE GUN--
THE SELECTOR SWITCH ON THE 9MM--
--STILL HAD ITS SAFETY ON.
BOLTED IN THE LOCKED POSITION...
...
YOU'RE BLUFFIN'.
INDEED HE IS!
@#$&%!!!
THOK
MFF!!
TRINA!
BUT HE CALLED MINE AS WELL... WASN'T SHOOTING HIM IN THE BACK.

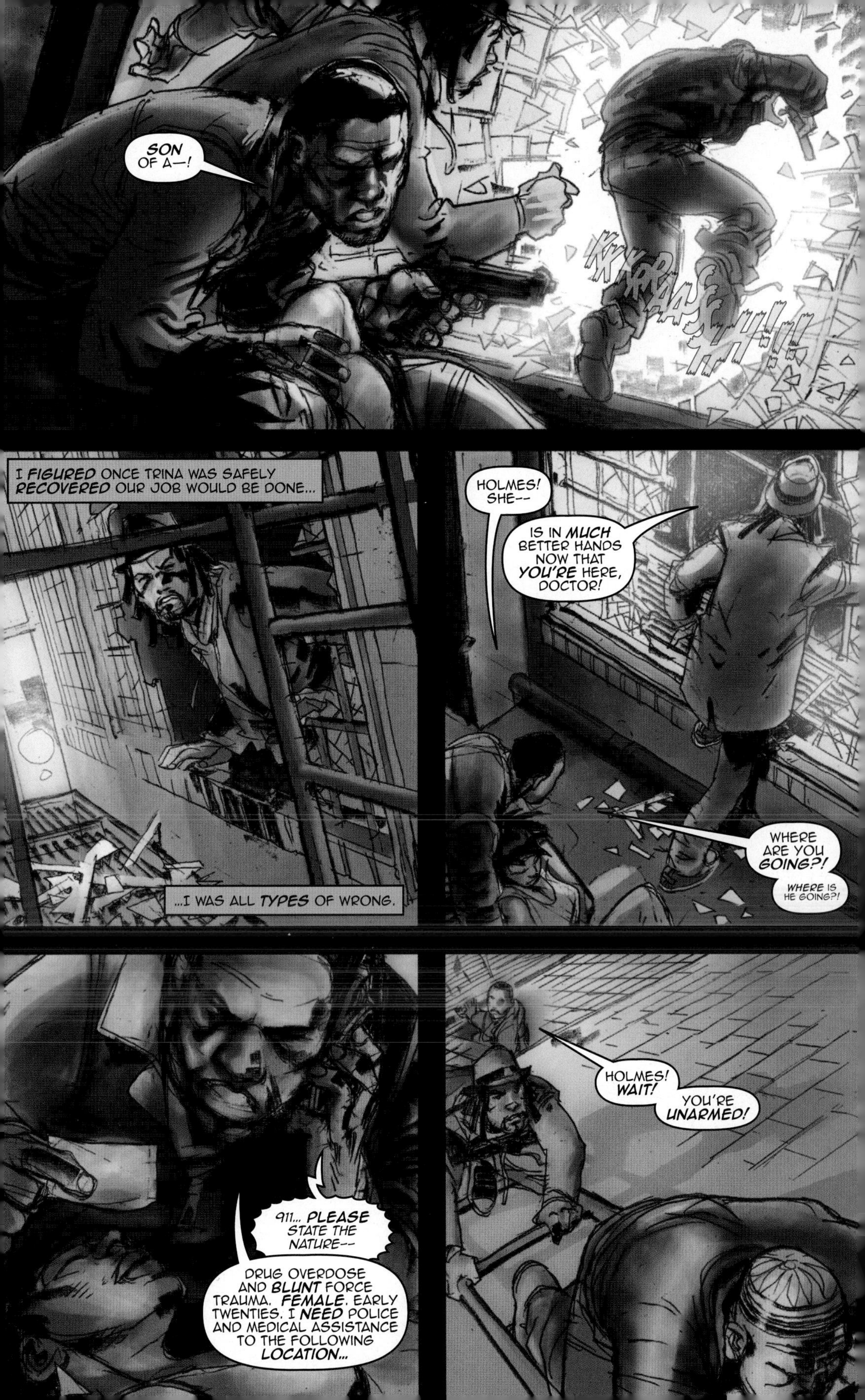
SON OF A—!
KKRRAASSHH!!!
I FIGURED ONCE TRINA WAS SAFELY RECOVERED OUR JOB WOULD BE DONE...
...I WAS ALL TYPES OF WRONG.
HOLMES! SHE--
IS IN MUCH BETTER HANDS NOW THAT YOU'RE HERE, DOCTOR!
WHERE ARE YOU GOING?!
WHERE IS HE GOING?!
911... PLEASE STATE THE NATURE--
DRUG OVERDOSE AND BLUNT FORCE TRAUMA. FEMALE. EARLY TWENTIES. I NEED POLICE AND MEDICAL ASSISTANCE TO THE FOLLOWING LOCATION...
HOLMES! WAIT!
YOU'RE UNARMED!

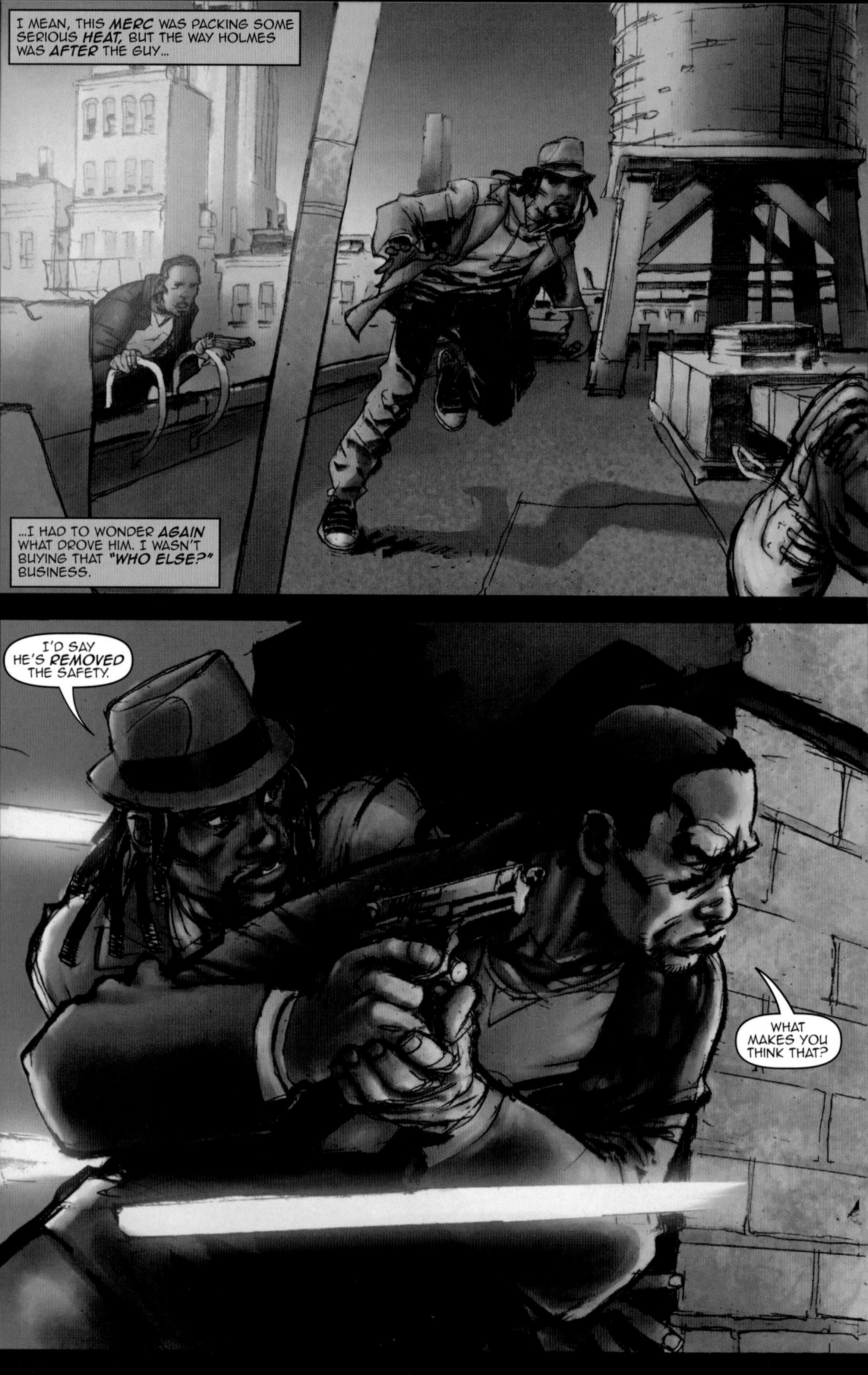
I MEAN, THIS MERC WAS PACKING SOME SERIOUS HEAT, BUT THE WAY HOLMES WAS AFTER THE GUY...
...I HAD TO WONDER AGAIN WHAT DROVE HIM. I WASN'T BUYING THAT "WHO ELSE?" BUSINESS.
I'D SAY HE'S REMOVED THE SAFETY.
WHAT MAKES YOU THINK THAT?

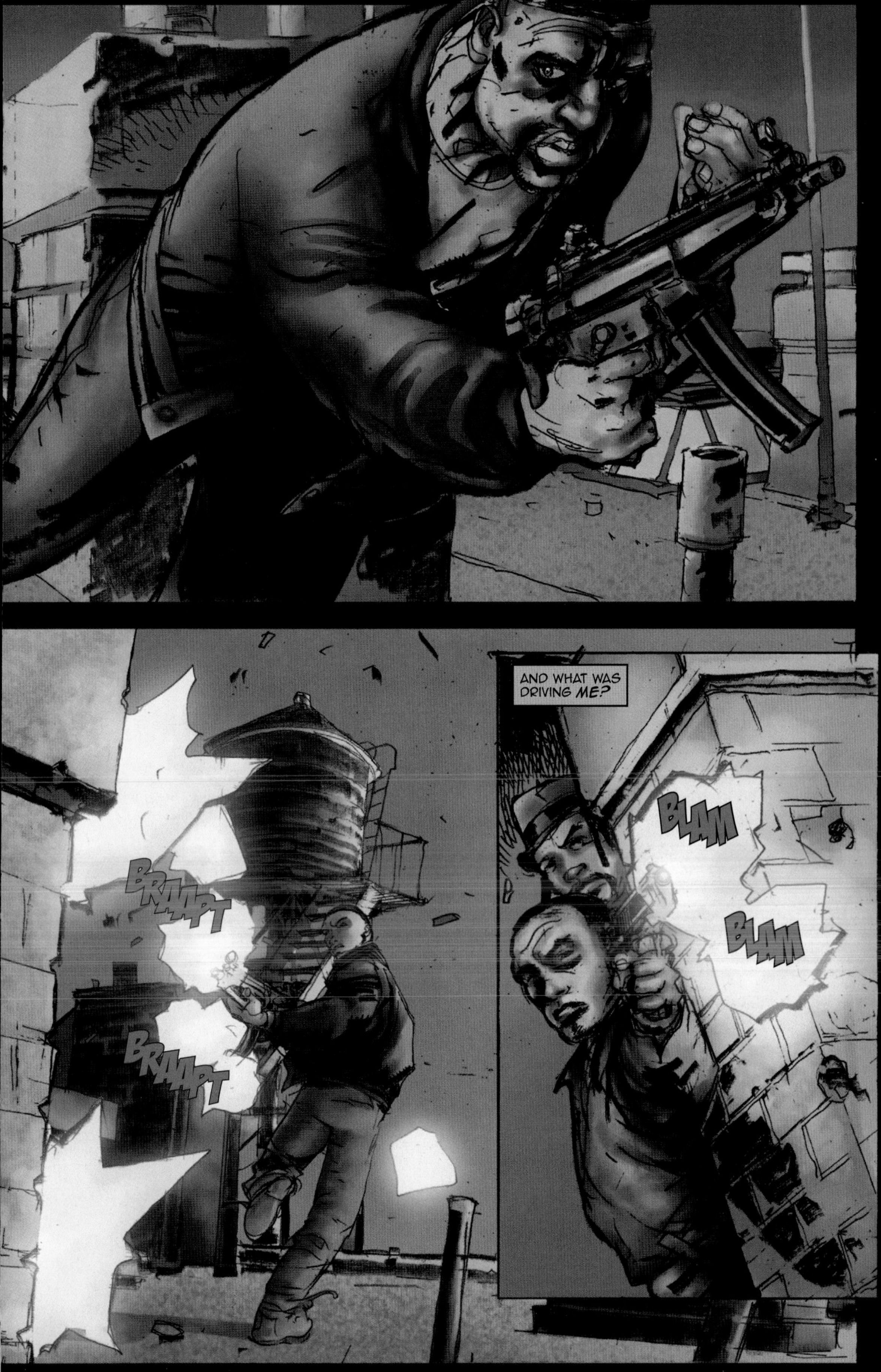
BRAAAPT
BRAAAPT
AND WHAT WAS DRIVING ME?
BLAM
BLAM

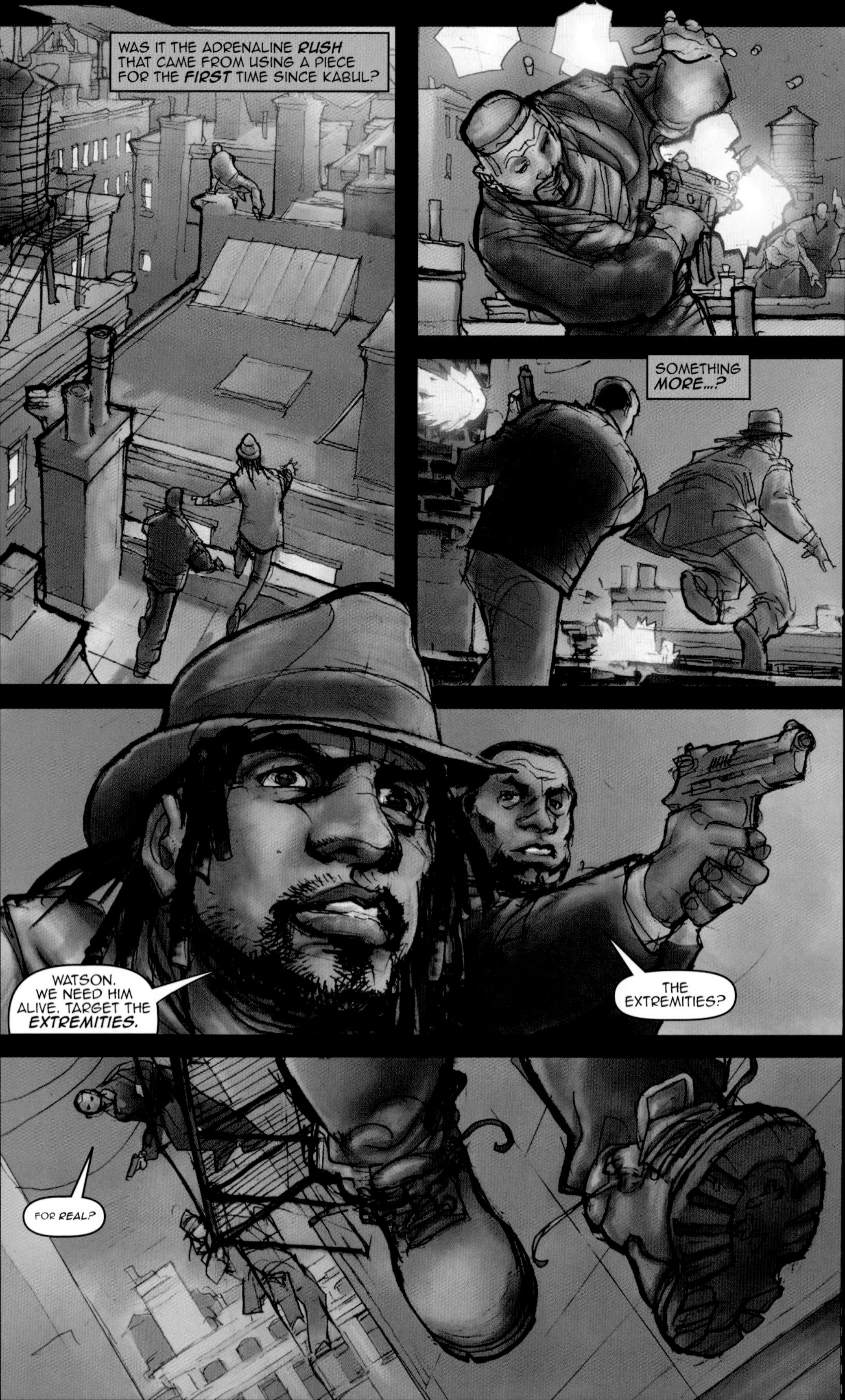
WAS IT THE ADRENALINE RUSH THAT CAME FROM USING A PIECE FOR THE FIRST TIME SINCE KABUL?
SOMETHING MORE...?
WATSON. WE NEED HIM ALIVE. TARGET THE EXTREMITIES.
THE EXTREMITIES?
FOR REAL?

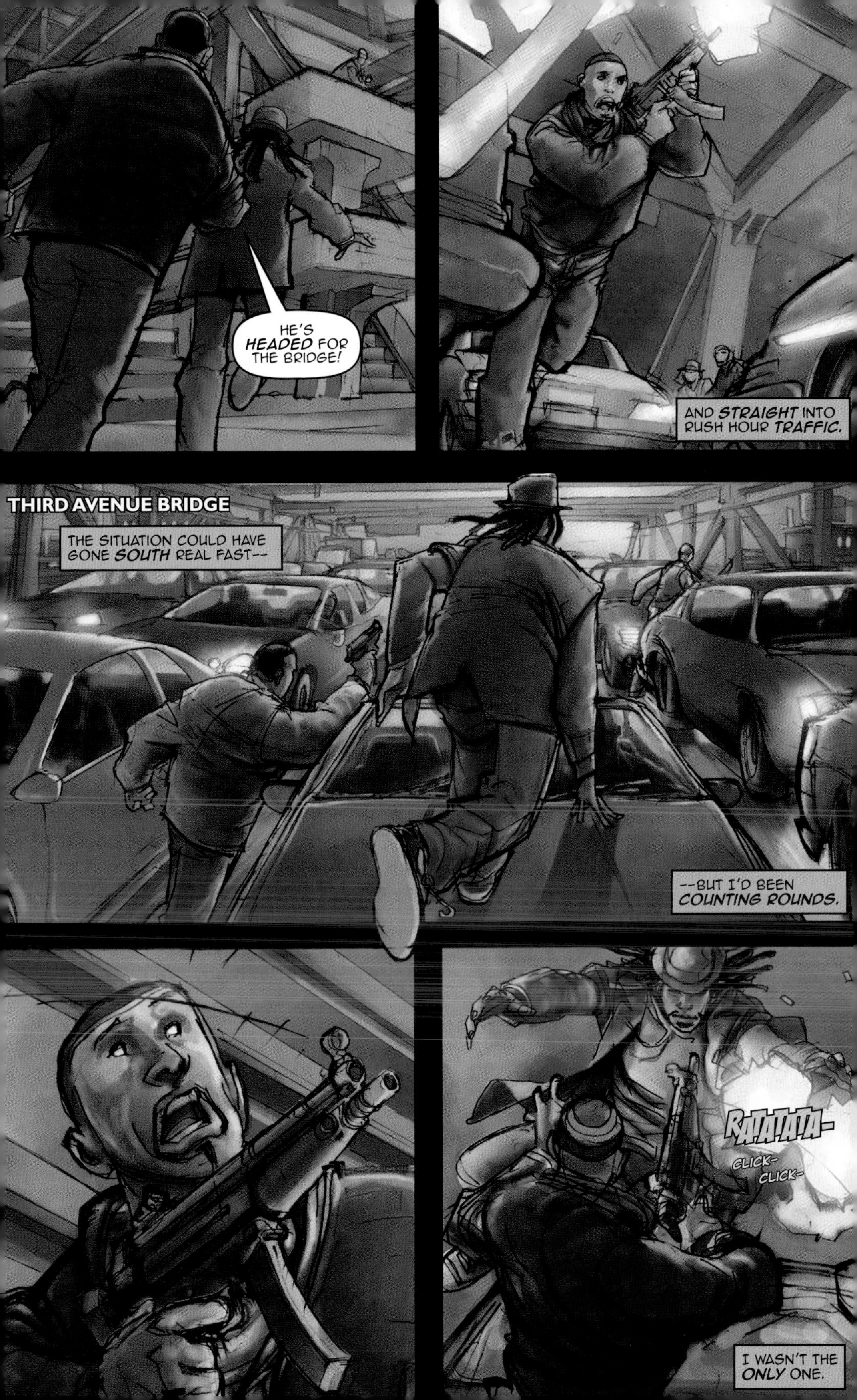
HE'S HEADED FOR THE BRIDGE!
AND STRAIGHT INTO RUSH HOUR TRAFFIC.
THIRD AVENUE BRIDGE
THE SITUATION COULD HAVE GONE SOUTH REAL FAST--
--BUT I'D BEEN COUNTING ROUNDS.
RATATATA-
CLICK-
CLICK-
I WASN'T THE ONLY ONE.

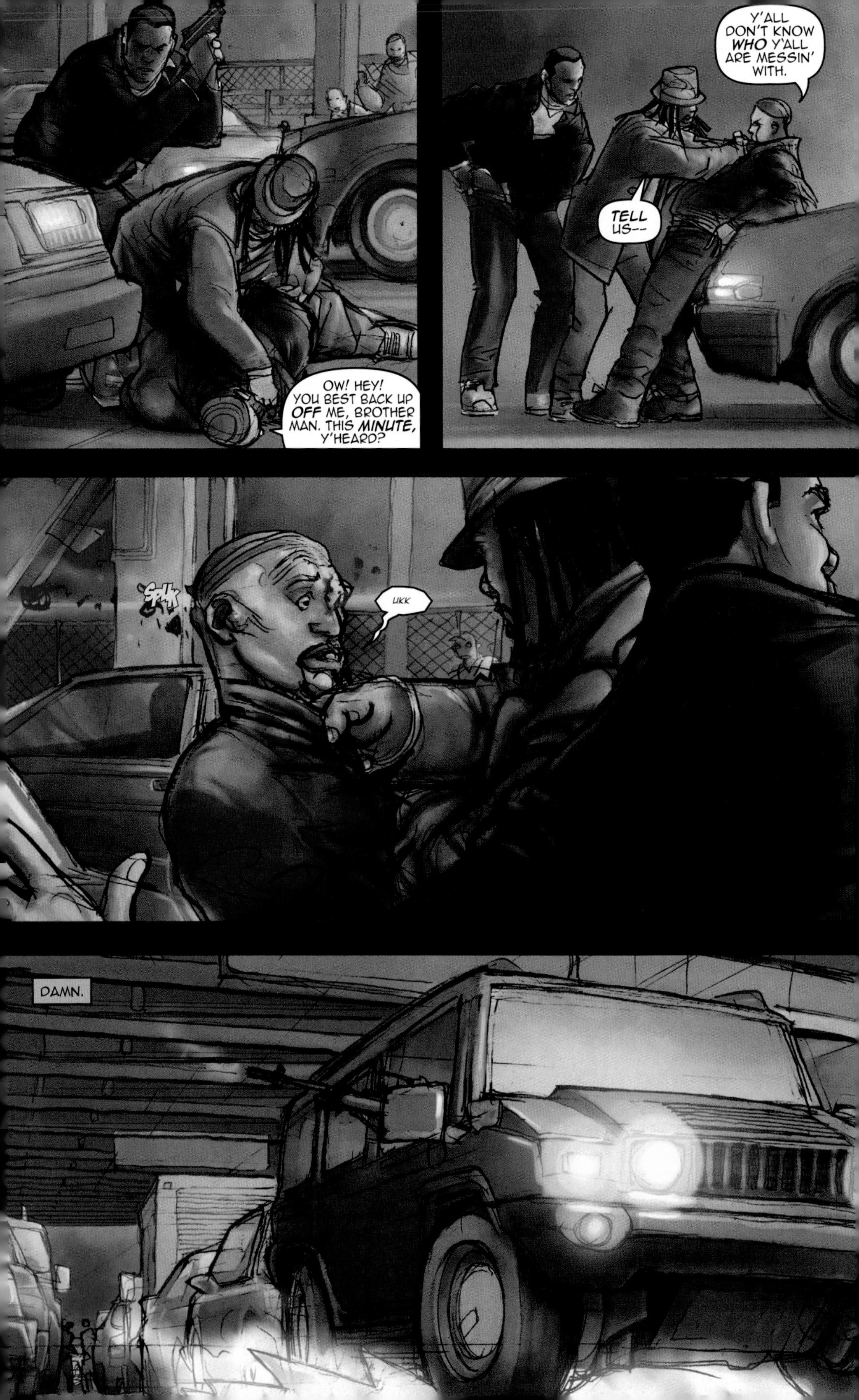
OW! HEY! YOU BEST BACK UP OFF ME, BROTHER MAN. THIS MINUTE, Y'HEARD?
Y'ALL DON'T KNOW WHO Y'ALL ARE MESSIN' WITH.
TELL US--
SPLKK
UKK
DAMN.

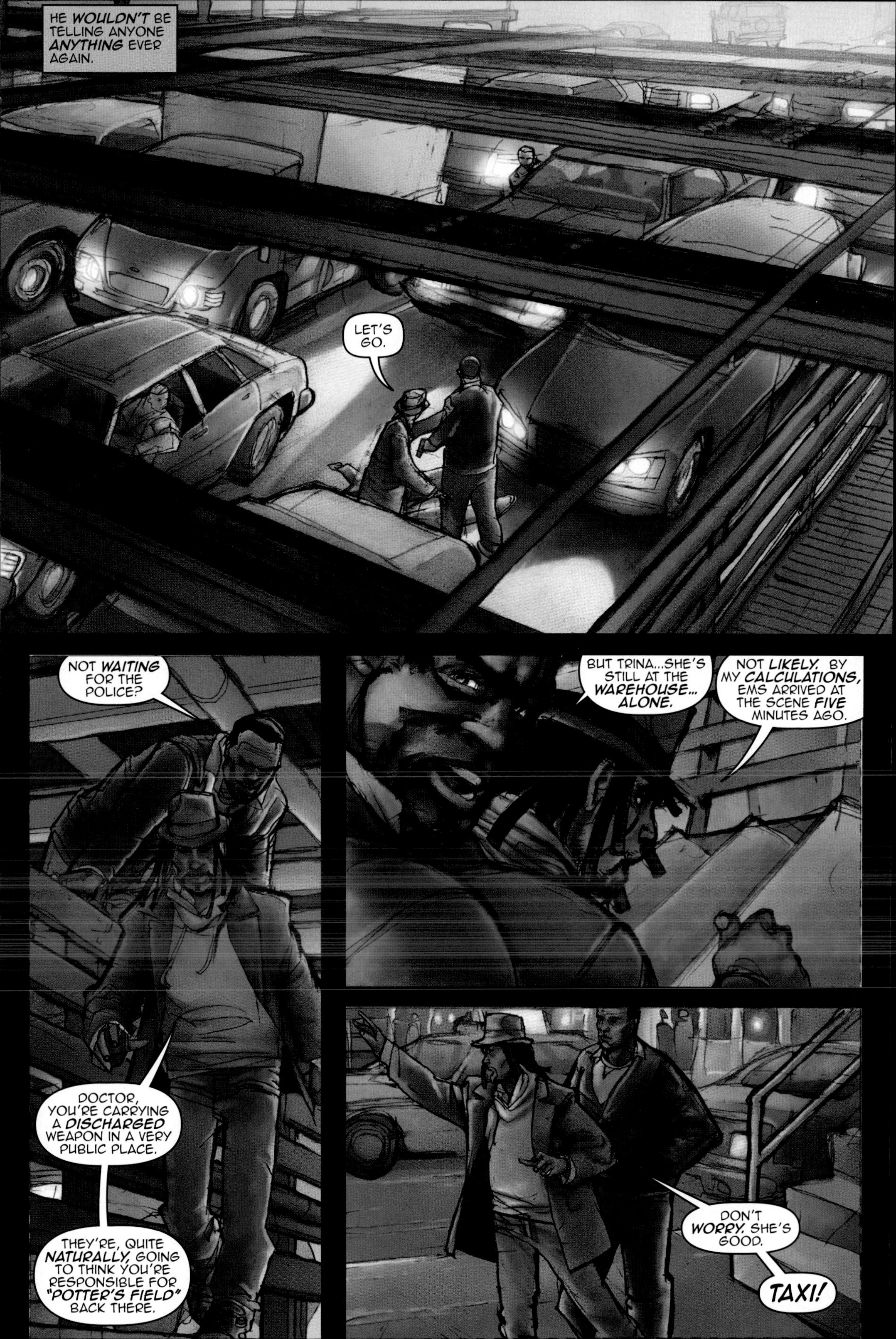
HE WOULDN'T BE TELLING ANYONE ANYTHING EVER AGAIN.
LET'S GO.
NOT WAITING FOR THE POLICE?
DOCTOR, YOU'RE CARRYING A DISCHARGED WEAPON IN A VERY PUBLIC PLACE.
THEY'RE, QUITE NATURALLY, GOING TO THINK YOU'RE RESPONSIBLE FOR "POTTER'S FIELD" BACK THERE.
BUT TRINA...SHE'S STILL AT THE WAREHOUSE... ALONE.
NOT LIKELY. BY MY CALCULATIONS, EMS ARRIVED AT THE SCENE FIVE MINUTES AGO.
DON'T WORRY. SHE'S GOOD.
TAXI!

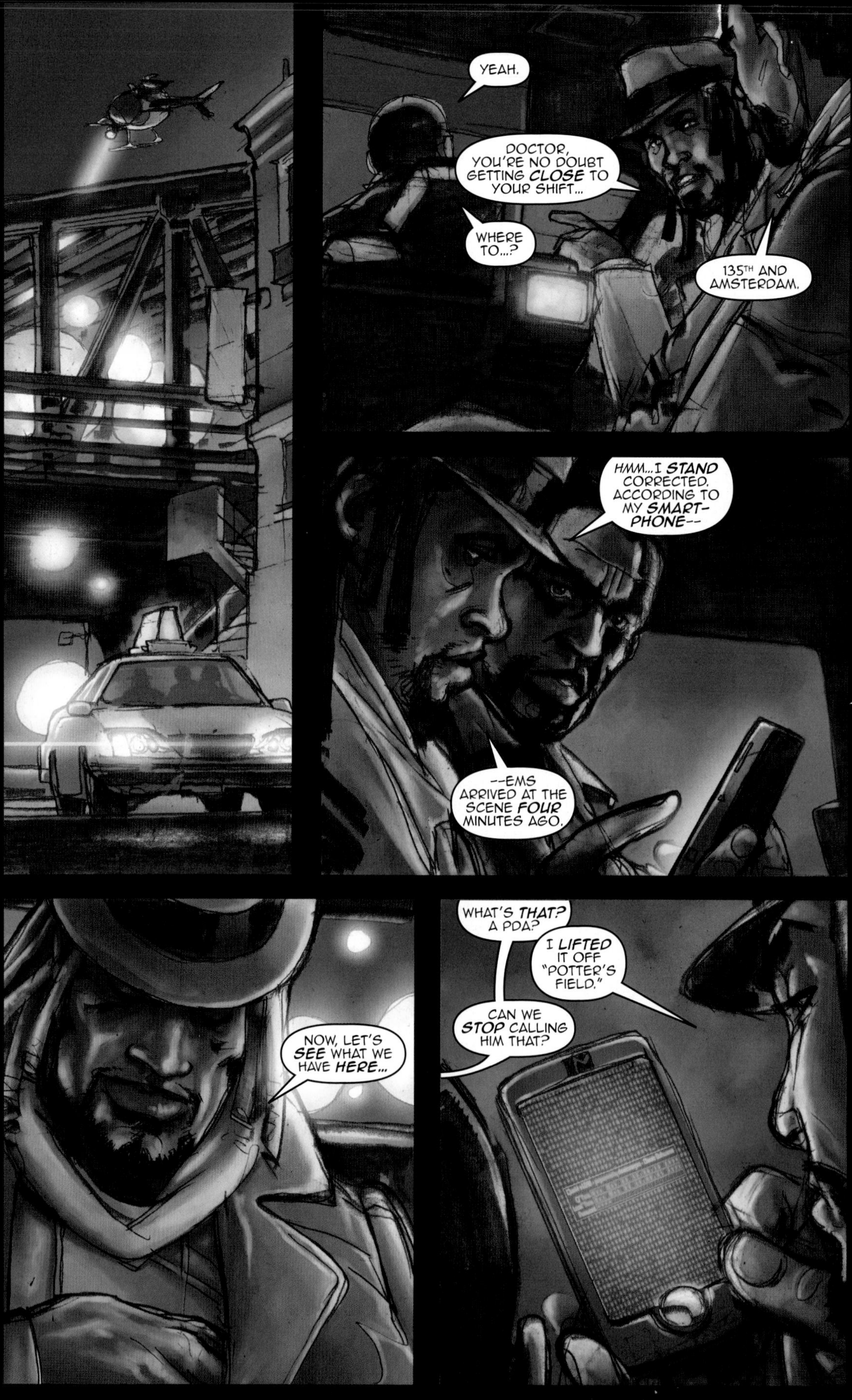
YEAH.
DOCTOR, YOU'RE NO DOUBT GETTING CLOSE TO YOUR SHIFT...
WHERE TO...?
135TH AND AMSTERDAM.
HMM...I STAND CORRECTED. ACCORDING TO MY SMART-PHONE--
--EMS ARRIVED AT THE SCENE FOUR MINUTES AGO.
NOW, LET'S SEE WHAT WE HAVE HERE...
WHAT'S THAT? A PDA?
I LIFTED IT OFF "POTTER'S FIELD."
CAN WE STOP CALLING HIM THAT?

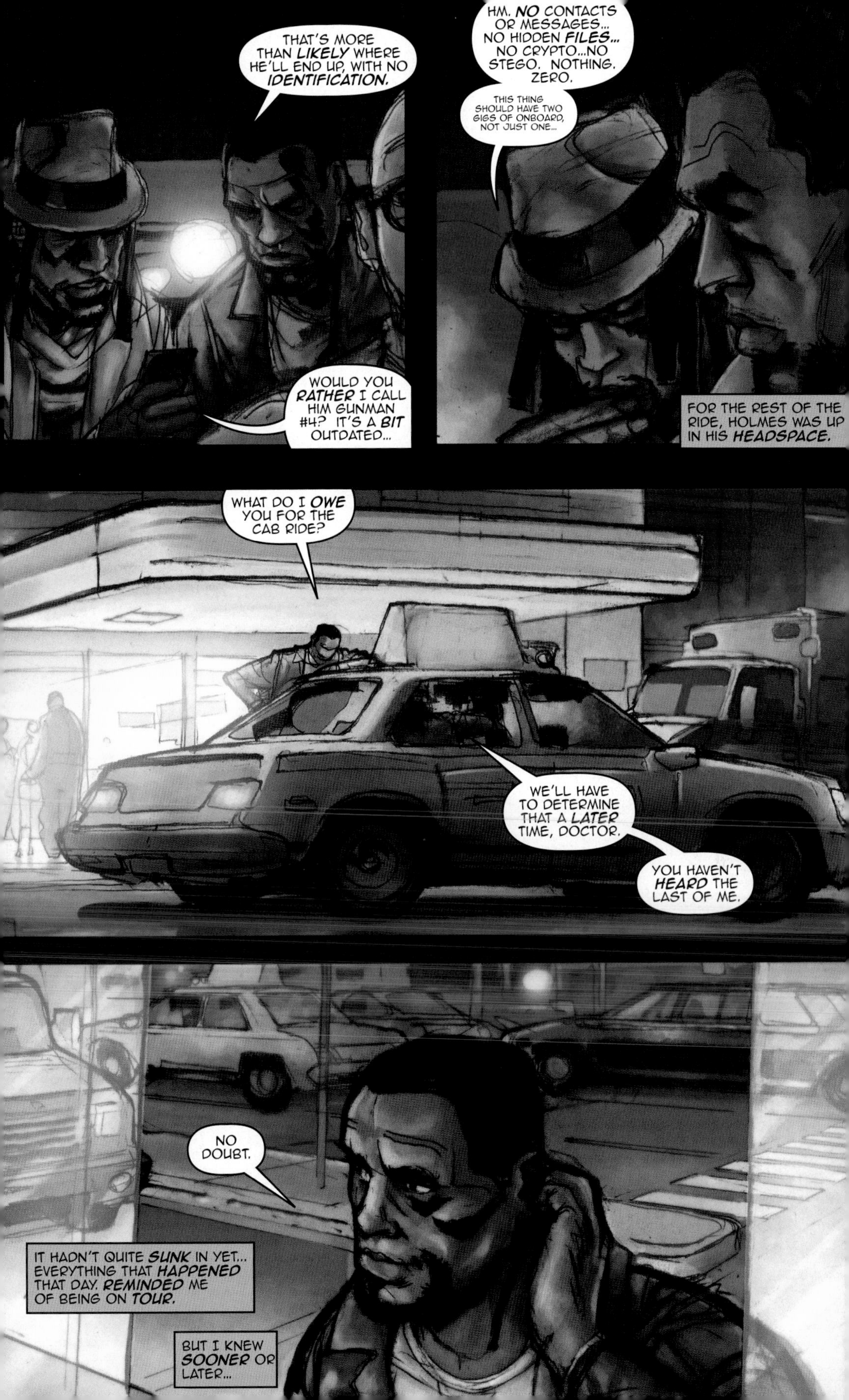
THAT'S MORE THAN LIKELY WHERE HE'LL END UP, WITH NO IDENTIFICATION.
WOULD YOU RATHER I CALL HIM GUNMAN #4? IT'S A BIT OUTDATED...
HM. NO CONTACTS OR MESSAGES... NO HIDDEN FILES... NO CRYPTO...NO STEGO. NOTHING. ZERO.
THIS THING SHOULD HAVE TWO GIGS OF ONBOARD, NOT JUST ONE...
FOR THE REST OF THE RIDE, HOLMES WAS UP IN HIS HEADSPACE.
WHAT DO I OWE YOU FOR THE CAB RIDE?
WE'LL HAVE TO DETERMINE THAT A LATER TIME, DOCTOR.
YOU HAVEN'T HEARD THE LAST OF ME.
NO DOUBT.
IT HADN'T QUITE SUNK IN YET... EVERYTHING THAT HAPPENED THAT DAY. REMINDED ME OF BEING ON TOUR.
BUT I KNEW SOONER OR LATER...

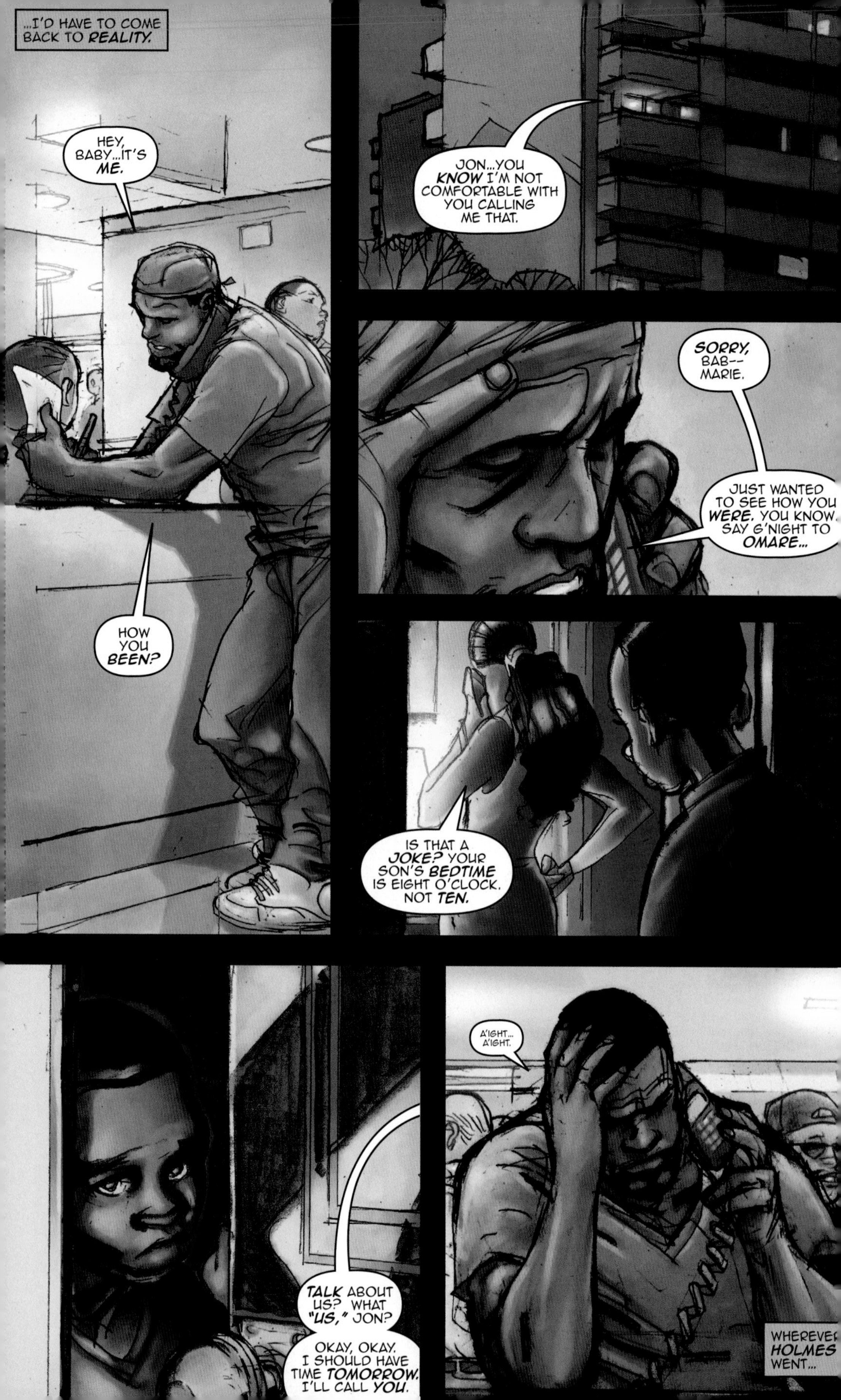

...I'D HAVE TO COME BACK TO *REALITY.*
HEY, BABY...IT'S *ME.*
HOW YOU *BEEN?*
JON...YOU *KNOW* I'M NOT COMFORTABLE WITH YOU CALLING ME THAT.
SORRY, BAB-- MARIE.
JUST WANTED TO SEE HOW YOU *WERE.* YOU KNOW. SAY G'NIGHT TO *OMARE...*
IS THAT A *JOKE?* YOUR SON'S *BEDTIME* IS EIGHT O'CLOCK. NOT *TEN.*
TALK ABOUT US? WHAT *"US,"* JON?
OKAY, OKAY. I SHOULD HAVE TIME *TOMORROW.* I'LL CALL *YOU.*
A'IGHT... A'IGHT.
WHEREVER *HOLMES* WENT...

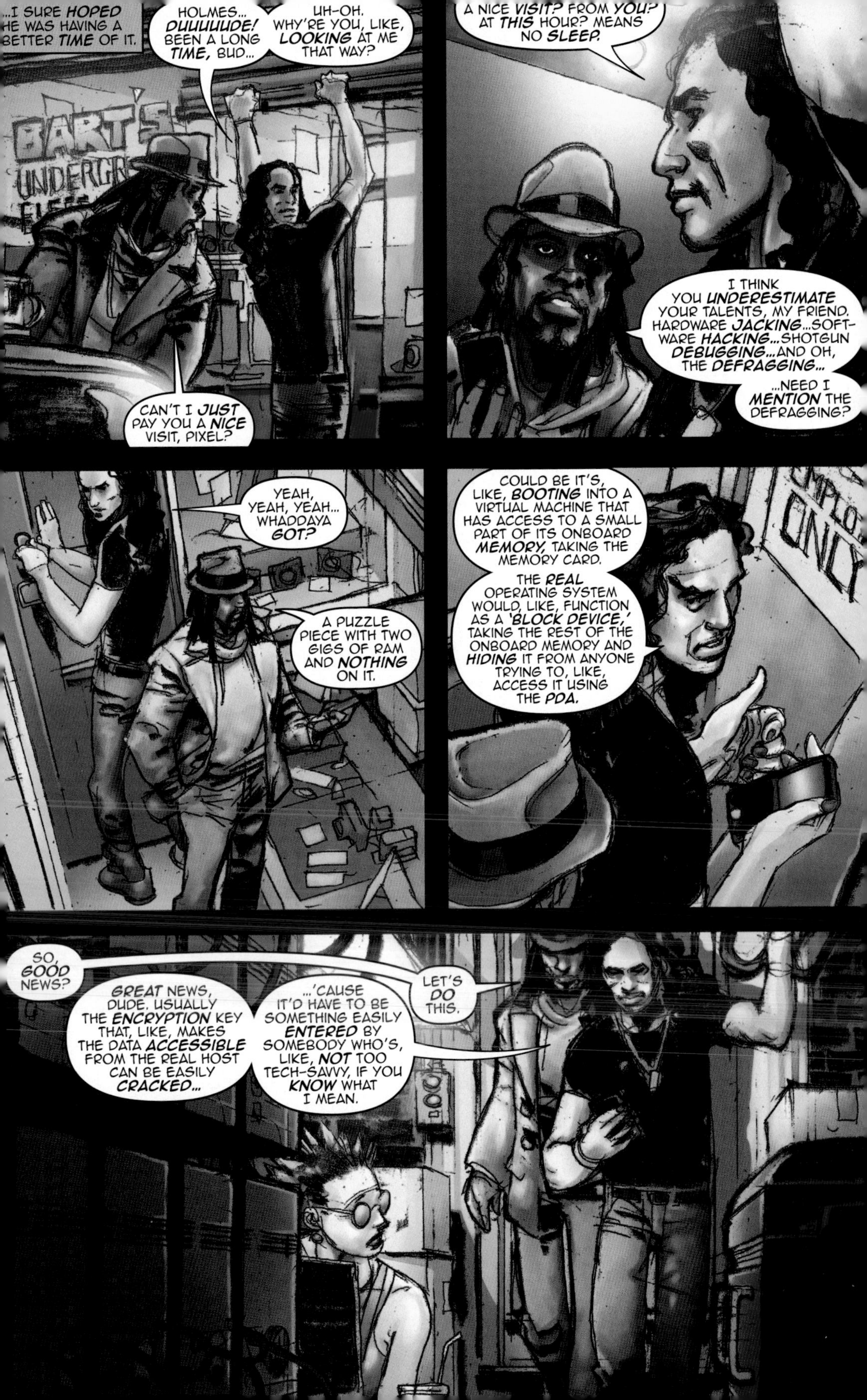
...I SURE HOPED HE WAS HAVING A BETTER TIME OF IT.
HOLMES... DUUUUUDE! BEEN A LONG TIME, BUD...
UH-OH. WHY'RE YOU, LIKE, LOOKING AT ME THAT WAY?
CAN'T I JUST PAY YOU A NICE VISIT, PIXEL?
BART'S UNDERGR
A NICE VISIT? FROM YOU? AT THIS HOUR? MEANS NO SLEEP.
I THINK YOU UNDERESTIMATE YOUR TALENTS, MY FRIEND. HARDWARE JACKING...SOFTWARE HACKING...SHOTGUN DEBUGGING...AND OH, THE DEFRAGGING...
...NEED I MENTION THE DEFRAGGING?
YEAH, YEAH, YEAH... WHADDAYA GOT?
A PUZZLE PIECE WITH TWO GIGS OF RAM AND NOTHING ON IT.
COULD BE IT'S, LIKE, BOOTING INTO A VIRTUAL MACHINE THAT HAS ACCESS TO A SMALL PART OF ITS ONBOARD MEMORY, TAKING THE MEMORY CARD.
THE REAL OPERATING SYSTEM WOULD, LIKE, FUNCTION AS A 'BLOCK DEVICE,' TAKING THE REST OF THE ONBOARD MEMORY AND HIDING IT FROM ANYONE TRYING TO, LIKE, ACCESS IT USING THE PDA.
SO, GOOD NEWS?
GREAT NEWS, DUDE. USUALLY THE ENCRYPTION KEY THAT, LIKE, MAKES THE DATA ACCESSIBLE FROM THE REAL HOST CAN BE EASILY CRACKED...
...'CAUSE IT'D HAVE TO BE SOMETHING EASILY ENTERED BY SOMEBODY WHO'S, LIKE, NOT TOO TECH-SAVVY, IF YOU KNOW WHAT I MEAN.
LET'S DO THIS.

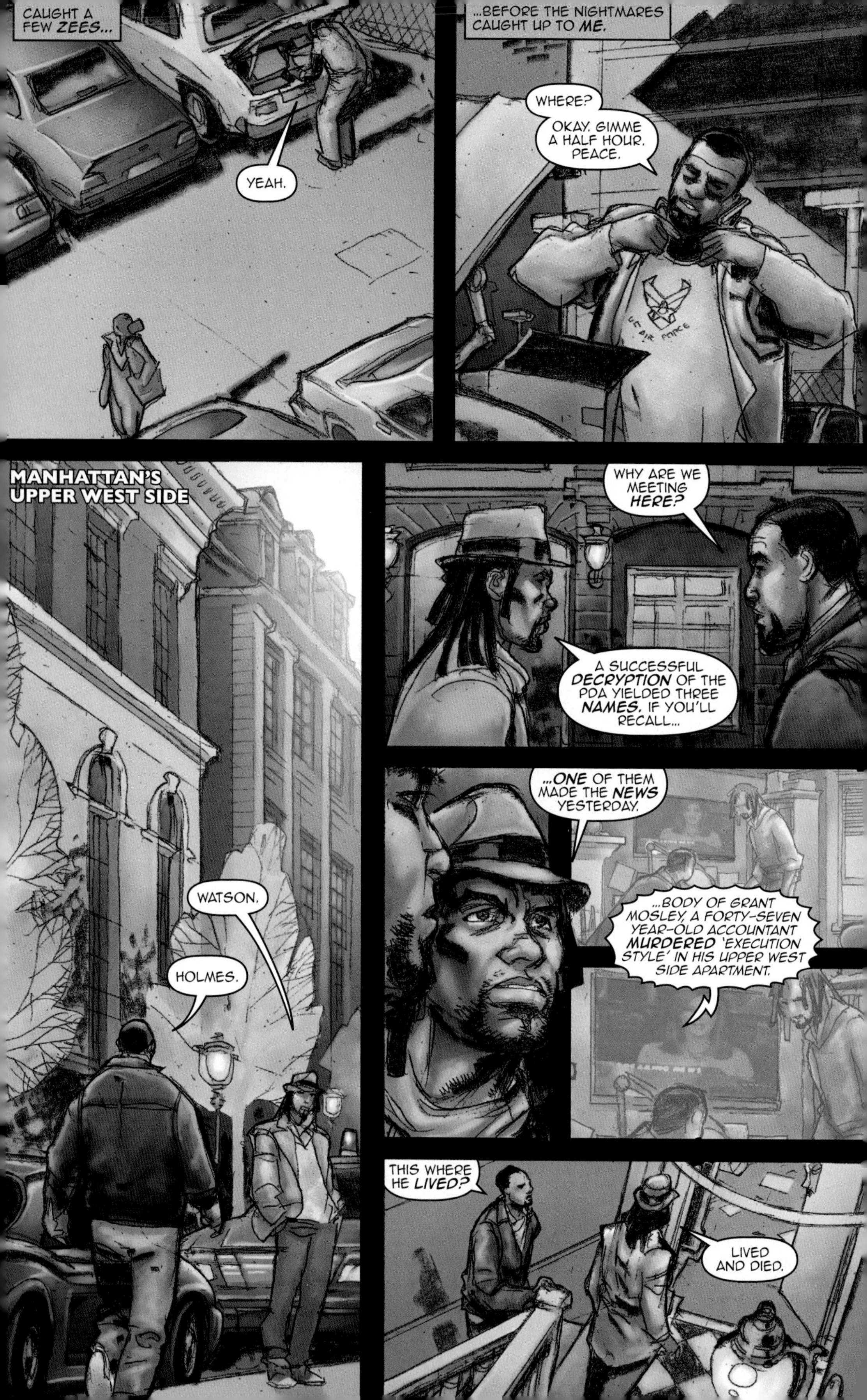
CAUGHT A FEW ZEES...
YEAH.
...BEFORE THE NIGHTMARES CAUGHT UP TO ME.
WHERE?
OKAY. GIMME A HALF HOUR. PEACE.
MANHATTAN'S UPPER WEST SIDE
WATSON.
HOLMES.
WHY ARE WE MEETING HERE?
A SUCCESSFUL DECRYPTION OF THE PDA YIELDED THREE NAMES. IF YOU'LL RECALL...
...ONE OF THEM MADE THE NEWS YESTERDAY.
...BODY OF GRANT MOSLEY, A FORTY-SEVEN YEAR-OLD ACCOUNTANT MURDERED 'EXECUTION STYLE' IN HIS UPPER WEST SIDE APARTMENT.
THIS WHERE HE LIVED?
LIVED AND DIED.

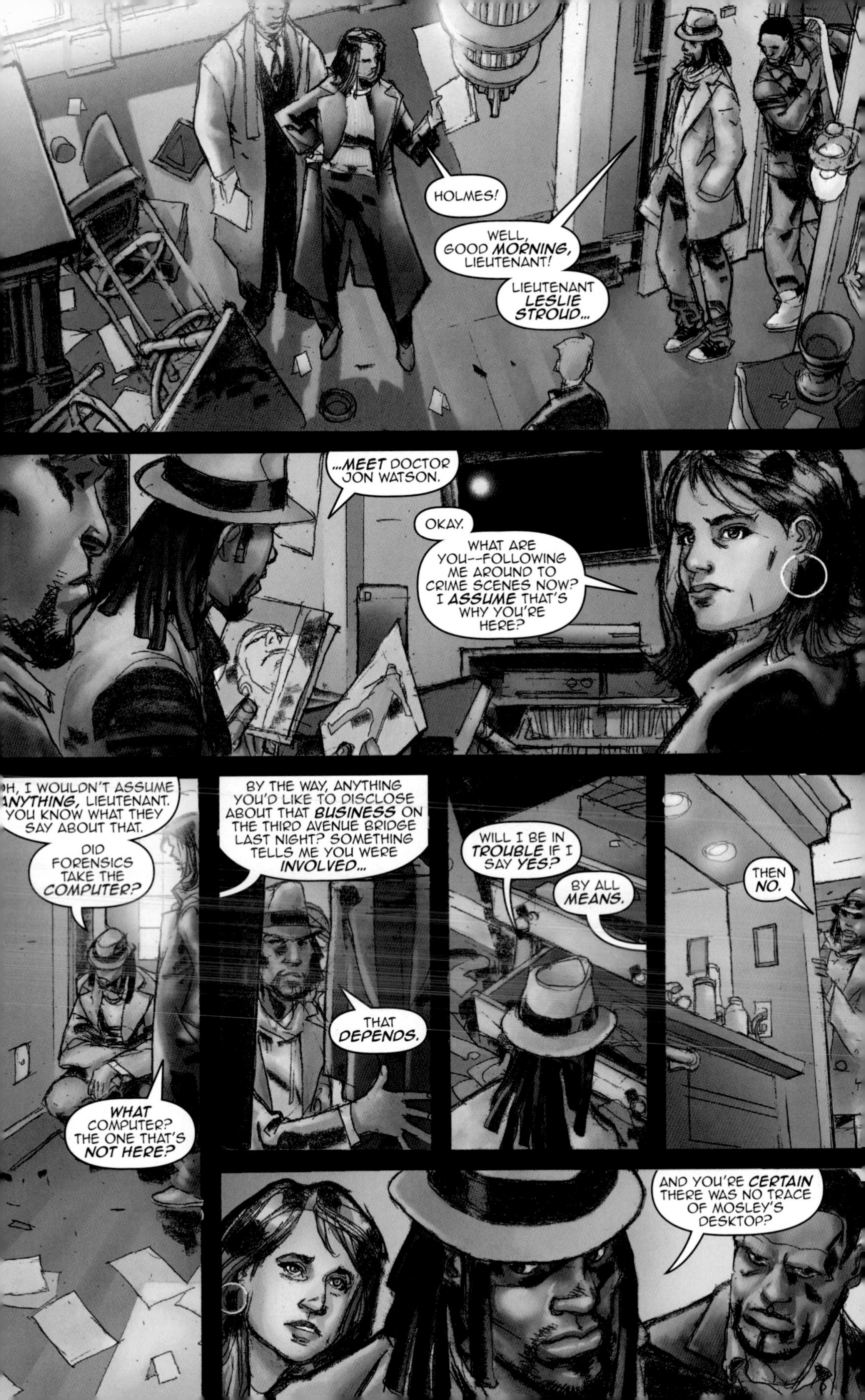
HOLMES!
WELL, GOOD MORNING, LIEUTENANT!
LIEUTENANT LESLIE STROUD...
...MEET DOCTOR JON WATSON.
OKAY.
WHAT ARE YOU--FOLLOWING ME AROUND TO CRIME SCENES NOW? I ASSUME THAT'S WHY YOU'RE HERE?
OH, I WOULDN'T ASSUME ANYTHING, LIEUTENANT. YOU KNOW WHAT THEY SAY ABOUT THAT.
DID FORENSICS TAKE THE COMPUTER?
WHAT COMPUTER? THE ONE THAT'S NOT HERE?
BY THE WAY, ANYTHING YOU'D LIKE TO DISCLOSE ABOUT THAT BUSINESS ON THE THIRD AVENUE BRIDGE LAST NIGHT? SOMETHING TELLS ME YOU WERE INVOLVED...
THAT DEPENDS.
WILL I BE IN TROUBLE IF I SAY YES?
BY ALL MEANS.
THEN NO.
AND YOU'RE CERTAIN THERE WAS NO TRACE OF MOSLEY'S DESKTOP?

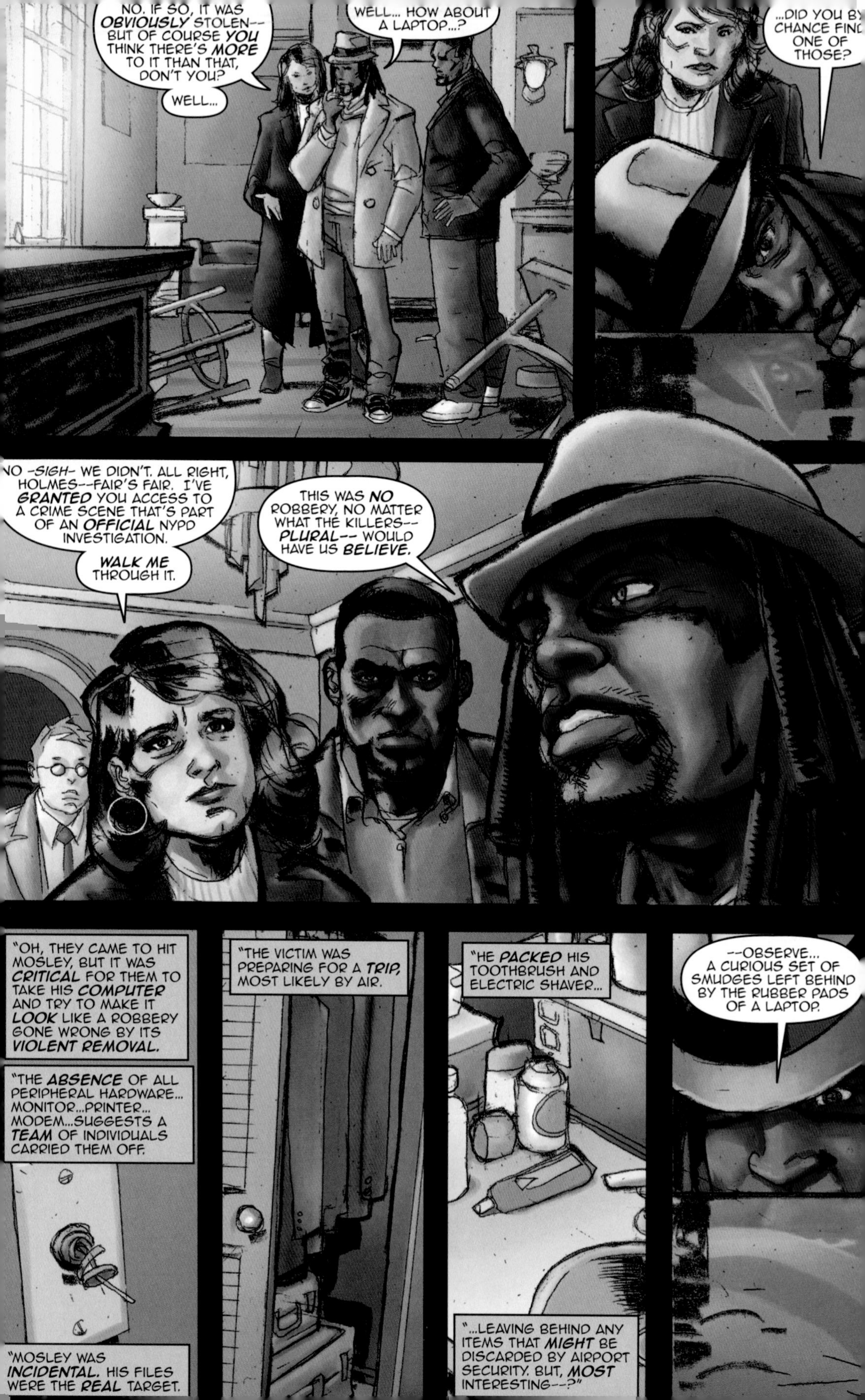
NO. IF SO, IT WAS OBVIOUSLY STOLEN-- BUT OF COURSE YOU THINK THERE'S MORE TO IT THAN THAT, DON'T YOU?
WELL...
WELL... HOW ABOUT A LAPTOP...?
...DID YOU BY CHANCE FIND ONE OF THOSE?
NO -SIGH- WE DIDN'T. ALL RIGHT, HOLMES--FAIR'S FAIR. I'VE GRANTED YOU ACCESS TO A CRIME SCENE THAT'S PART OF AN OFFICIAL NYPD INVESTIGATION.
WALK ME THROUGH IT.
THIS WAS NO ROBBERY, NO MATTER WHAT THE KILLERS-- PLURAL-- WOULD HAVE US BELIEVE.
"OH, THEY CAME TO HIT MOSLEY, BUT IT WAS CRITICAL FOR THEM TO TAKE HIS COMPUTER AND TRY TO MAKE IT LOOK LIKE A ROBBERY GONE WRONG BY ITS VIOLENT REMOVAL.
"THE ABSENCE OF ALL PERIPHERAL HARDWARE... MONITOR...PRINTER... MODEM...SUGGESTS A TEAM OF INDIVIDUALS CARRIED THEM OFF.
"MOSLEY WAS INCIDENTAL. HIS FILES WERE THE REAL TARGET.
"THE VICTIM WAS PREPARING FOR A TRIP, MOST LIKELY BY AIR.
"HE PACKED HIS TOOTHBRUSH AND ELECTRIC SHAVER...
"...LEAVING BEHIND ANY ITEMS THAT MIGHT BE DISCARDED BY AIRPORT SECURITY. BUT, MOST INTERESTING--?"
--OBSERVE... A CURIOUS SET OF SMUDGES LEFT BEHIND BY THE RUBBER PADS OF A LAPTOP.

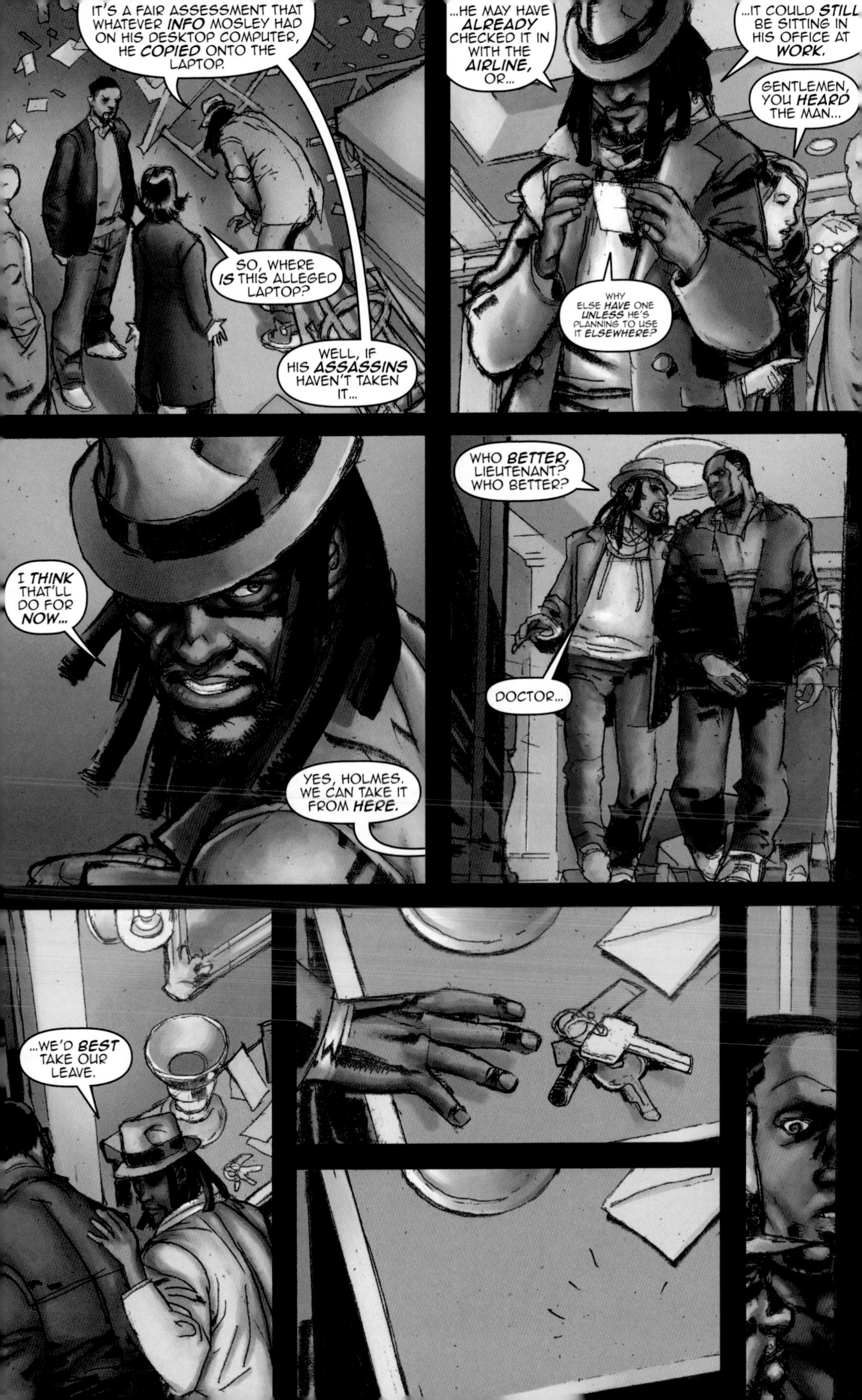
IT'S A FAIR ASSESSMENT THAT WHATEVER INFO MOSLEY HAD ON HIS DESKTOP COMPUTER, HE COPIED ONTO THE LAPTOP.
SO, WHERE IS THIS ALLEGED LAPTOP?
WELL, IF HIS ASSASSINS HAVEN'T TAKEN IT...
...HE MAY HAVE ALREADY CHECKED IT IN WITH THE AIRLINE, OR...
WHY ELSE HAVE ONE UNLESS HE'S PLANNING TO USE IT ELSEWHERE?
...IT COULD STILL BE SITTING IN HIS OFFICE AT WORK.
GENTLEMEN, YOU HEARD THE MAN...
I THINK THAT'LL DO FOR NOW...
YES, HOLMES. WE CAN TAKE IT FROM HERE.
WHO BETTER, LIEUTENANT? WHO BETTER?
DOCTOR...
...WE'D BEST TAKE OUR LEAVE.

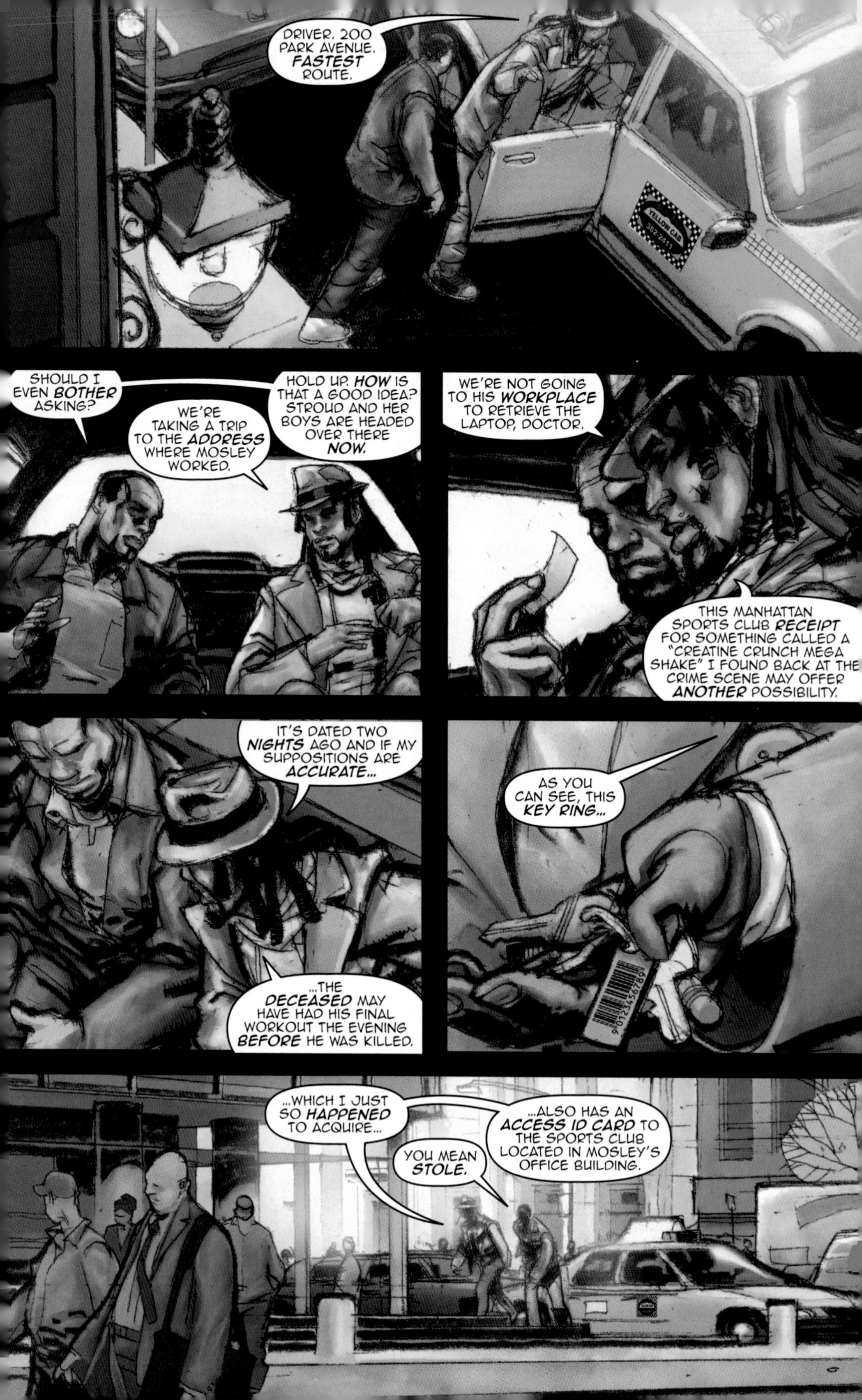
DRIVER. 200 PARK AVENUE. FASTEST ROUTE.
SHOULD I EVEN BOTHER ASKING?
WE'RE TAKING A TRIP TO THE ADDRESS WHERE MOSLEY WORKED.
HOLD UP. HOW IS THAT A GOOD IDEA? STROUD AND HER BOYS ARE HEADED OVER THERE NOW.
WE'RE NOT GOING TO HIS WORKPLACE TO RETRIEVE THE LAPTOP, DOCTOR.
THIS MANHATTAN SPORTS CLUB RECEIPT FOR SOMETHING CALLED A "CREATINE CRUNCH MEGA SHAKE" I FOUND BACK AT THE CRIME SCENE MAY OFFER ANOTHER POSSIBILITY.
IT'S DATED TWO NIGHTS AGO AND IF MY SUPPOSITIONS ARE ACCURATE...
...THE DECEASED MAY HAVE HAD HIS FINAL WORKOUT THE EVENING BEFORE HE WAS KILLED.
AS YOU CAN SEE, THIS KEY RING...
...WHICH I JUST SO HAPPENED TO ACQUIRE...
YOU MEAN STOLE.
...ALSO HAS AN ACCESS ID CARD TO THE SPORTS CLUB LOCATED IN MOSLEY'S OFFICE BUILDING.

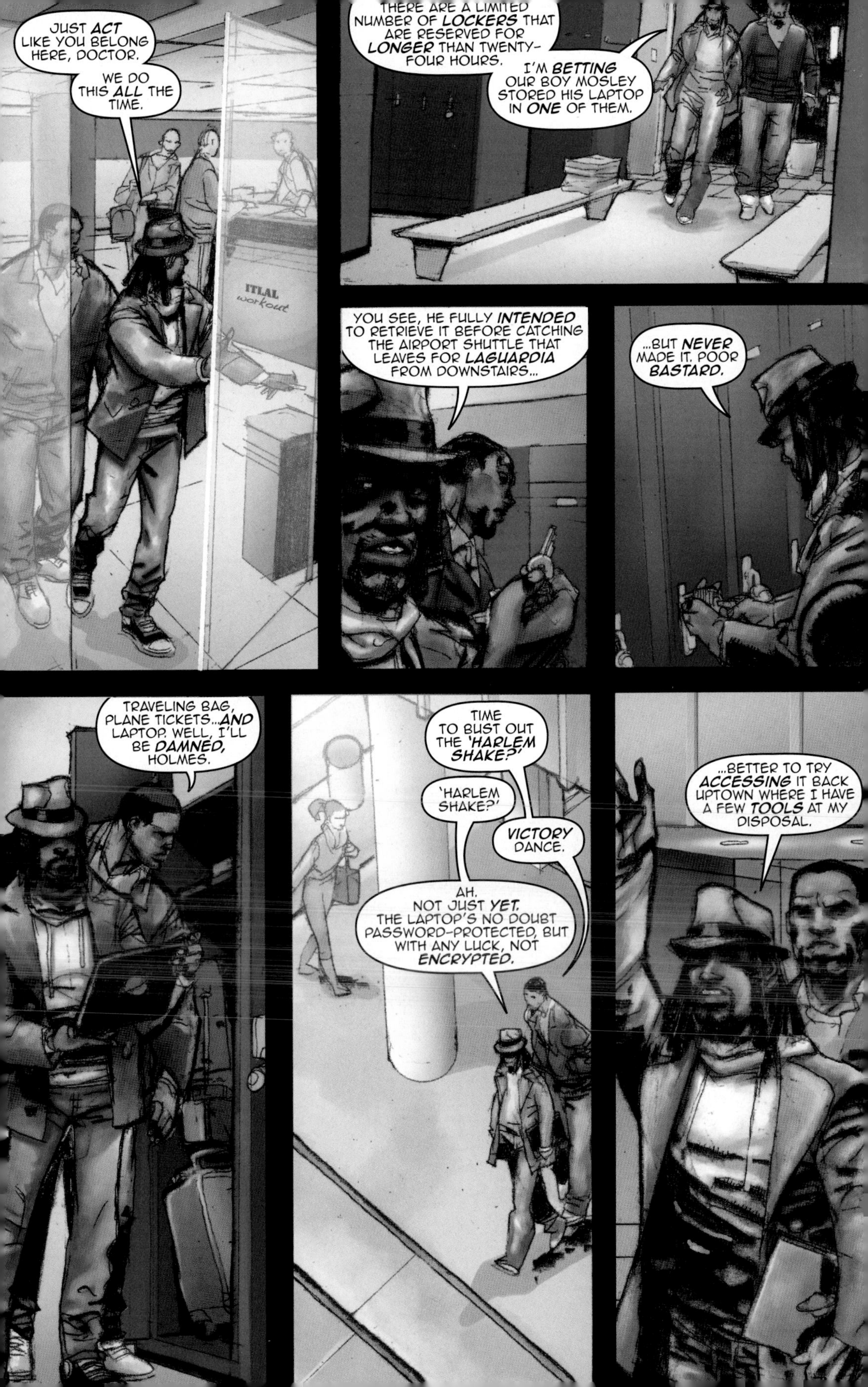
JUST **ACT** LIKE YOU BELONG HERE, DOCTOR.
WE DO THIS **ALL** THE TIME.
ITLAL workout
THERE ARE A LIMITED NUMBER OF **LOCKERS** THAT ARE RESERVED FOR **LONGER** THAN TWENTY-FOUR HOURS.
I'M **BETTING** OUR BOY MOSLEY STORED HIS LAPTOP IN **ONE** OF THEM.
YOU SEE, HE FULLY **INTENDED** TO RETRIEVE IT BEFORE CATCHING THE AIRPORT SHUTTLE THAT LEAVES FOR **LAGUARDIA** FROM DOWNSTAIRS...
...BUT **NEVER** MADE IT. POOR **BASTARD.**
TRAVELING BAG, PLANE TICKETS...**AND** LAPTOP. WELL, I'LL BE **DAMNED,** HOLMES.
TIME TO BUST OUT THE **'HARLEM SHAKE?'**
'HARLEM SHAKE?'
VICTORY DANCE.
AH. NOT JUST **YET.** THE LAPTOP'S NO DOUBT PASSWORD-PROTECTED, BUT WITH ANY LUCK, NOT **ENCRYPTED.**
...BETTER TO TRY **ACCESSING** IT BACK UPTOWN WHERE I HAVE A FEW **TOOLS** AT MY DISPOSAL.

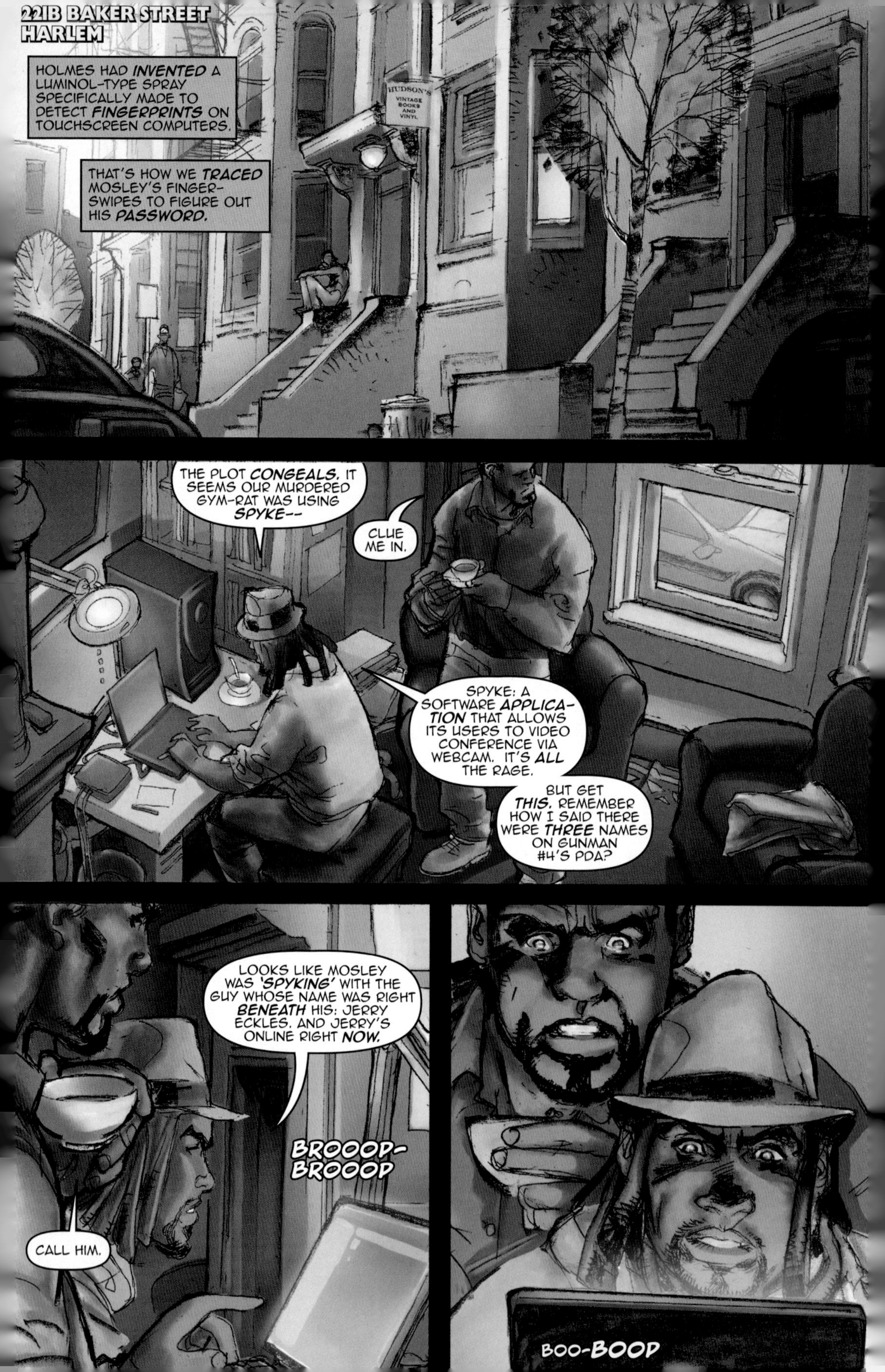
22IB BAKER STREET
HARLEM
HOLMES HAD INVENTED A LUMINOL-TYPE SPRAY SPECIFICALLY MADE TO DETECT FINGERPRINTS ON TOUCHSCREEN COMPUTERS.
THAT'S HOW WE TRACED MOSLEY'S FINGER-SWIPES TO FIGURE OUT HIS PASSWORD.
HUDSON'S VINTAGE BOOKS AND VINYL
THE PLOT CONGEALS. IT SEEMS OUR MURDERED GYM-RAT WAS USING SPYKE--
CLUE ME IN.
SPYKE: A SOFTWARE APPLICATION THAT ALLOWS ITS USERS TO VIDEO CONFERENCE VIA WEBCAM. IT'S ALL THE RAGE.
BUT GET THIS. REMEMBER HOW I SAID THERE WERE THREE NAMES ON GUNMAN #4'S PDA?
LOOKS LIKE MOSLEY WAS 'SPYKING' WITH THE GUY WHOSE NAME WAS RIGHT BENEATH HIS: JERRY ECKLES. AND JERRY'S ONLINE RIGHT NOW.
BROOOP-BROOOP
CALL HIM.
BOO-BOOD

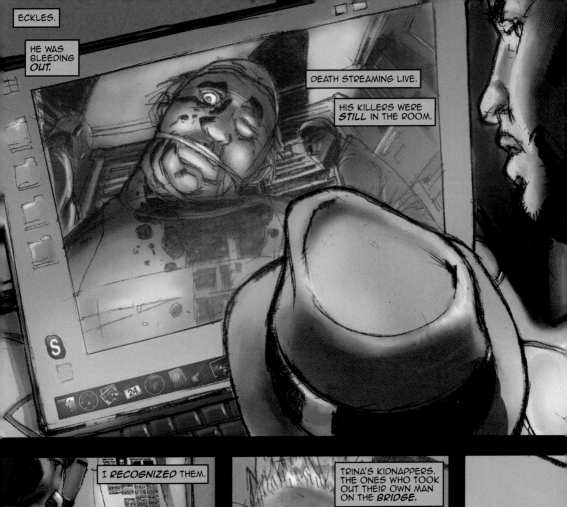

ECKLES.

HE WAS BLEEDING **OUT.**

DEATH STREAMING LIVE.

HIS KILLERS WERE **STILL** IN THE ROOM.

I **RECOGNIZED** THEM.

TRINA'S KIDNAPPERS. THE ONES WHO TOOK OUT THEIR OWN MAN ON THE **BRIDGE.**

GAME ON.

I DON'T **THINK** SO.

THE GUNMEN MUST HAVE **UPLOADED** SOME TYPE OF MALWARE TO MOSLEY'S LAPTOP AFTER **ANSWERING** OUR CALL!

IT WON'T LET ME TURN IT **OFF.**

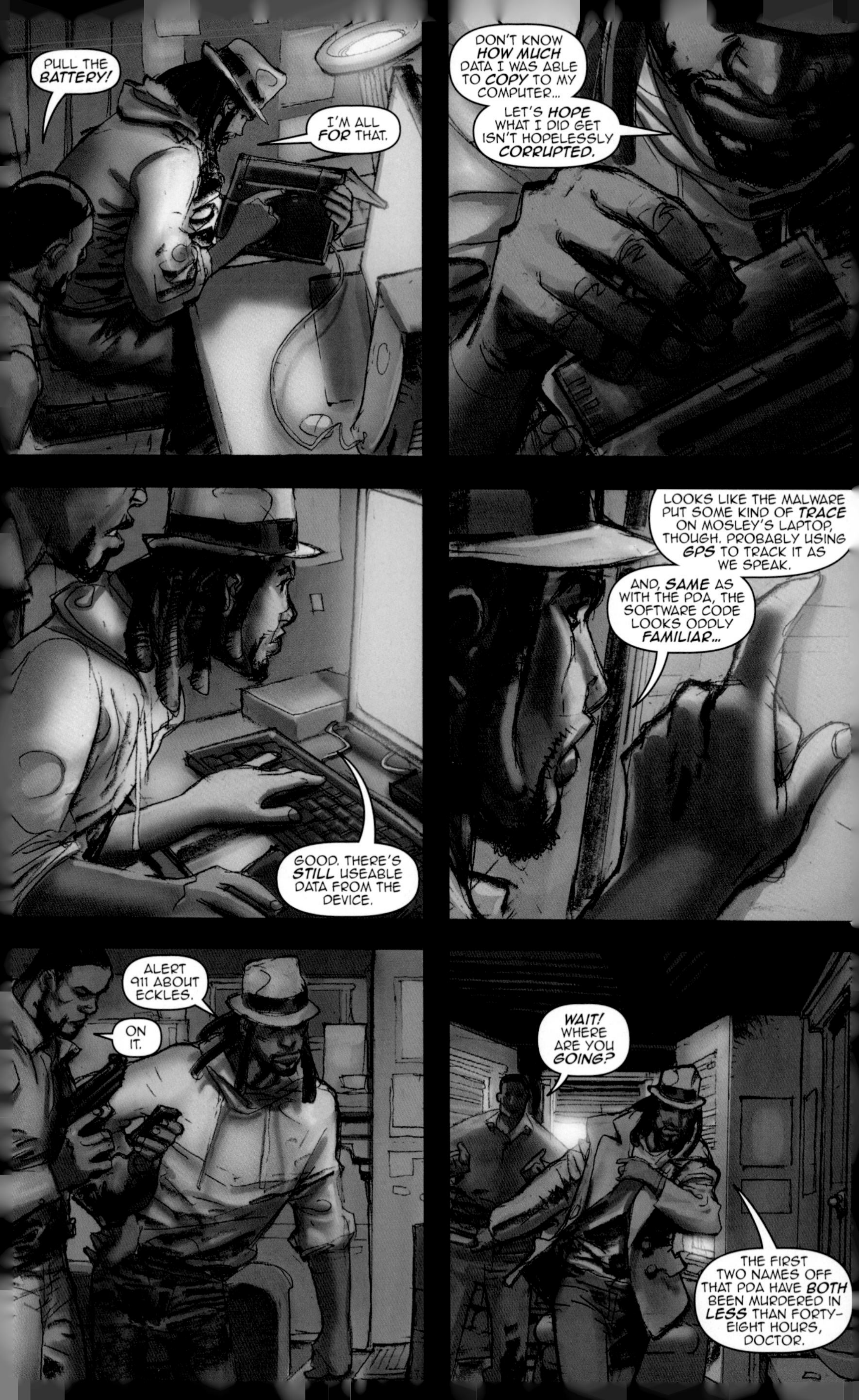
PULL THE BATTERY!
I'M ALL FOR THAT.
DON'T KNOW HOW MUCH DATA I WAS ABLE TO COPY TO MY COMPUTER...
LET'S HOPE WHAT I DID GET ISN'T HOPELESSLY CORRUPTED.
GOOD. THERE'S STILL USEABLE DATA FROM THE DEVICE.
LOOKS LIKE THE MALWARE PUT SOME KIND OF TRACE ON MOSLEY'S LAPTOP, THOUGH. PROBABLY USING GPS TO TRACK IT AS WE SPEAK.
AND, SAME AS WITH THE PDA, THE SOFTWARE CODE LOOKS ODDLY FAMILIAR...
ALERT 911 ABOUT ECKLES.
ON IT.
WAIT! WHERE ARE YOU GOING?
THE FIRST TWO NAMES OFF THAT PDA HAVE BOTH BEEN MURDERED IN LESS THAN FORTY-EIGHT HOURS, DOCTOR.

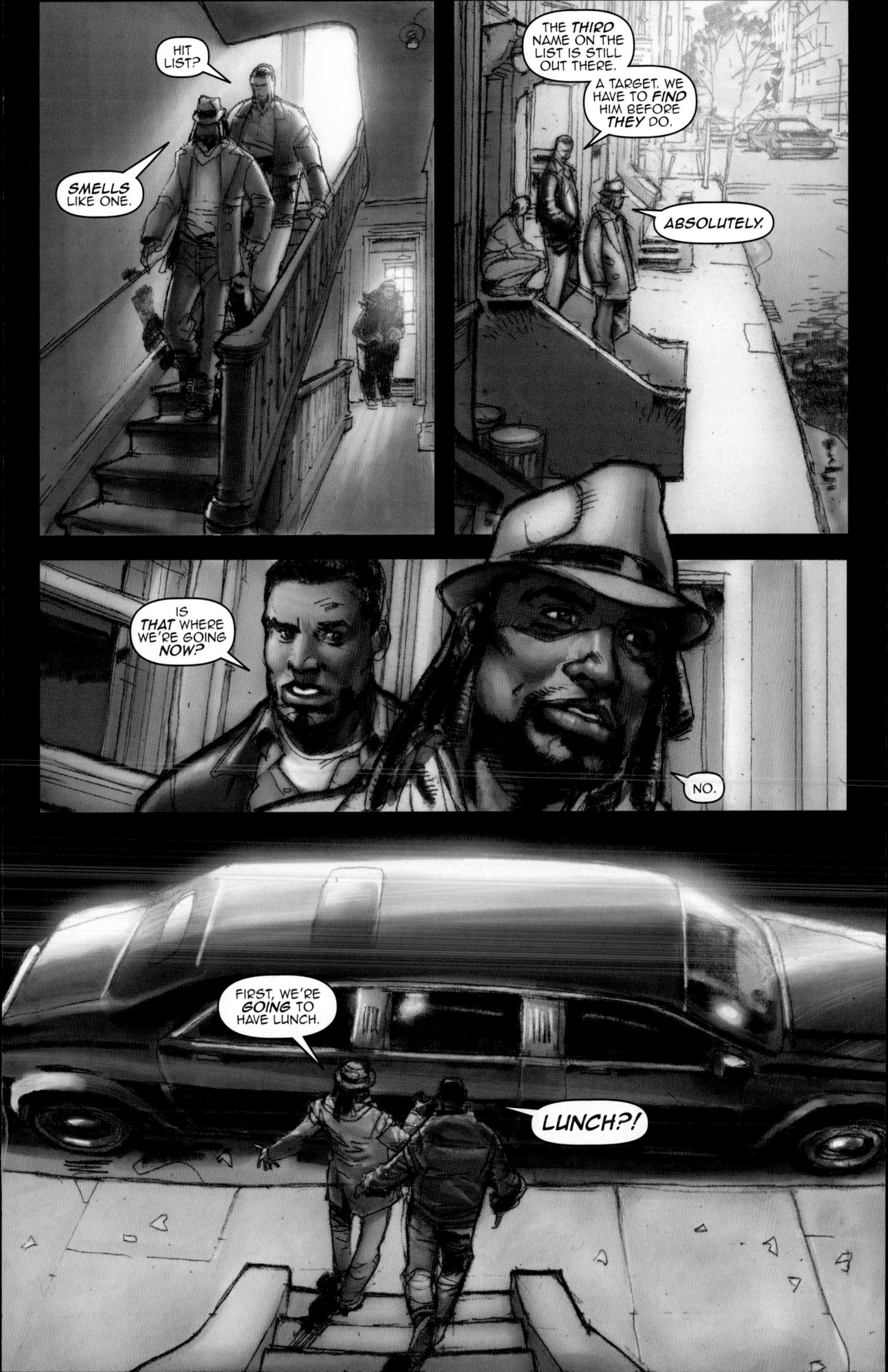
HIT LIST?
SMELLS LIKE ONE.
THE THIRD NAME ON THE LIST IS STILL OUT THERE.
A TARGET. WE HAVE TO FIND HIM BEFORE THEY DO.
ABSOLUTELY.
IS THAT WHERE WE'RE GOING NOW?
NO.
FIRST, WE'RE GOING TO HAVE LUNCH.
LUNCH?!

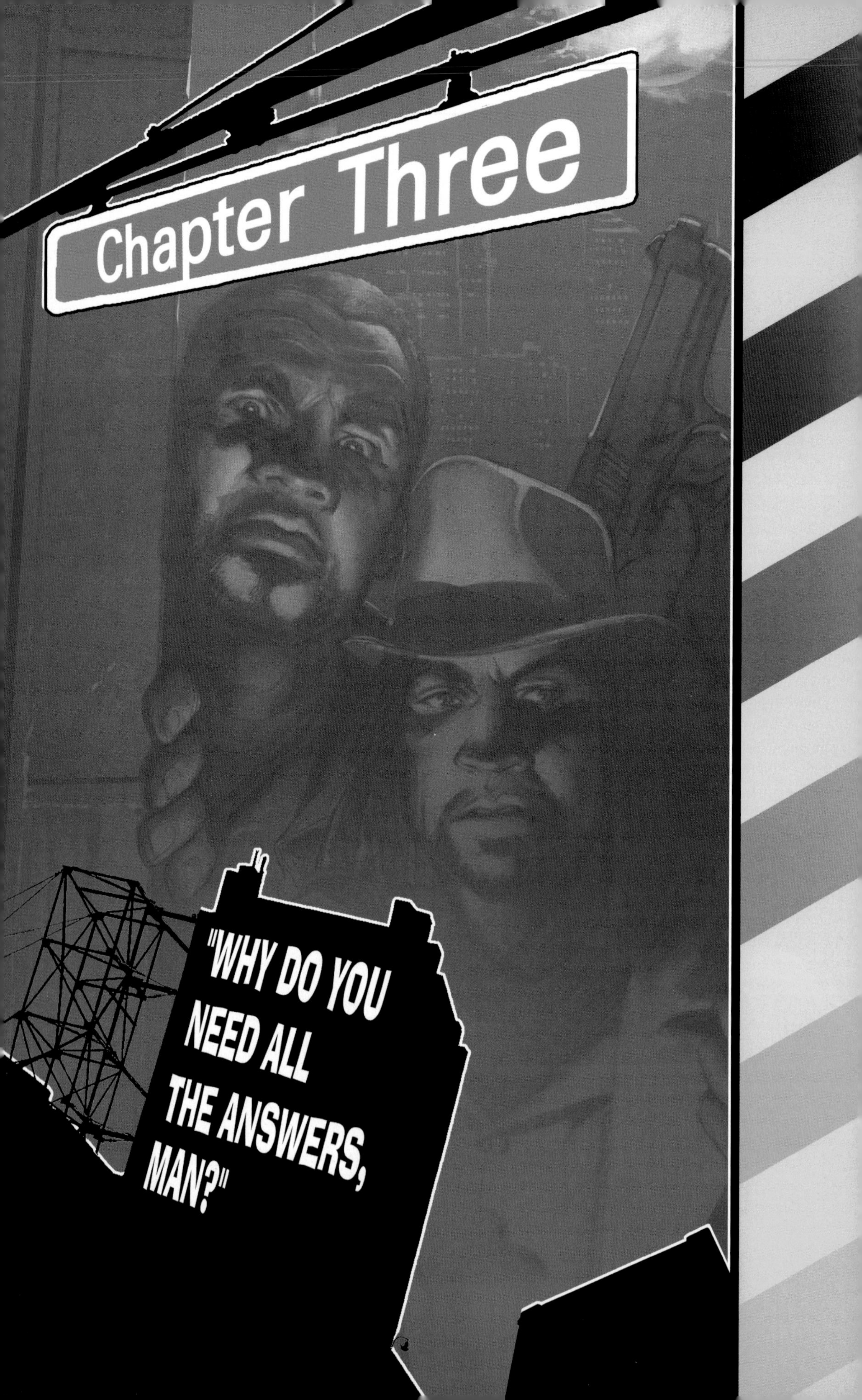
Chapter Three
"WHY DO YOU NEED ALL THE ANSWERS, MAN?"

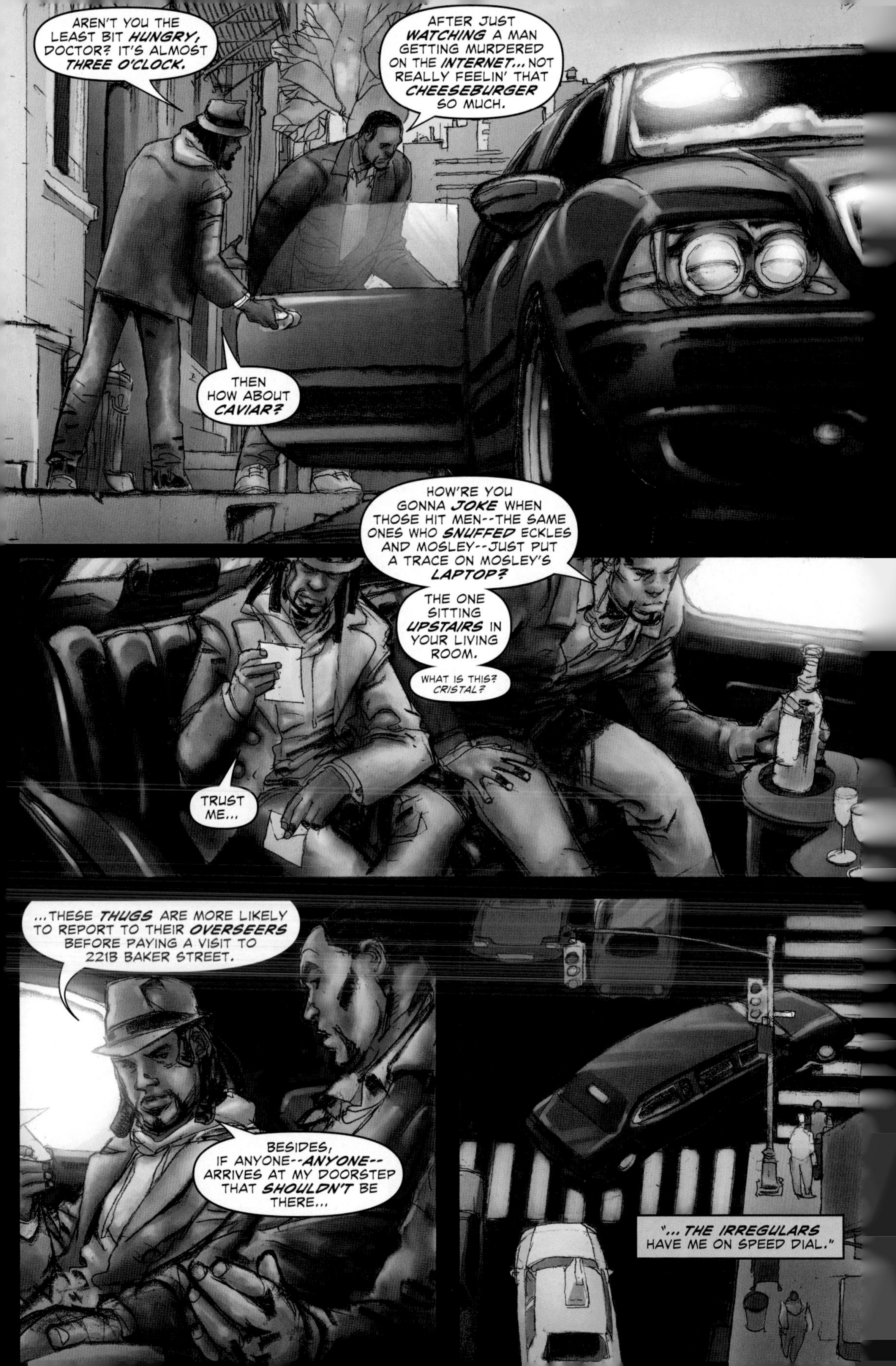
AREN'T YOU THE LEAST BIT HUNGRY, DOCTOR? IT'S ALMOST THREE O'CLOCK.
AFTER JUST WATCHING A MAN GETTING MURDERED ON THE INTERNET... NOT REALLY FEELIN' THAT CHEESEBURGER SO MUCH.
THEN HOW ABOUT CAVIAR?
HOW'RE YOU GONNA JOKE WHEN THOSE HIT MEN--THE SAME ONES WHO SNUFFED ECKLES AND MOSLEY--JUST PUT A TRACE ON MOSLEY'S LAPTOP?
THE ONE SITTING UPSTAIRS IN YOUR LIVING ROOM.
WHAT IS THIS? CRISTAL?
TRUST ME...
...THESE THUGS ARE MORE LIKELY TO REPORT TO THEIR OVERSEERS BEFORE PAYING A VISIT TO 221B BAKER STREET.
BESIDES, IF ANYONE--ANYONE--ARRIVES AT MY DOORSTEP THAT SHOULDN'T BE THERE...
"...THE IRREGULARS HAVE ME ON SPEED DIAL."

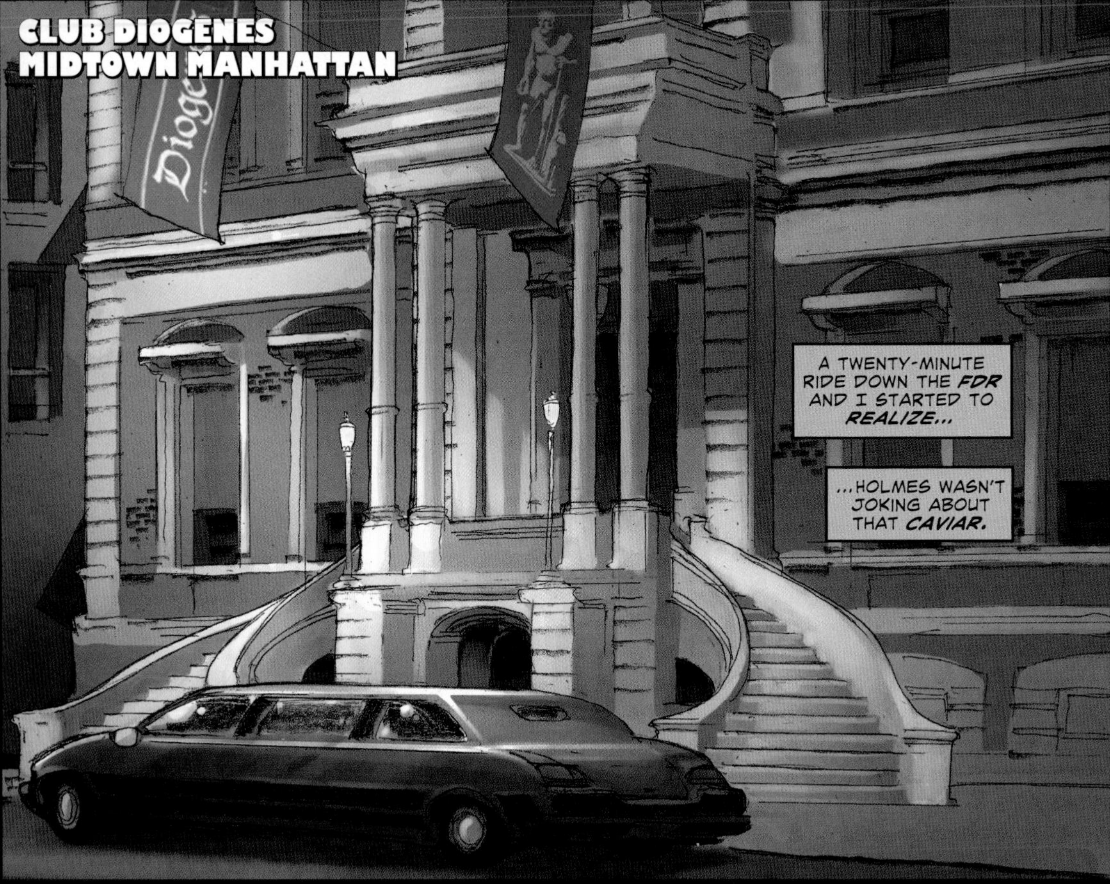
CLUB DIOGENES
MIDTOWN MANHATTAN
A TWENTY-MINUTE RIDE DOWN THE FDR AND I STARTED TO REALIZE...
...HOLMES WASN'T JOKING ABOUT THAT CAVIAR.

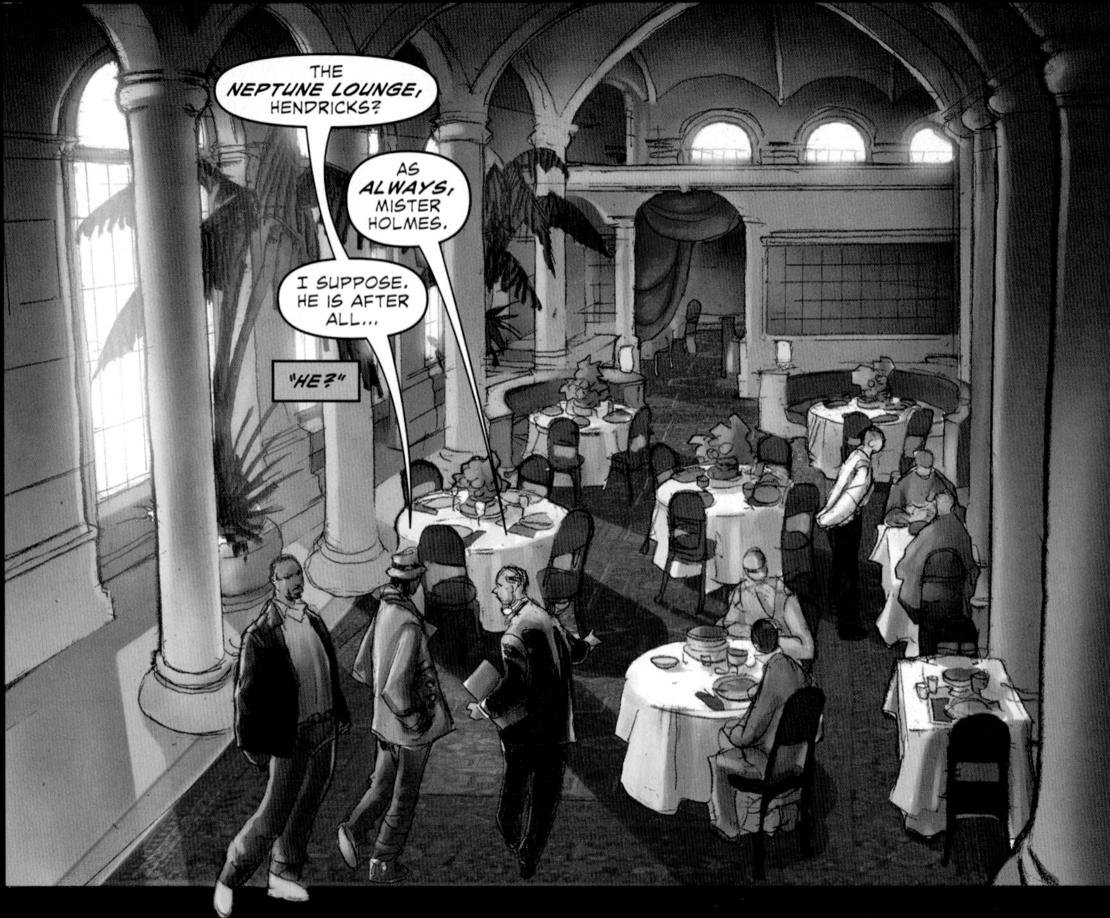
THE NEPTUNE LOUNGE, HENDRICKS?
AS ALWAYS, MISTER HOLMES.
I SUPPOSE. HE IS AFTER ALL...
"HE?"

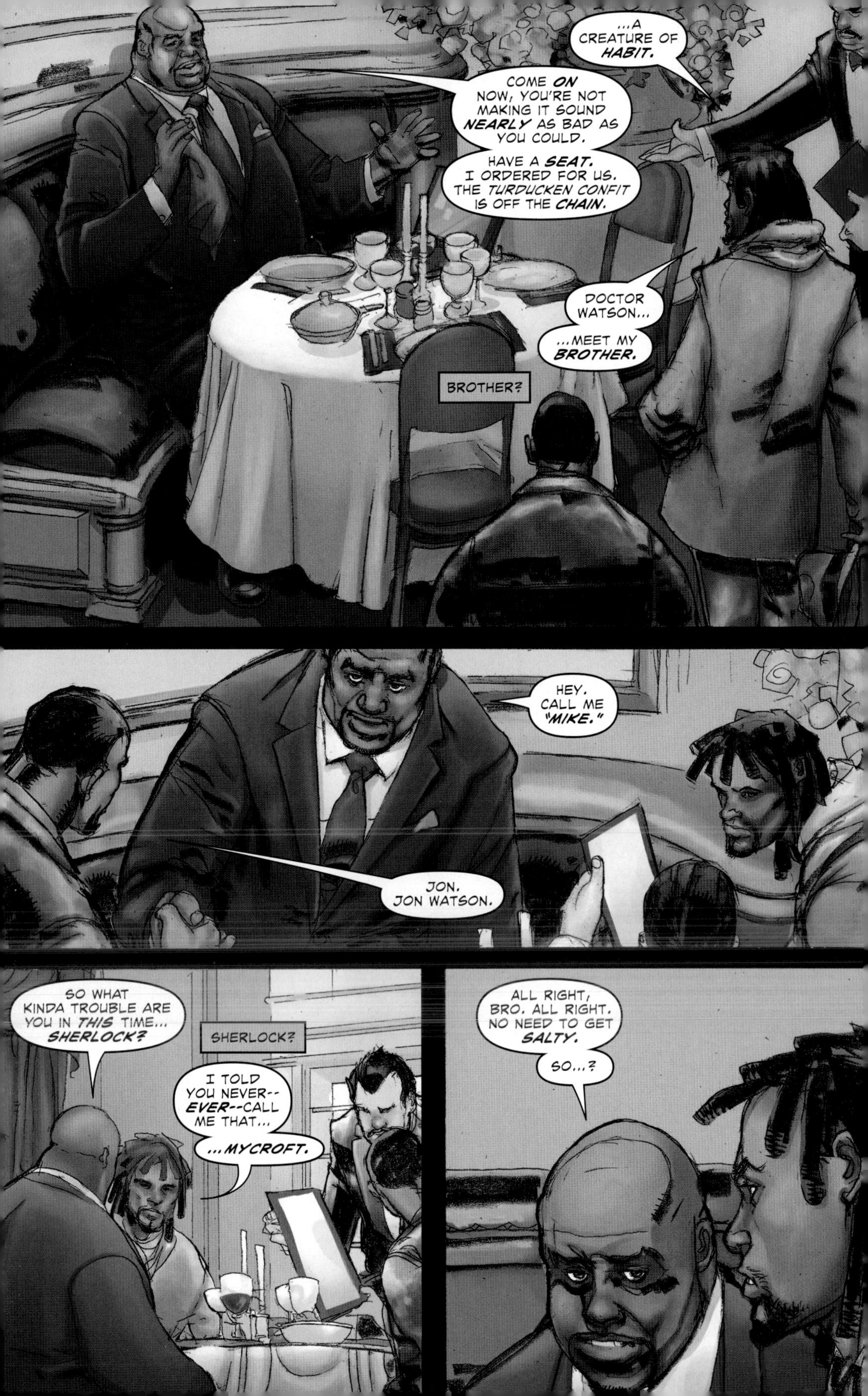
...A CREATURE OF HABIT.
COME ON NOW, YOU'RE NOT MAKING IT SOUND NEARLY AS BAD AS YOU COULD.
HAVE A SEAT. I ORDERED FOR US. THE TURDUCKEN CONFIT IS OFF THE CHAIN.
DOCTOR WATSON...
...MEET MY BROTHER.
BROTHER?
HEY. CALL ME "MIKE."
JON. JON WATSON.
SO WHAT KINDA TROUBLE ARE YOU IN THIS TIME... SHERLOCK?
SHERLOCK?
I TOLD YOU NEVER--EVER--CALL ME THAT...
...MYCROFT.
ALL RIGHT, BRO. ALL RIGHT. NO NEED TO GET SALTY.
SO...?

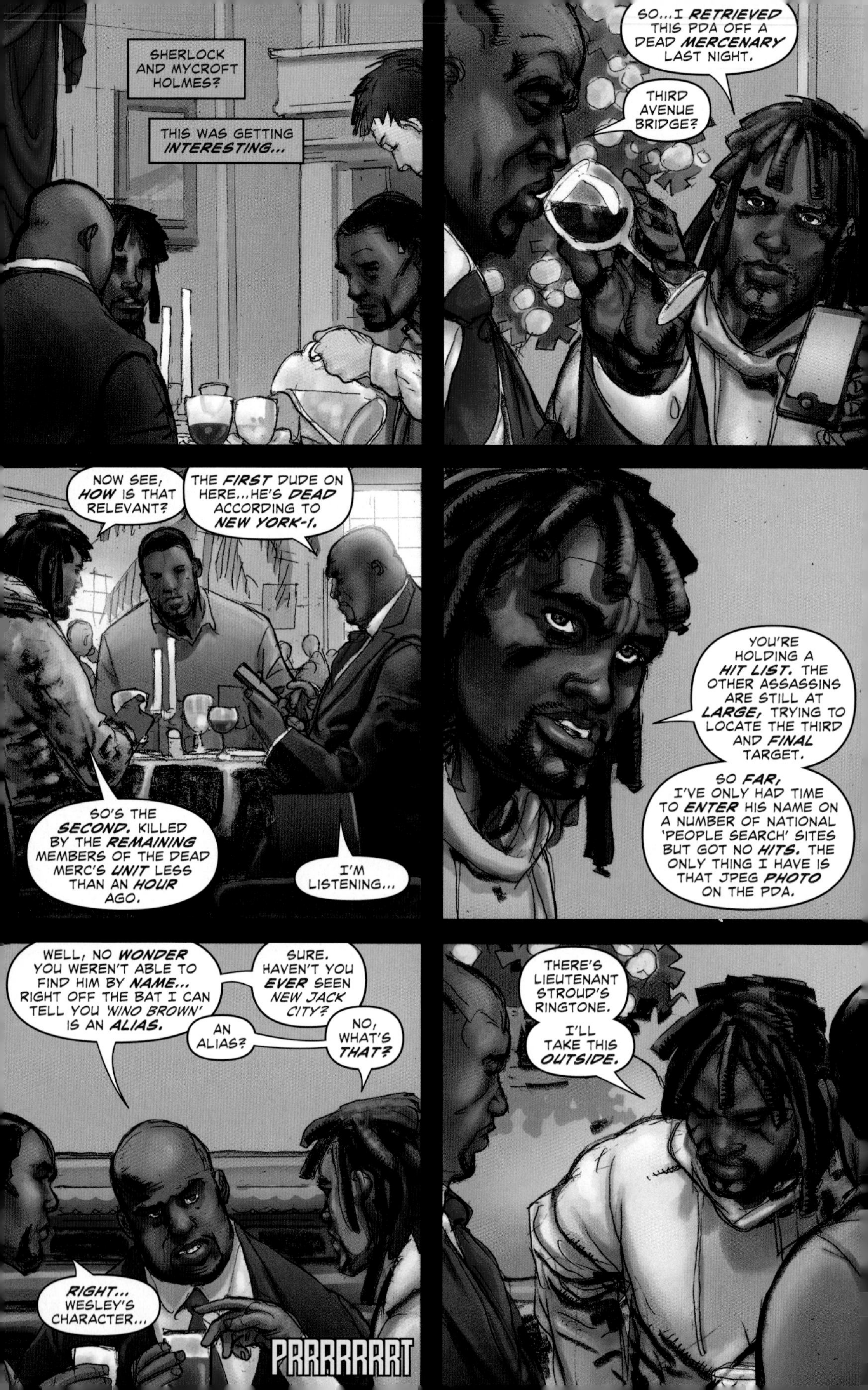
SHERLOCK AND MYCROFT HOLMES?
THIS WAS GETTING INTERESTING...
SO...I RETRIEVED THIS PDA OFF A DEAD MERCENARY LAST NIGHT.
THIRD AVENUE BRIDGE?
NOW SEE, HOW IS THAT RELEVANT?
THE FIRST DUDE ON HERE...HE'S DEAD ACCORDING TO NEW YORK-1.
SO'S THE SECOND. KILLED BY THE REMAINING MEMBERS OF THE DEAD MERC'S UNIT LESS THAN AN HOUR AGO.
I'M LISTENING...
YOU'RE HOLDING A HIT LIST. THE OTHER ASSASSINS ARE STILL AT LARGE, TRYING TO LOCATE THE THIRD AND FINAL TARGET.
SO FAR, I'VE ONLY HAD TIME TO ENTER HIS NAME ON A NUMBER OF NATIONAL 'PEOPLE SEARCH' SITES BUT GOT NO HITS. THE ONLY THING I HAVE IS THAT JPEG PHOTO ON THE PDA.
WELL, NO WONDER YOU WEREN'T ABLE TO FIND HIM BY NAME... RIGHT OFF THE BAT I CAN TELL YOU 'WINO BROWN' IS AN ALIAS.
AN ALIAS?
SURE. HAVEN'T YOU EVER SEEN NEW JACK CITY?
NO, WHAT'S THAT?
RIGHT... WESLEY'S CHARACTER...
PRRRRRRRT
THERE'S LIEUTENANT STROUD'S RINGTONE.
I'LL TAKE THIS OUTSIDE.

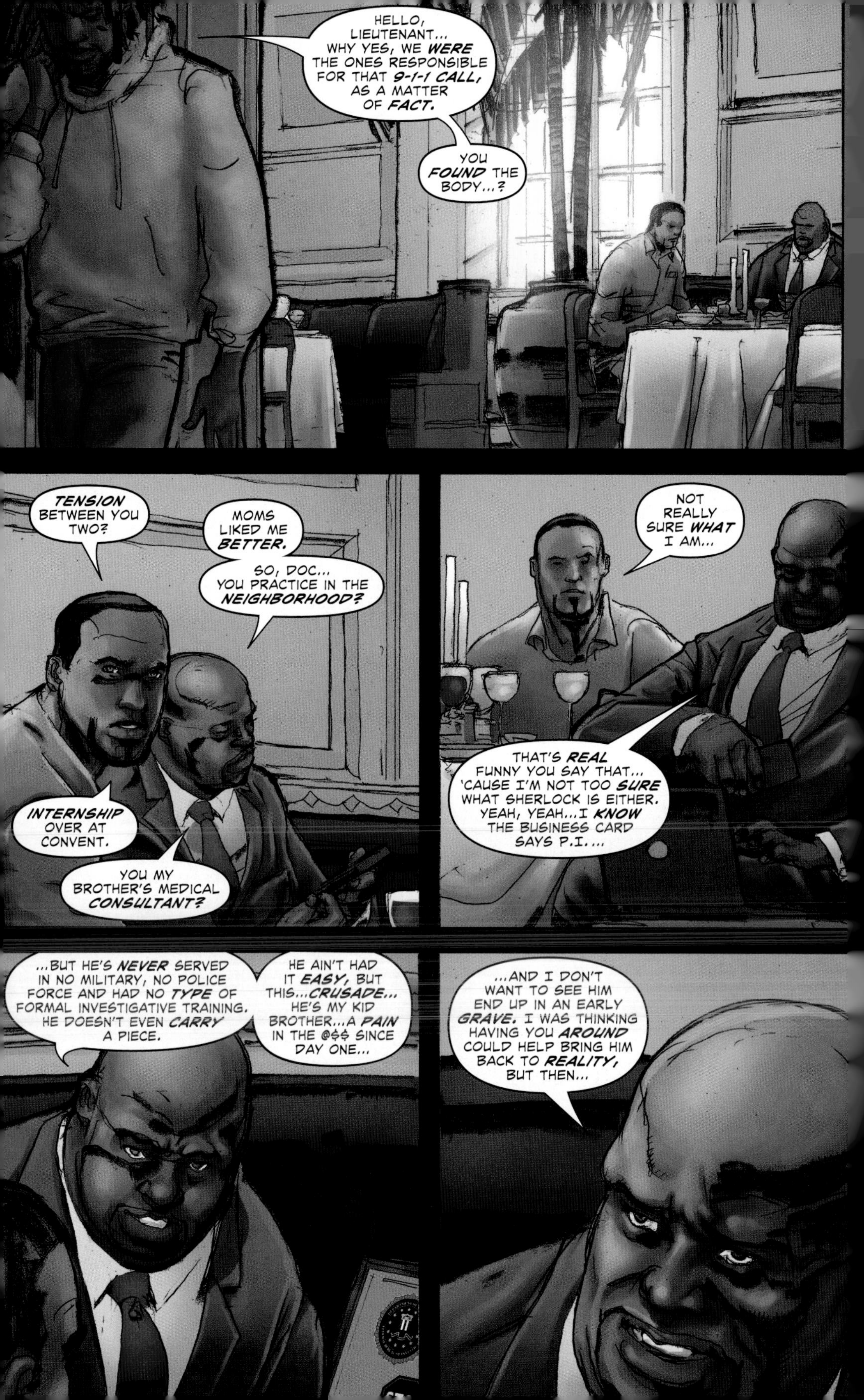
HELLO, LIEUTENANT... WHY YES, WE WERE THE ONES RESPONSIBLE FOR THAT 9-1-1 CALL, AS A MATTER OF FACT.
YOU FOUND THE BODY...?
TENSION BETWEEN YOU TWO?
MOMS LIKED ME BETTER.
SO, DOC... YOU PRACTICE IN THE NEIGHBORHOOD?
INTERNSHIP OVER AT CONVENT.
YOU MY BROTHER'S MEDICAL CONSULTANT?
NOT REALLY SURE WHAT I AM...
THAT'S REAL FUNNY YOU SAY THAT... 'CAUSE I'M NOT TOO SURE WHAT SHERLOCK IS EITHER. YEAH, YEAH...I KNOW THE BUSINESS CARD SAYS P.I. ...
...BUT HE'S NEVER SERVED IN NO MILITARY, NO POLICE FORCE AND HAD NO TYPE OF FORMAL INVESTIGATIVE TRAINING. HE DOESN'T EVEN CARRY A PIECE.
HE AIN'T HAD IT EASY, BUT THIS...CRUSADE... HE'S MY KID BROTHER...A PAIN IN THE @$$ SINCE DAY ONE...
...AND I DON'T WANT TO SEE HIM END UP IN AN EARLY GRAVE. I WAS THINKING HAVING YOU AROUND COULD HELP BRING HIM BACK TO REALITY, BUT THEN...

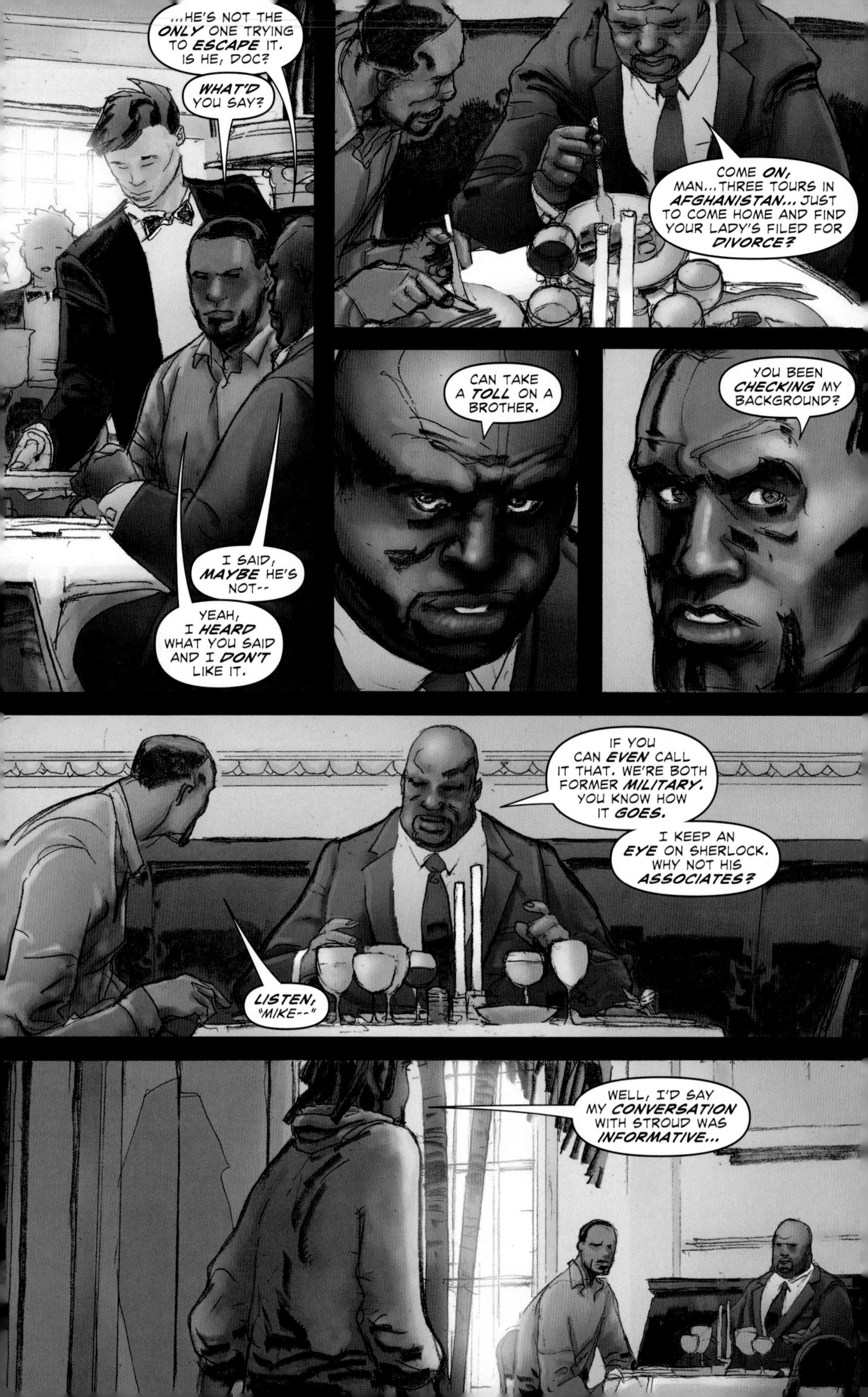
...HE'S NOT THE ONLY ONE TRYING TO ESCAPE IT. IS HE, DOC?
WHAT'D YOU SAY?
I SAID, MAYBE HE'S NOT--
YEAH, I HEARD WHAT YOU SAID AND I DON'T LIKE IT.
COME ON, MAN...THREE TOURS IN AFGHANISTAN... JUST TO COME HOME AND FIND YOUR LADY'S FILED FOR DIVORCE?
CAN TAKE A TOLL ON A BROTHER.
YOU BEEN CHECKING MY BACKGROUND?
IF YOU CAN EVEN CALL IT THAT. WE'RE BOTH FORMER MILITARY. YOU KNOW HOW IT GOES.
I KEEP AN EYE ON SHERLOCK. WHY NOT HIS ASSOCIATES?
LISTEN, "MIKE--"
WELL, I'D SAY MY CONVERSATION WITH STROUD WAS INFORMATIVE...

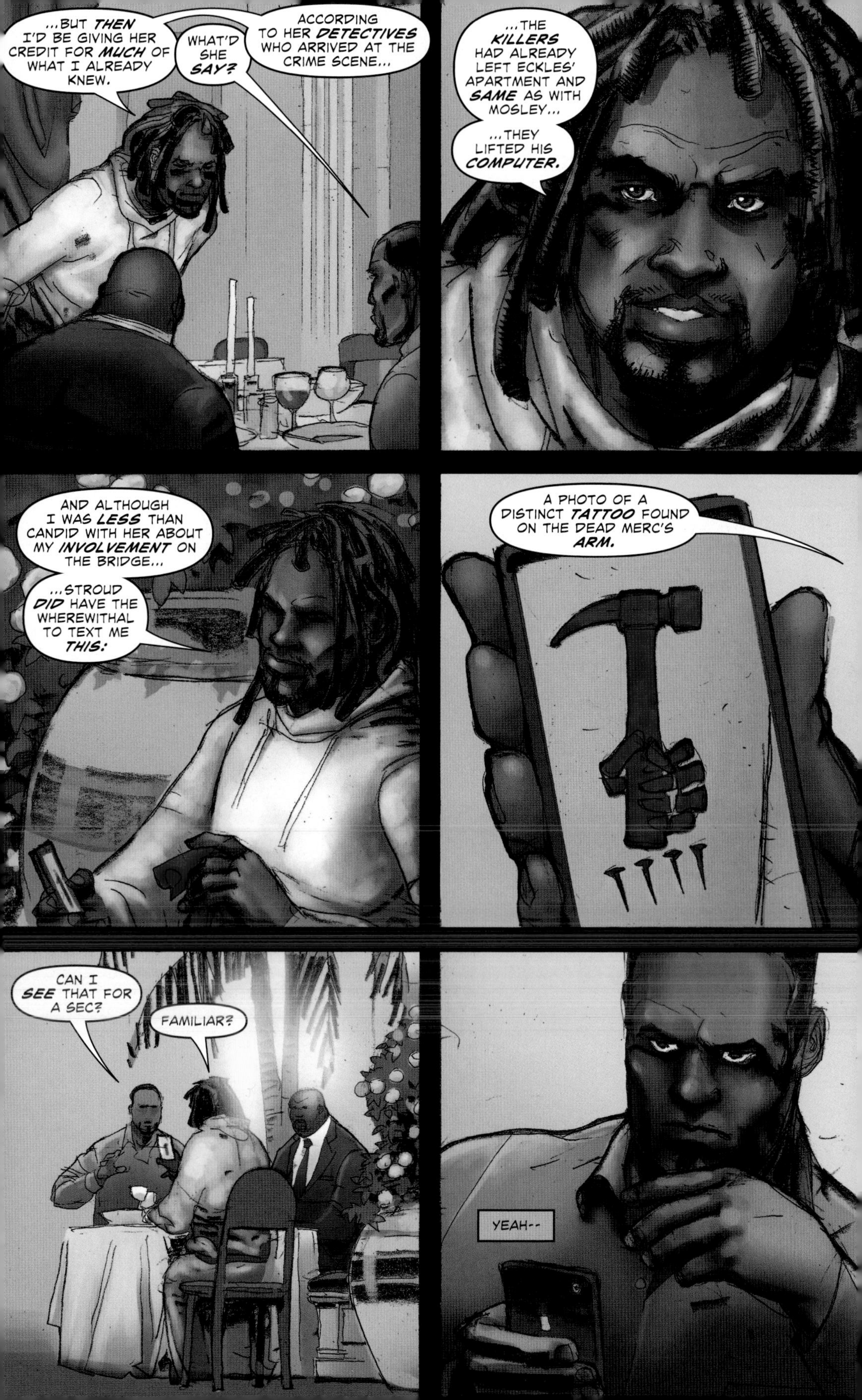
...BUT THEN I'D BE GIVING HER CREDIT FOR MUCH OF WHAT I ALREADY KNEW.
WHAT'D SHE SAY?
ACCORDING TO HER DETECTIVES WHO ARRIVED AT THE CRIME SCENE...
...THE KILLERS HAD ALREADY LEFT ECKLES' APARTMENT AND SAME AS WITH MOSLEY...
...THEY LIFTED HIS COMPUTER.
AND ALTHOUGH I WAS LESS THAN CANDID WITH HER ABOUT MY INVOLVEMENT ON THE BRIDGE...
...STROUD DID HAVE THE WHEREWITHAL TO TEXT ME THIS:
A PHOTO OF A DISTINCT TATTOO FOUND ON THE DEAD MERC'S ARM.
CAN I SEE THAT FOR A SEC?
FAMILIAR?
YEAH--

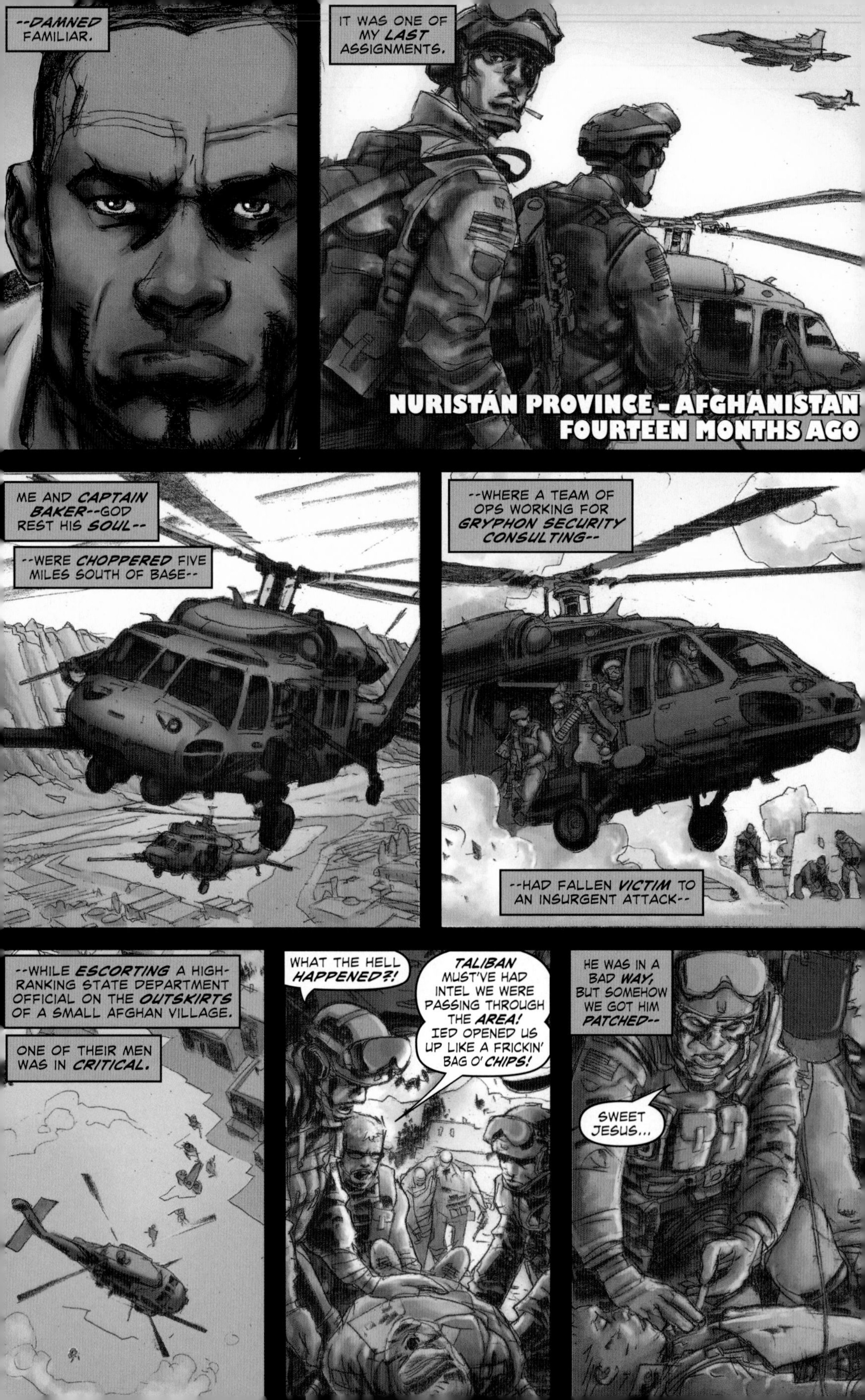
--DAMNED FAMILIAR.
IT WAS ONE OF MY LAST ASSIGNMENTS.
NURISTÁN PROVINCE - AFGHANISTAN
FOURTEEN MONTHS AGO
ME AND CAPTAIN BAKER--GOD REST HIS SOUL--
--WERE CHOPPERED FIVE MILES SOUTH OF BASE--
--WHERE A TEAM OF OPS WORKING FOR GRYPHON SECURITY CONSULTING--
--HAD FALLEN VICTIM TO AN INSURGENT ATTACK--
--WHILE ESCORTING A HIGH-RANKING STATE DEPARTMENT OFFICIAL ON THE OUTSKIRTS OF A SMALL AFGHAN VILLAGE.
ONE OF THEIR MEN WAS IN CRITICAL.
WHAT THE HELL HAPPENED?!
TALIBAN MUST'VE HAD INTEL WE WERE PASSING THROUGH THE AREA! IED OPENED US UP LIKE A FRICKIN' BAG O' CHIPS!
HE WAS IN A BAD WAY, BUT SOMEHOW WE GOT HIM PATCHED--
SWEET JESUS...

--AND GOT THE HELL *OUT* OF THERE.

WAIT. THAT *VILLAGE.* THERE ARE *BODIES...*

YUP. WE WENT GUNNING FOR THE *SUMBITCHES* WHO EFFED UP ORTIZ.

THERE WERE *WOMEN... CHILDREN...*

YOU THINK I *GIVE* A GOOD GODDAMN? FAR AS *I'M* CONCERNED...

...ANYTHING WEARING A *TURBAN* IS FAIR GAME.

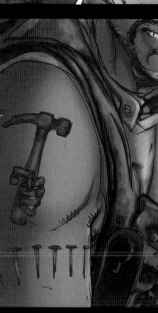

THESE *MERCS.* THEY'RE EITHER WORKING *FOR,* OR WERE ONCE CONTRACTED *TO,* GRYPHON.

THE PRIVATE *SECURITY* FIRM?

CORPORATE SOLDIERS.

A LOT OF THEIR GUYS BORE THAT *SAME* TAT.

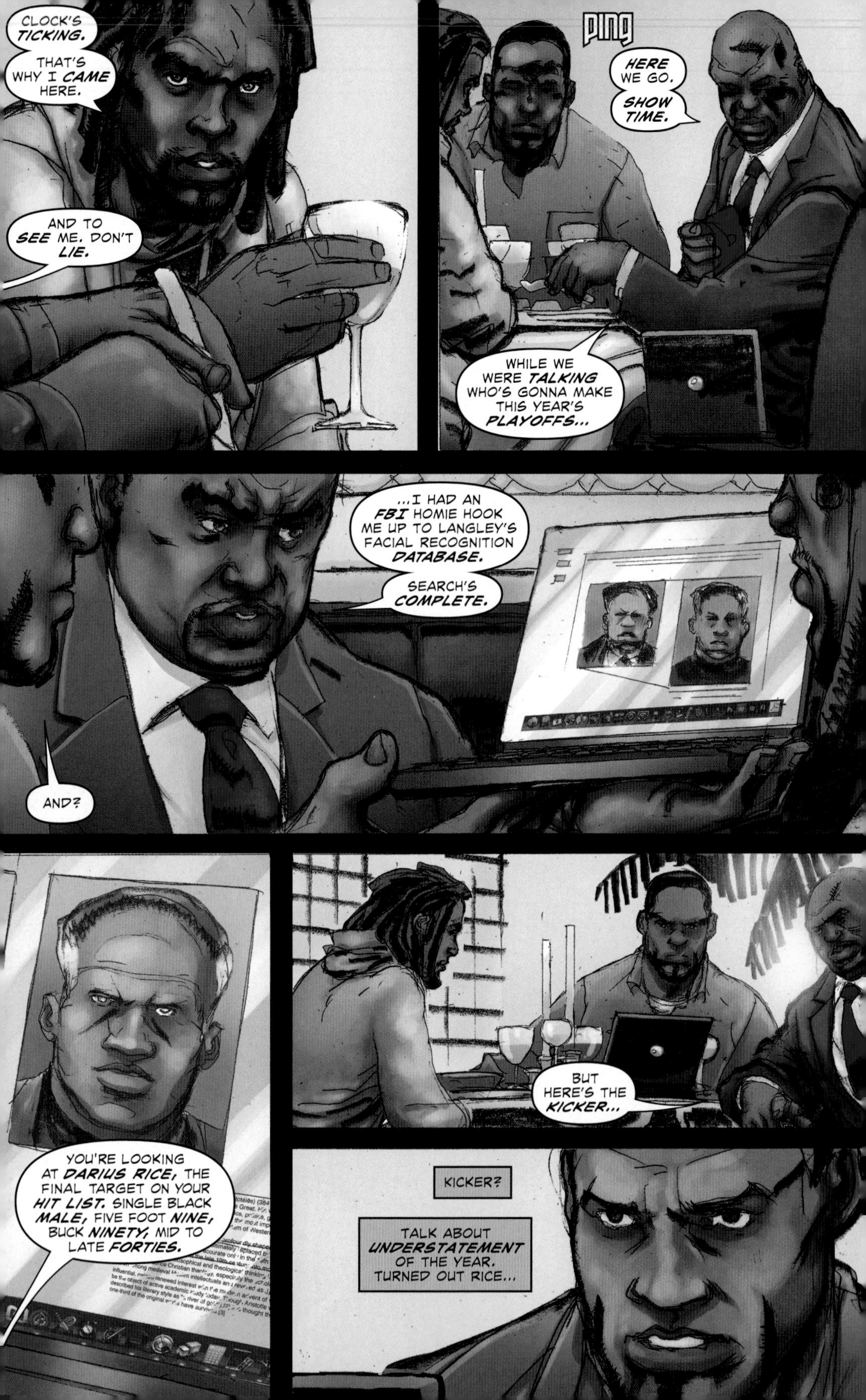
CLOCK'S TICKING.
THAT'S WHY I CAME HERE.
AND TO SEE ME. DON'T LIE.
PING
HERE WE GO. SHOW TIME.
WHILE WE WERE TALKING WHO'S GONNA MAKE THIS YEAR'S PLAYOFFS...
...I HAD AN FBI HOMIE HOOK ME UP TO LANGLEY'S FACIAL RECOGNITION DATABASE.
SEARCH'S COMPLETE.
AND?
YOU'RE LOOKING AT DARIUS RICE, THE FINAL TARGET ON YOUR HIT LIST. SINGLE BLACK MALE, FIVE FOOT NINE, BUCK NINETY, MID TO LATE FORTIES.
BUT HERE'S THE KICKER...
KICKER?
TALK ABOUT UNDERSTATEMENT OF THE YEAR. TURNED OUT RICE...

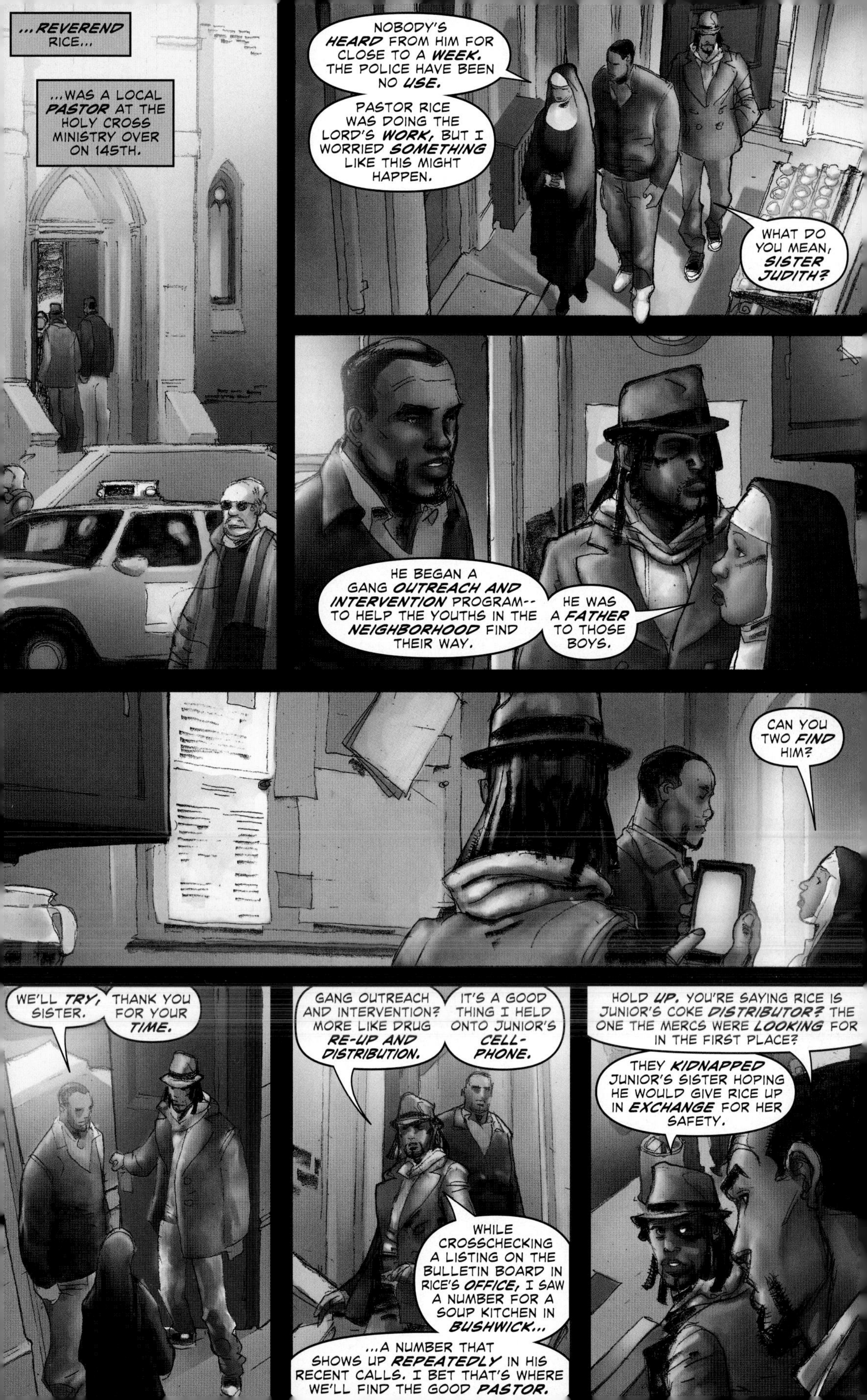
...REVEREND RICE...
...WAS A LOCAL PASTOR AT THE HOLY CROSS MINISTRY OVER ON 145TH.
NOBODY'S HEARD FROM HIM FOR CLOSE TO A WEEK. THE POLICE HAVE BEEN NO USE.
PASTOR RICE WAS DOING THE LORD'S WORK, BUT I WORRIED SOMETHING LIKE THIS MIGHT HAPPEN.
WHAT DO YOU MEAN, SISTER JUDITH?
HE BEGAN A GANG OUTREACH AND INTERVENTION PROGRAM-- TO HELP THE YOUTHS IN THE NEIGHBORHOOD FIND THEIR WAY.
HE WAS A FATHER TO THOSE BOYS.
CAN YOU TWO FIND HIM?
WE'LL TRY, SISTER.
THANK YOU FOR YOUR TIME.
GANG OUTREACH AND INTERVENTION? MORE LIKE DRUG RE-UP AND DISTRIBUTION.
IT'S A GOOD THING I HELD ONTO JUNIOR'S CELL-PHONE.
WHILE CROSSCHECKING A LISTING ON THE BULLETIN BOARD IN RICE'S OFFICE, I SAW A NUMBER FOR A SOUP KITCHEN IN BUSHWICK...
...A NUMBER THAT SHOWS UP REPEATEDLY IN HIS RECENT CALLS. I BET THAT'S WHERE WE'LL FIND THE GOOD PASTOR.
HOLD UP. YOU'RE SAYING RICE IS JUNIOR'S COKE DISTRIBUTOR? THE ONE THE MERCS WERE LOOKING FOR IN THE FIRST PLACE?
THEY KIDNAPPED JUNIOR'S SISTER HOPING HE WOULD GIVE RICE UP IN EXCHANGE FOR HER SAFETY.

SO **WHAT** NOW? YOU'RE HEADING OUT TO **BROOKLYN** TO FIND HIM?

HIS LIFE IS IN **DANGER**.

SO WHY NOT LET THE **POLICE** HANDLE IT?

THAT WON'T TELL ME **WHY** THE MERCS WANT HIM AND THE OTHER MEN **DEAD**. OR WHAT CONNECTS THEM ALL **BESIDES** THE HIT LIST.

HOLMES... I GOT **INVOLVED** IN THIS TO FIND A MISSING **GIRL**.

MISSION ACCOMPLISHED. I ADMIT, HELPING YOU UNCOVER ALL THE CLUES WAS... KINDA COOL.

BUT WE DON'T **NEED** TO TAKE IT ANY FURTHER. SAVING TRINA WAS **ONE** THING...

...BUT **NOW** THIS IS ABOUT DRUGS, HIT SQUADS AND LOST SOULS. I'VE **SEEN** WHAT THESE **DUDES** ARE CAPABLE OF...AND MY **SON** NEEDS A FATHER. YOU **FEEL** ME? WHY DO YOU NEED ALL THE **ANSWERS**, MAN?

BECAUSE I **HAVE** TO KNOW.

DAMN YOU, HOLMES...

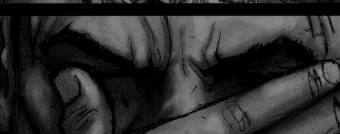

OKAY, I'LL **GO** WITH YOU.

TAXI!

BUT ON **ONE** CONDITION...

I HAVE ZERO **OBJECTION** TO STOPPING BY THE HOSPITAL FIRST.

HOW'D YOU KNOW I WAS GONNA **SAY** THAT?

REALLY, DOCTOR? ≡SIGH≡

OKAY, FROM THE **TOP**...

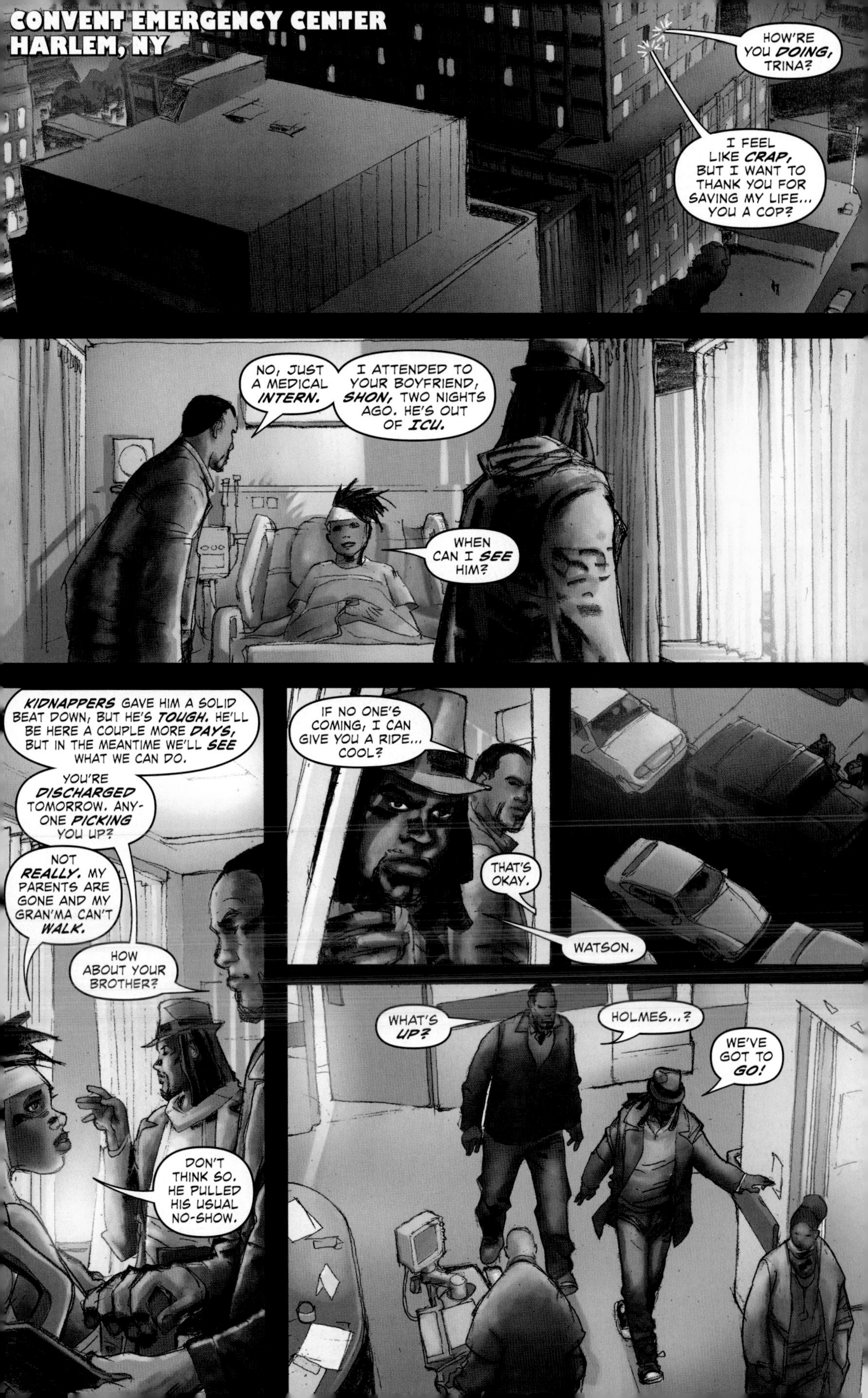
CONVENT EMERGENCY CENTER
HARLEM, NY
HOW'RE YOU DOING, TRINA?
I FEEL LIKE CRAP, BUT I WANT TO THANK YOU FOR SAVING MY LIFE... YOU A COP?
NO, JUST A MEDICAL INTERN.
I ATTENDED TO YOUR BOYFRIEND, SHON, TWO NIGHTS AGO. HE'S OUT OF ICU.
WHEN CAN I SEE HIM?
KIDNAPPERS GAVE HIM A SOLID BEAT DOWN, BUT HE'S TOUGH. HE'LL BE HERE A COUPLE MORE DAYS, BUT IN THE MEANTIME WE'LL SEE WHAT WE CAN DO.
YOU'RE DISCHARGED TOMORROW. ANY-ONE PICKING YOU UP?
NOT REALLY. MY PARENTS ARE GONE AND MY GRAN'MA CAN'T WALK.
HOW ABOUT YOUR BROTHER?
DON'T THINK SO. HE PULLED HIS USUAL NO-SHOW.
IF NO ONE'S COMING, I CAN GIVE YOU A RIDE... COOL?
THAT'S OKAY.
WATSON.
WHAT'S UP?
HOLMES...?
WE'VE GOT TO GO!

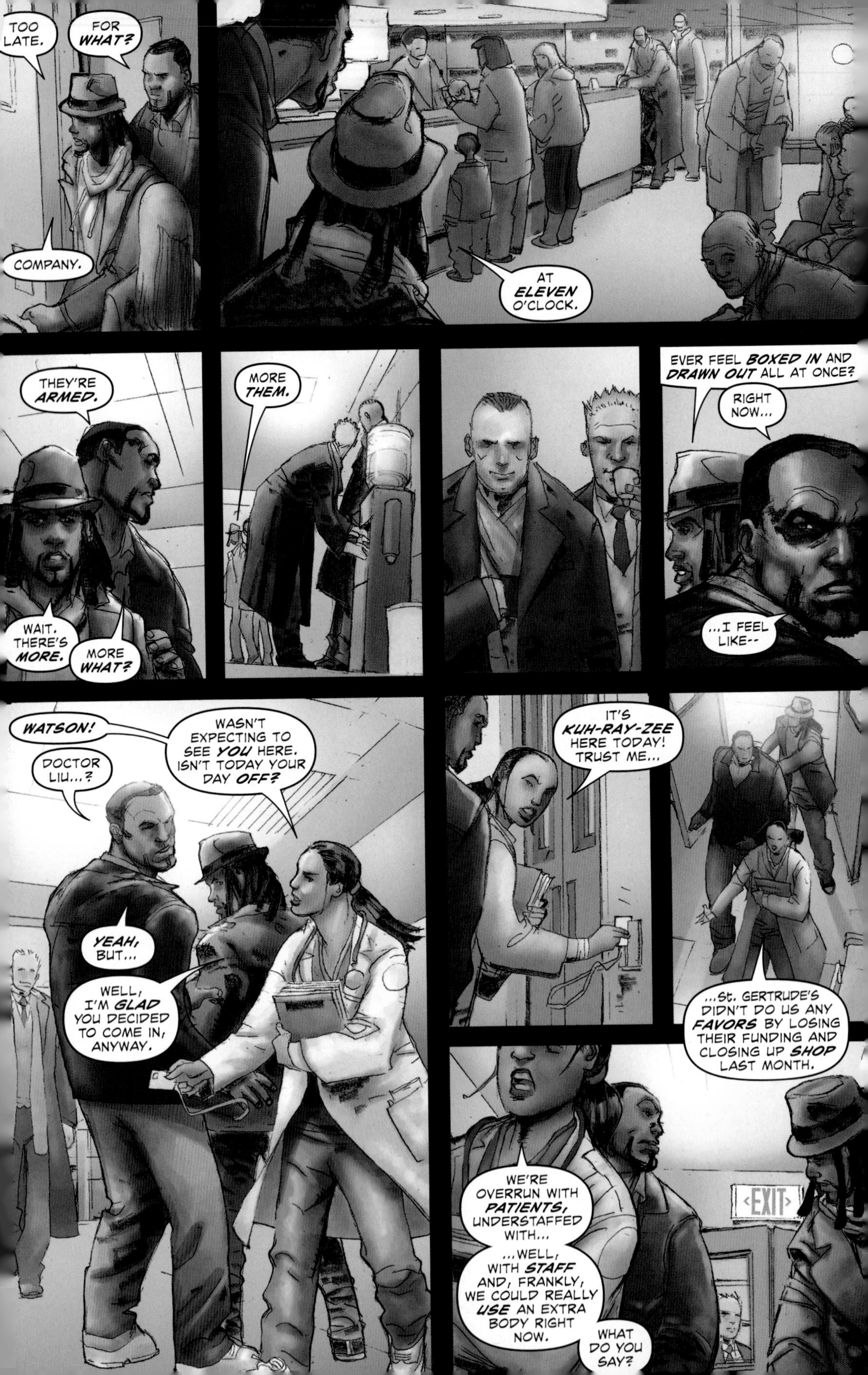
TOO LATE.
FOR WHAT?
COMPANY.
AT ELEVEN O'CLOCK.
THEY'RE ARMED.
WAIT. THERE'S MORE.
MORE WHAT?
MORE THEM.
EVER FEEL BOXED IN AND DRAWN OUT ALL AT ONCE?
RIGHT NOW...
...I FEEL LIKE--
WATSON!
WASN'T EXPECTING TO SEE YOU HERE. ISN'T TODAY YOUR DAY OFF?
DOCTOR LIU...?
YEAH, BUT...
WELL, I'M GLAD YOU DECIDED TO COME IN, ANYWAY.
IT'S KUH-RAY-ZEE HERE TODAY! TRUST ME...
...St. GERTRUDE'S DIDN'T DO US ANY FAVORS BY LOSING THEIR FUNDING AND CLOSING UP SHOP LAST MONTH.
WE'RE OVERRUN WITH PATIENTS, UNDERSTAFFED WITH...
...WELL, WITH STAFF AND, FRANKLY, WE COULD REALLY USE AN EXTRA BODY RIGHT NOW.
WHAT DO YOU SAY?
EXIT

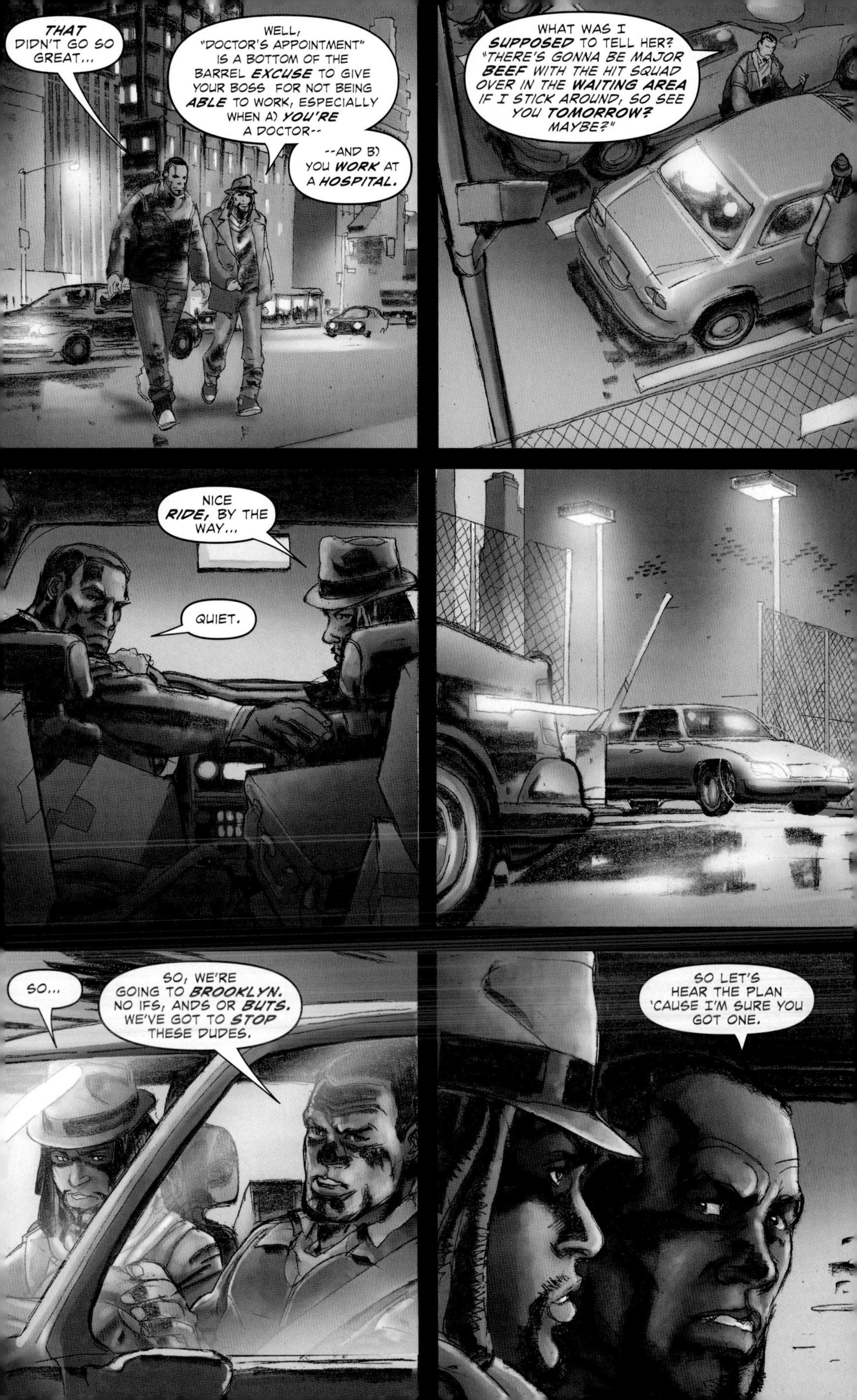
THAT DIDN'T GO SO GREAT...
WELL, "DOCTOR'S APPOINTMENT" IS A BOTTOM OF THE BARREL EXCUSE TO GIVE YOUR BOSS FOR NOT BEING ABLE TO WORK, ESPECIALLY WHEN A) YOU'RE A DOCTOR--
--AND B) YOU WORK AT A HOSPITAL.
WHAT WAS I SUPPOSED TO TELL HER? "THERE'S GONNA BE MAJOR BEEF WITH THE HIT SQUAD OVER IN THE WAITING AREA IF I STICK AROUND, SO SEE YOU TOMORROW? MAYBE?"
NICE RIDE, BY THE WAY...
QUIET.
SO...
SO, WE'RE GOING TO BROOKLYN. NO IFS, ANDS OR BUTS. WE'VE GOT TO STOP THESE DUDES.
SO LET'S HEAR THE PLAN 'CAUSE I'M SURE YOU GOT ONE.

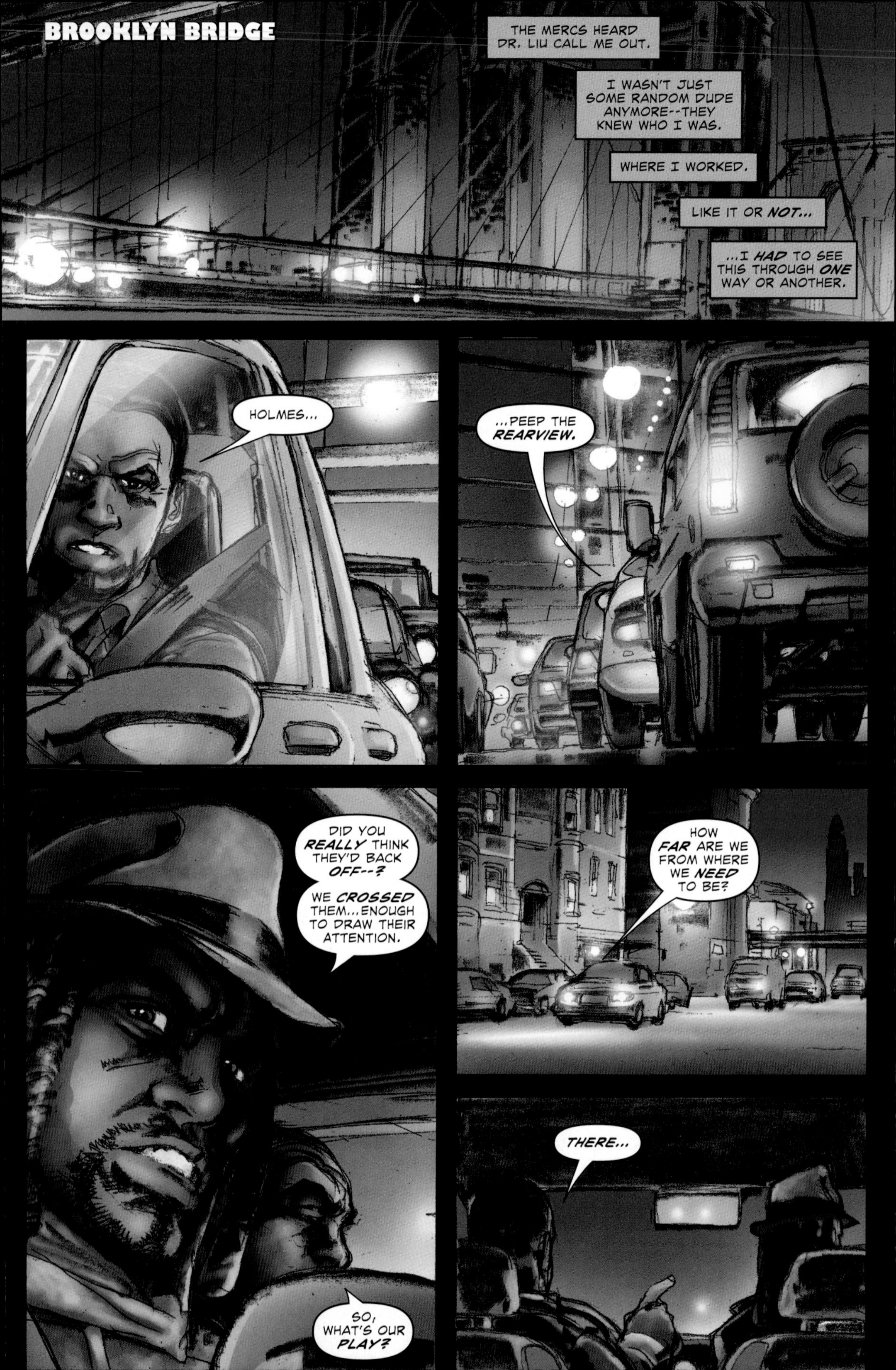
BROOKLYN BRIDGE
THE MERCS HEARD DR. LIU CALL ME OUT.
I WASN'T JUST SOME RANDOM DUDE ANYMORE--THEY KNEW WHO I WAS.
WHERE I WORKED.
LIKE IT OR NOT...
...I HAD TO SEE THIS THROUGH ONE WAY OR ANOTHER.
HOLMES...
...PEEP THE REARVIEW.
DID YOU REALLY THINK THEY'D BACK OFF--?
WE CROSSED THEM...ENOUGH TO DRAW THEIR ATTENTION.
SO, WHAT'S OUR PLAY?
HOW FAR ARE WE FROM WHERE WE NEED TO BE?
THERE...

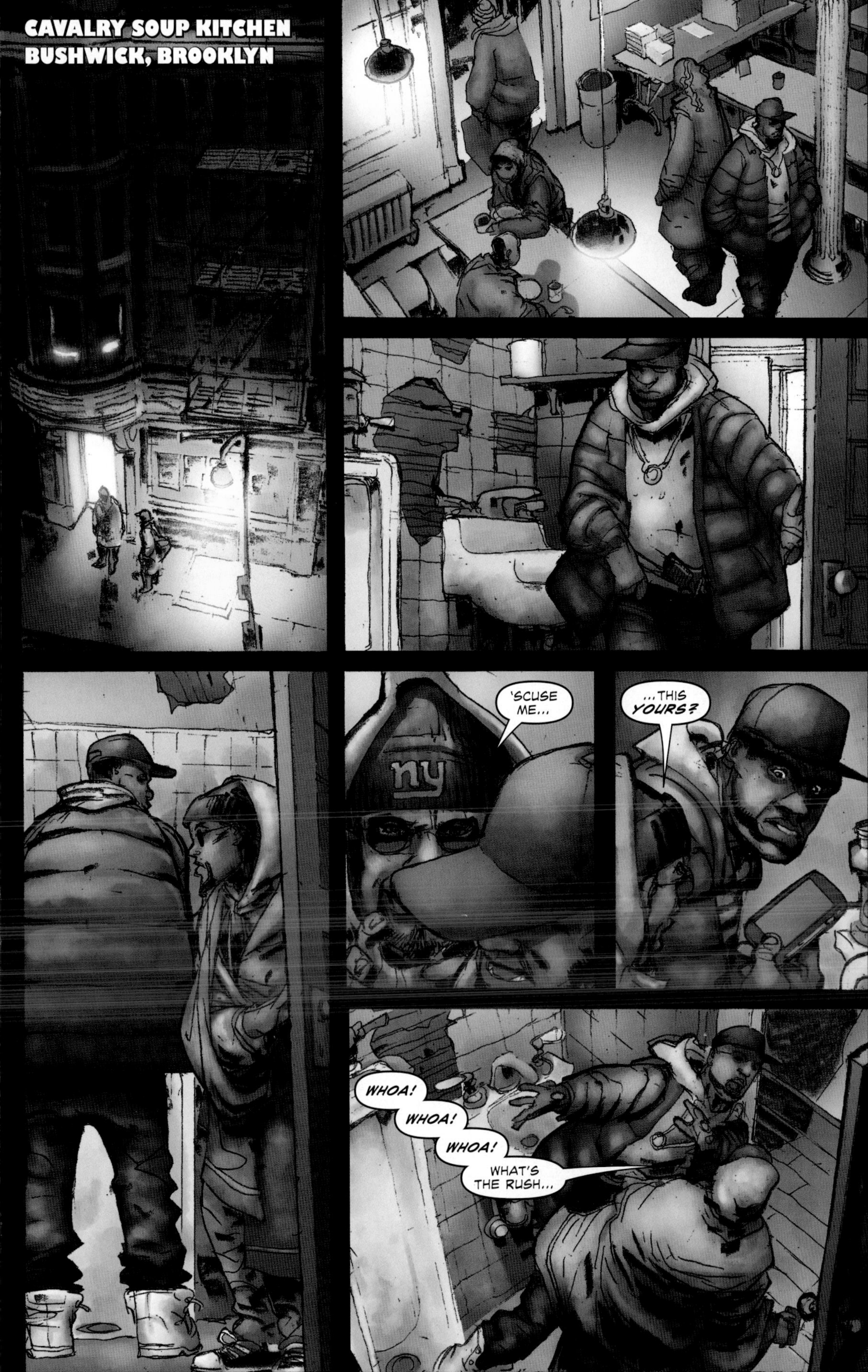
CAVALRY SOUP KITCHEN
BUSHWICK, BROOKLYN
'SCUSE ME...
...THIS *YOURS?*
WHOA!
WHOA!
WHOA!
WHAT'S THE RUSH...

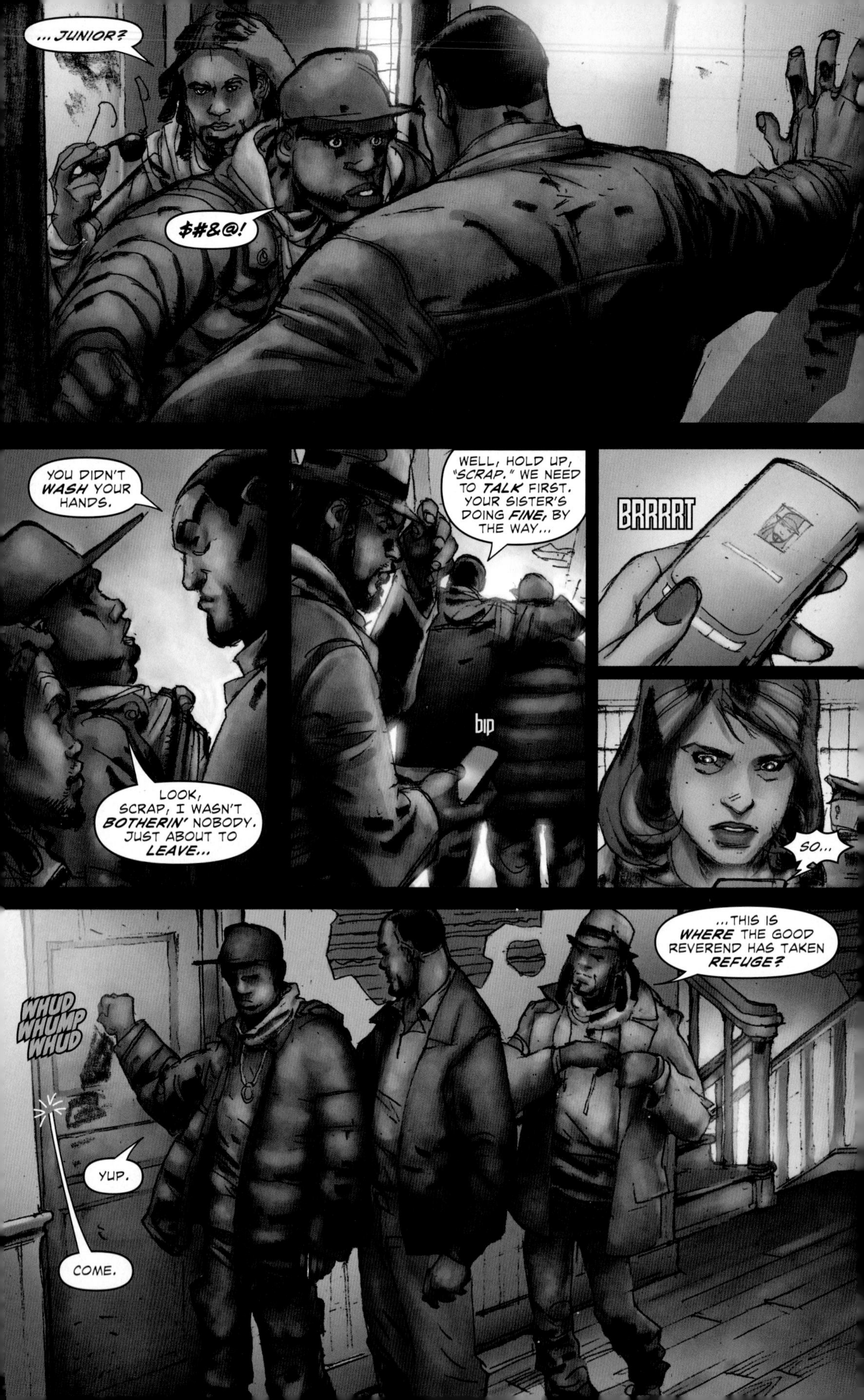

...JUNIOR?
$#&@!
YOU DIDN'T WASH YOUR HANDS.
LOOK, SCRAP, I WASN'T BOTHERIN' NOBODY. JUST ABOUT TO LEAVE...
WELL, HOLD UP, "SCRAP." WE NEED TO TALK FIRST. YOUR SISTER'S DOING FINE, BY THE WAY...
bip
BRRRRT
SO...
...THIS IS WHERE THE GOOD REVEREND HAS TAKEN REFUGE?
WHUD WHUMP WHUD
YUP.
COME.

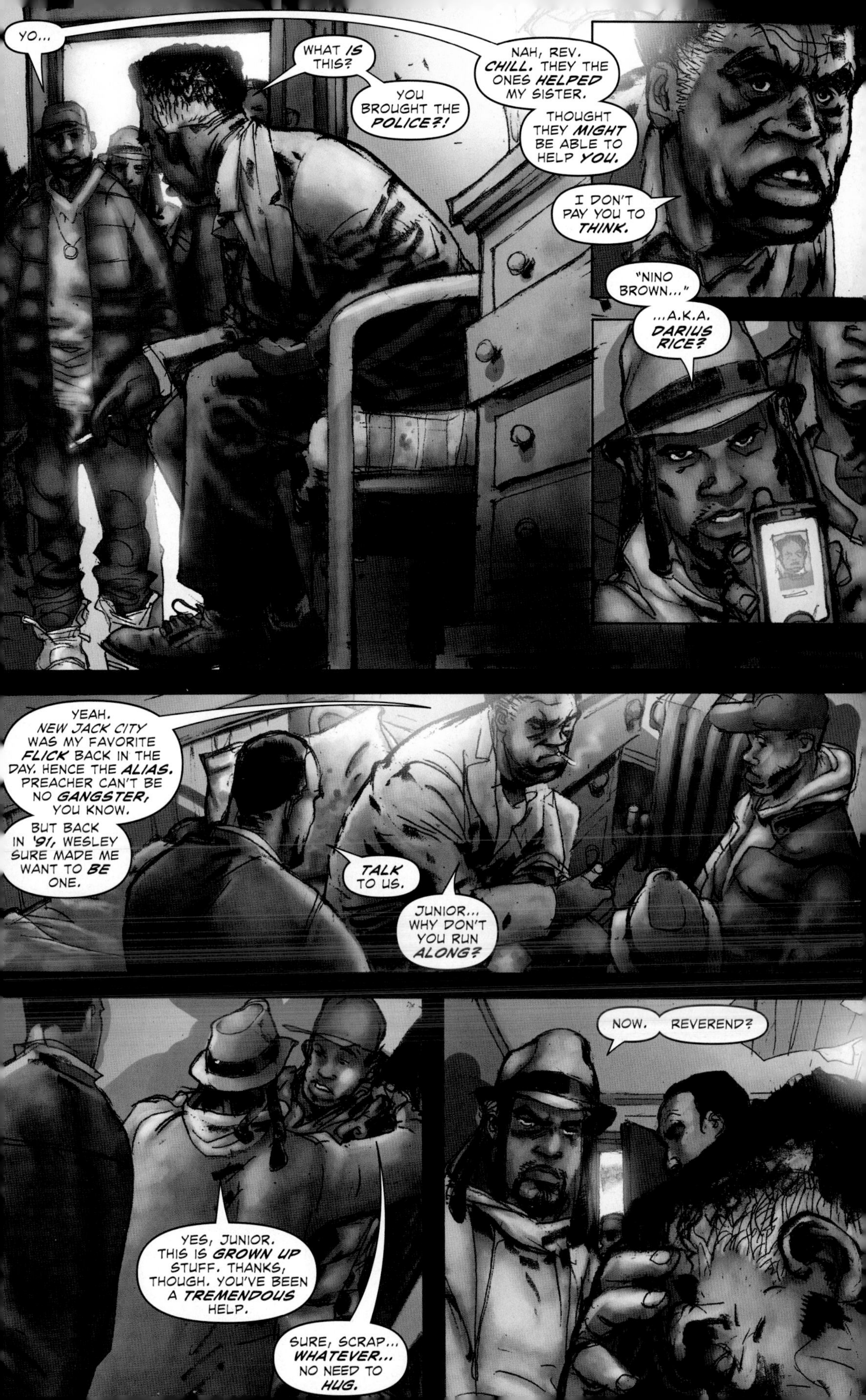

YO...
WHAT *IS* THIS?
YOU BROUGHT THE *POLICE?!*
NAH, REV. *CHILL.* THEY THE ONES *HELPED* MY SISTER.
THOUGHT THEY *MIGHT* BE ABLE TO HELP *YOU.*
I DON'T PAY YOU TO *THINK.*
"NINO BROWN..."
...A.K.A. *DARIUS RICE?*
YEAH. *NEW JACK CITY* WAS MY FAVORITE *FLICK* BACK IN THE DAY. HENCE THE *ALIAS.* PREACHER CAN'T BE NO *GANGSTER,* YOU KNOW.
BUT BACK IN *'91,* WESLEY SURE MADE ME WANT TO *BE* ONE.
TALK TO US.
JUNIOR... WHY DON'T YOU RUN *ALONG?*
YES, JUNIOR. THIS IS *GROWN UP* STUFF. THANKS, THOUGH. YOU'VE BEEN A *TREMENDOUS* HELP.
SURE, SCRAP... *WHATEVER...* NO NEED TO *HUG.*
NOW.
REVEREND?

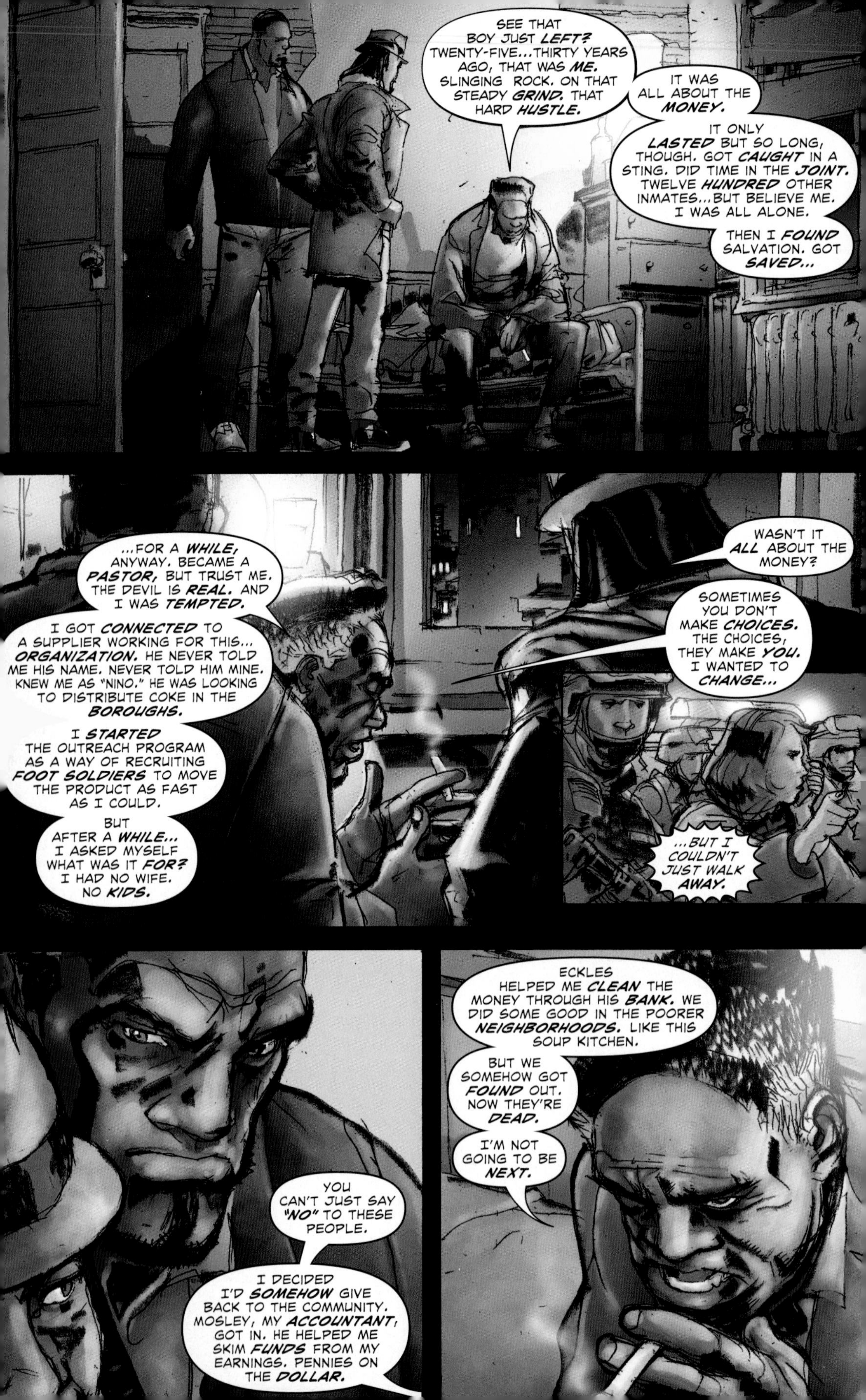
SEE THAT BOY JUST LEFT? TWENTY-FIVE...THIRTY YEARS AGO, THAT WAS ME. SLINGING ROCK. ON THAT STEADY GRIND. THAT HARD HUSTLE.
IT WAS ALL ABOUT THE MONEY.
IT ONLY LASTED BUT SO LONG, THOUGH. GOT CAUGHT IN A STING. DID TIME IN THE JOINT. TWELVE HUNDRED OTHER INMATES...BUT BELIEVE ME. I WAS ALL ALONE.
THEN I FOUND SALVATION. GOT SAVED...
...FOR A WHILE, ANYWAY. BECAME A PASTOR, BUT TRUST ME. THE DEVIL IS REAL. AND I WAS TEMPTED.
I GOT CONNECTED TO A SUPPLIER WORKING FOR THIS... ORGANIZATION. HE NEVER TOLD ME HIS NAME. NEVER TOLD HIM MINE. KNEW ME AS "NINO." HE WAS LOOKING TO DISTRIBUTE COKE IN THE BOROUGHS.
I STARTED THE OUTREACH PROGRAM AS A WAY OF RECRUITING FOOT SOLDIERS TO MOVE THE PRODUCT AS FAST AS I COULD.
BUT AFTER A WHILE... I ASKED MYSELF WHAT WAS IT FOR? I HAD NO WIFE. NO KIDS.
WASN'T IT ALL ABOUT THE MONEY?
SOMETIMES YOU DON'T MAKE CHOICES. THE CHOICES, THEY MAKE YOU. I WANTED TO CHANGE...
...BUT I COULDN'T JUST WALK AWAY.
YOU CAN'T JUST SAY "NO" TO THESE PEOPLE.
I DECIDED I'D SOMEHOW GIVE BACK TO THE COMMUNITY. MOSLEY, MY ACCOUNTANT, GOT IN. HE HELPED ME SKIM FUNDS FROM MY EARNINGS. PENNIES ON THE DOLLAR.
ECKLES HELPED ME CLEAN THE MONEY THROUGH HIS BANK. WE DID SOME GOOD IN THE POORER NEIGHBORHOODS. LIKE THIS SOUP KITCHEN.
BUT WE SOMEHOW GOT FOUND OUT. NOW THEY'RE DEAD.
I'M NOT GOING TO BE NEXT.

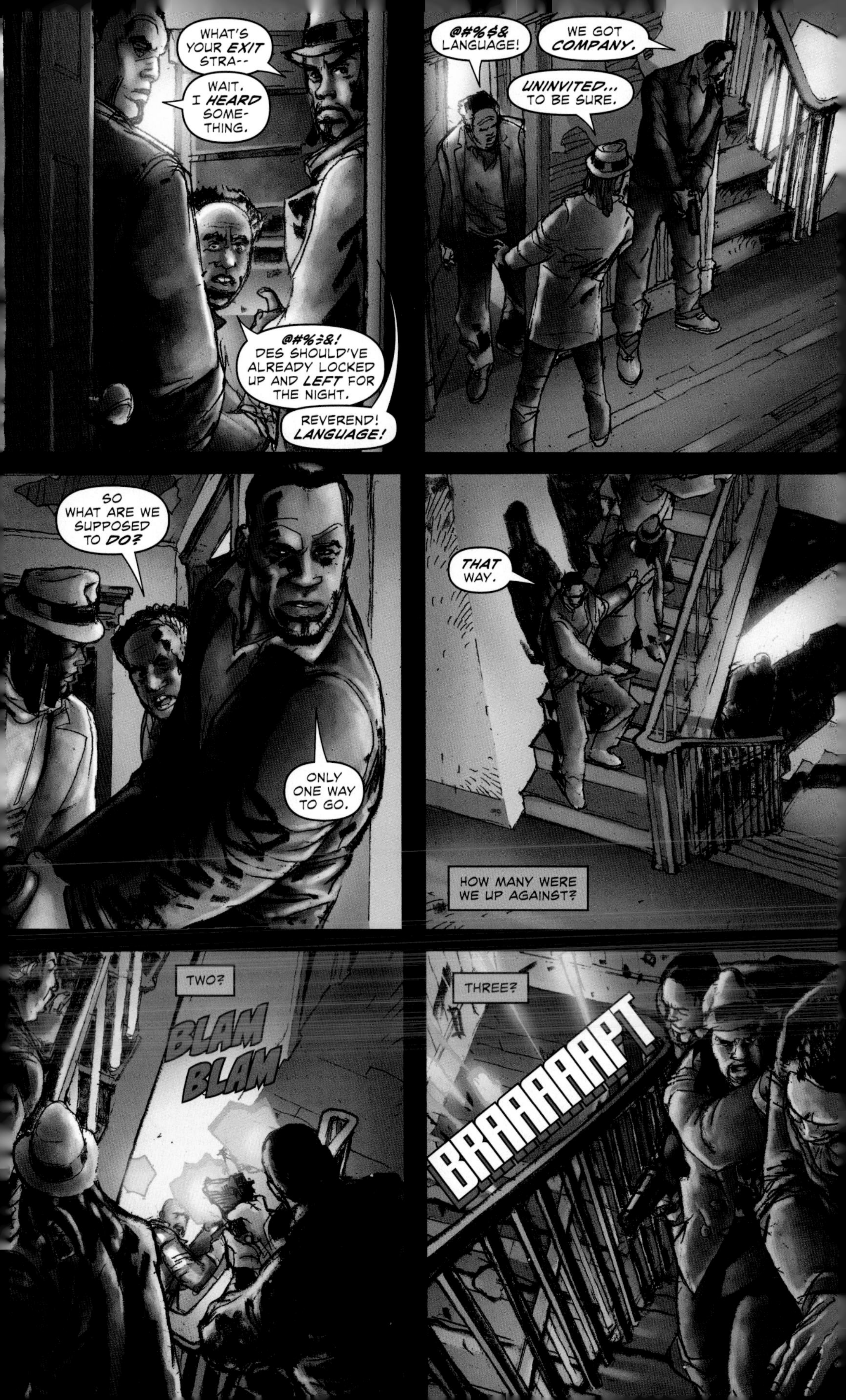
WHAT'S YOUR EXIT STRA--
WAIT. I HEARD SOME-THING.
@#%=&! DES SHOULD'VE ALREADY LOCKED UP AND LEFT FOR THE NIGHT.
REVEREND! LANGUAGE!
@#%$& LANGUAGE!
WE GOT COMPANY.
UNINVITED... TO BE SURE.
SO WHAT ARE WE SUPPOSED TO DO?
ONLY ONE WAY TO GO.
THAT WAY.
HOW MANY WERE WE UP AGAINST?
TWO?
BLAM BLAM
THREE?
BRAAAAAPT

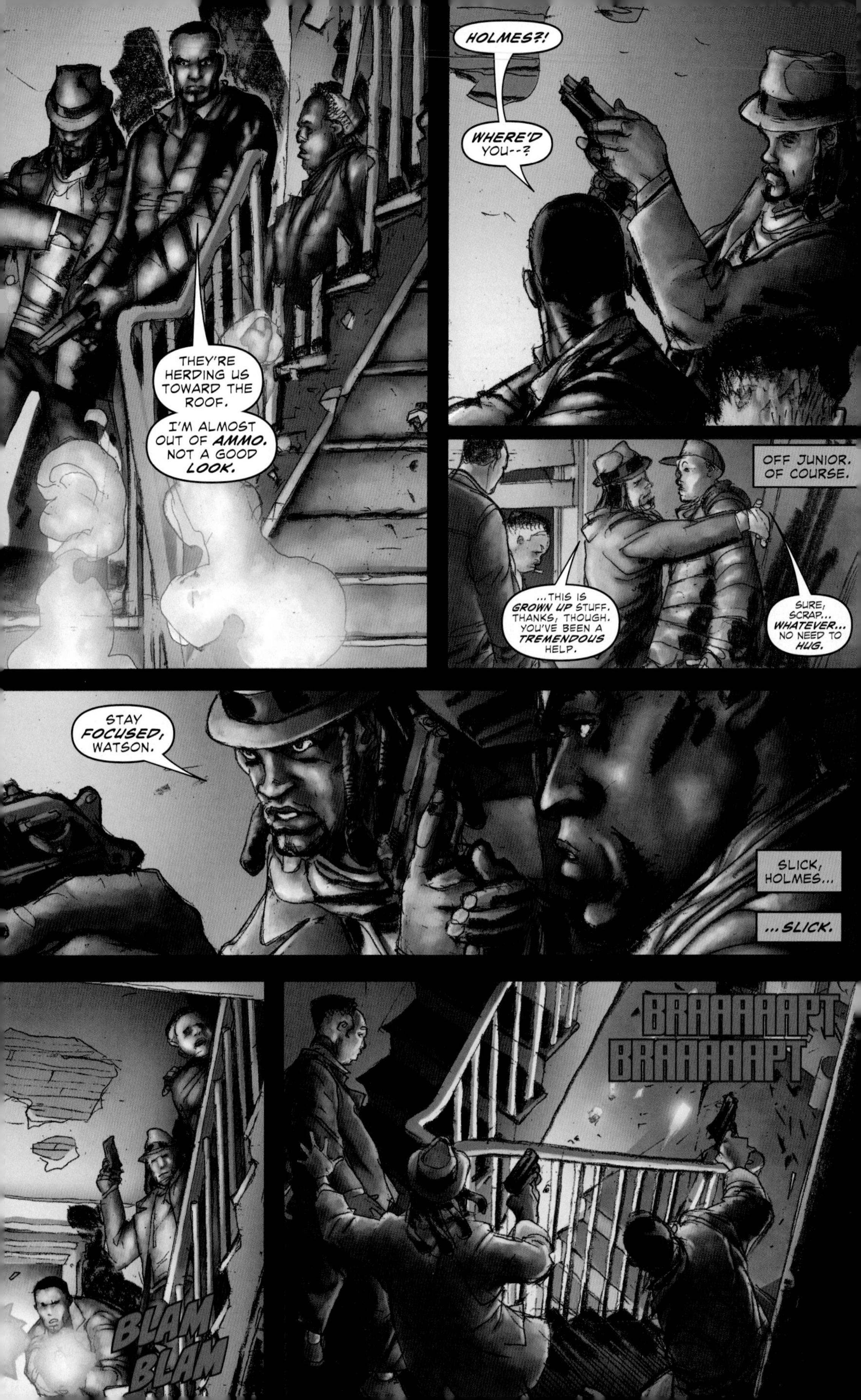
THEY'RE HERDING US TOWARD THE ROOF.
I'M ALMOST OUT OF AMMO. NOT A GOOD LOOK.
HOLMES?!
WHERE'D YOU--?
OFF JUNIOR OF COURSE.
...THIS IS GROWN UP STUFF. THANKS, THOUGH. YOU'VE BEEN A TREMENDOUS HELP.
SURE, SCRAP... WHATEVER... NO NEED TO HUG.
STAY FOCUSED, WATSON.
SLICK, HOLMES...
...SLICK.
BLAM BLAM
BRAAAAAPT
BRAAAAAPT

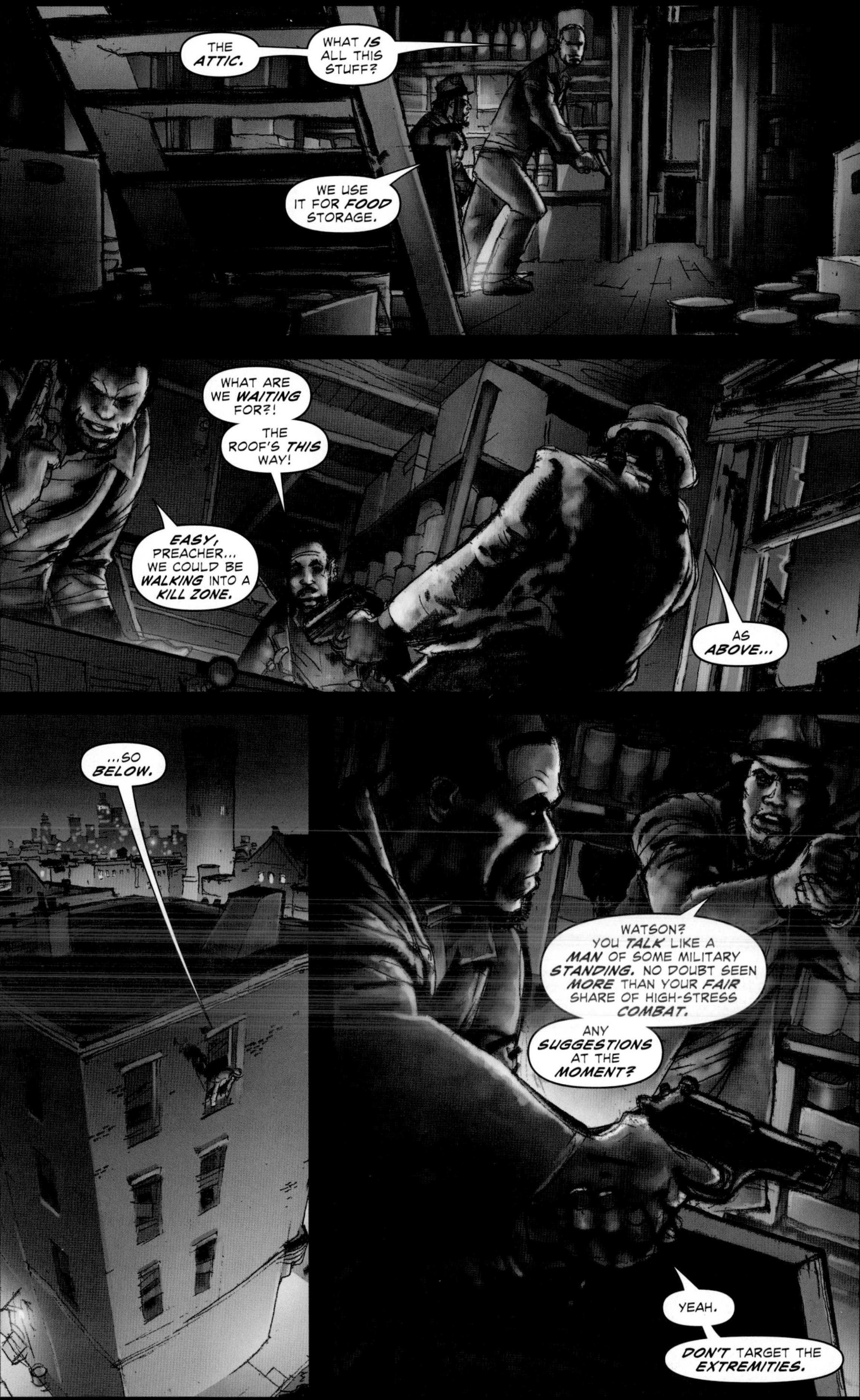
THE ATTIC.
WHAT IS ALL THIS STUFF?
WE USE IT FOR FOOD STORAGE.
WHAT ARE WE WAITING FOR?!
THE ROOF'S THIS WAY!
EASY, PREACHER... WE COULD BE WALKING INTO A KILL ZONE.
AS ABOVE...
...SO BELOW.
WATSON? YOU TALK LIKE A MAN OF SOME MILITARY STANDING. NO DOUBT SEEN MORE THAN YOUR FAIR SHARE OF HIGH-STRESS COMBAT.
ANY SUGGESTIONS AT THE MOMENT?
YEAH.
DON'T TARGET THE EXTREMITIES.

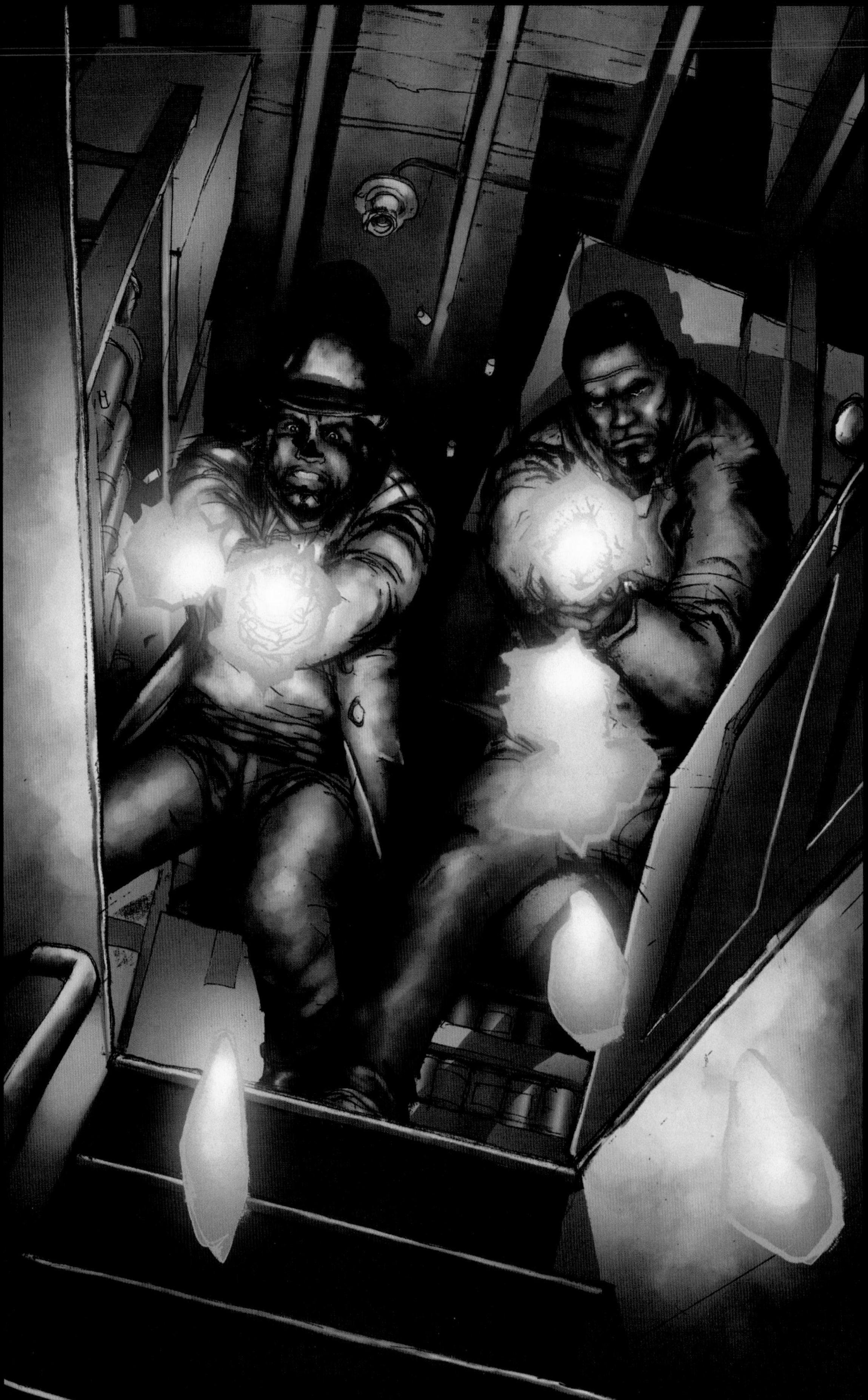

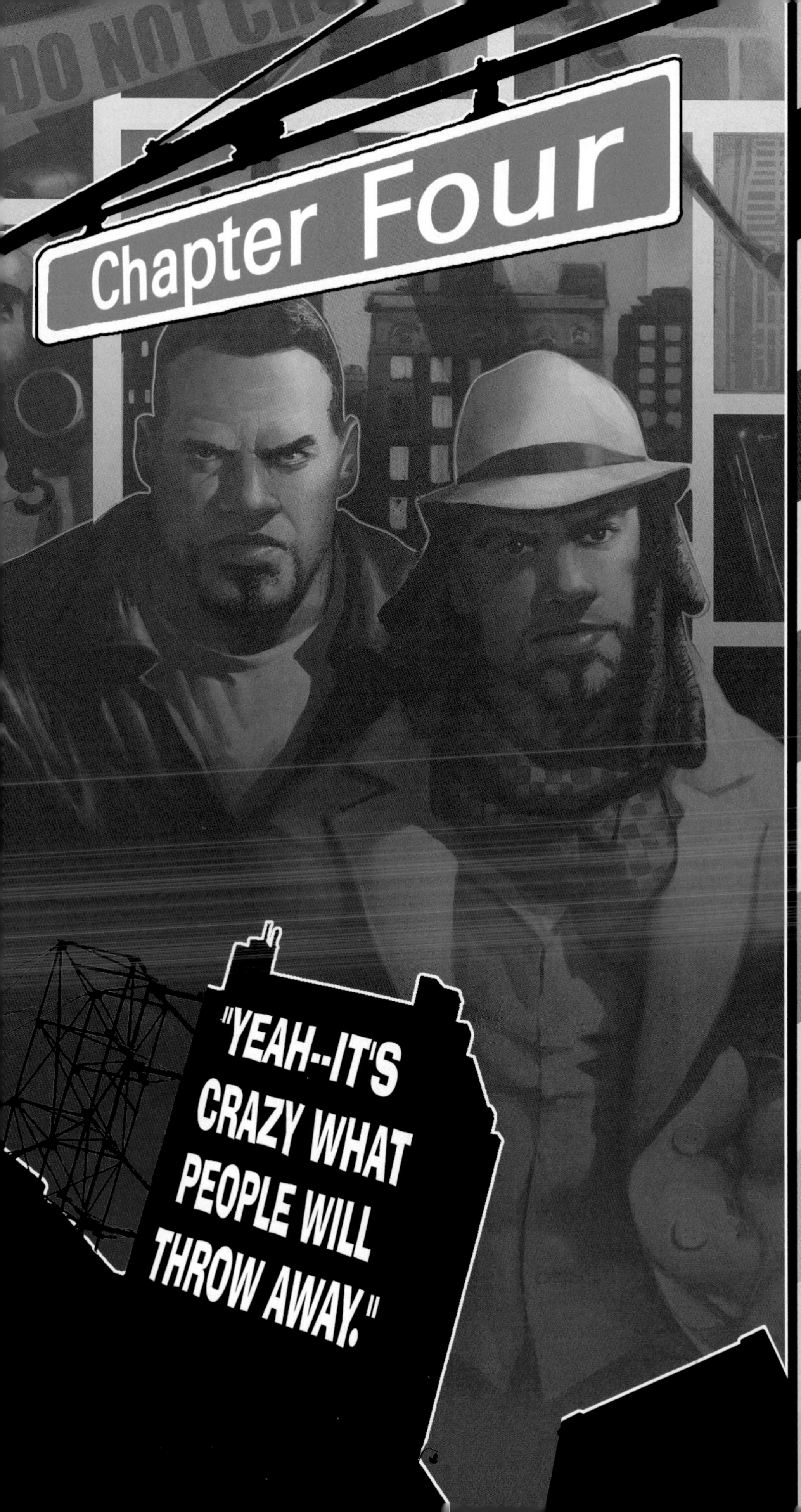
Chapter Four
"YEAH--IT'S CRAZY WHAT PEOPLE WILL THROW AWAY."

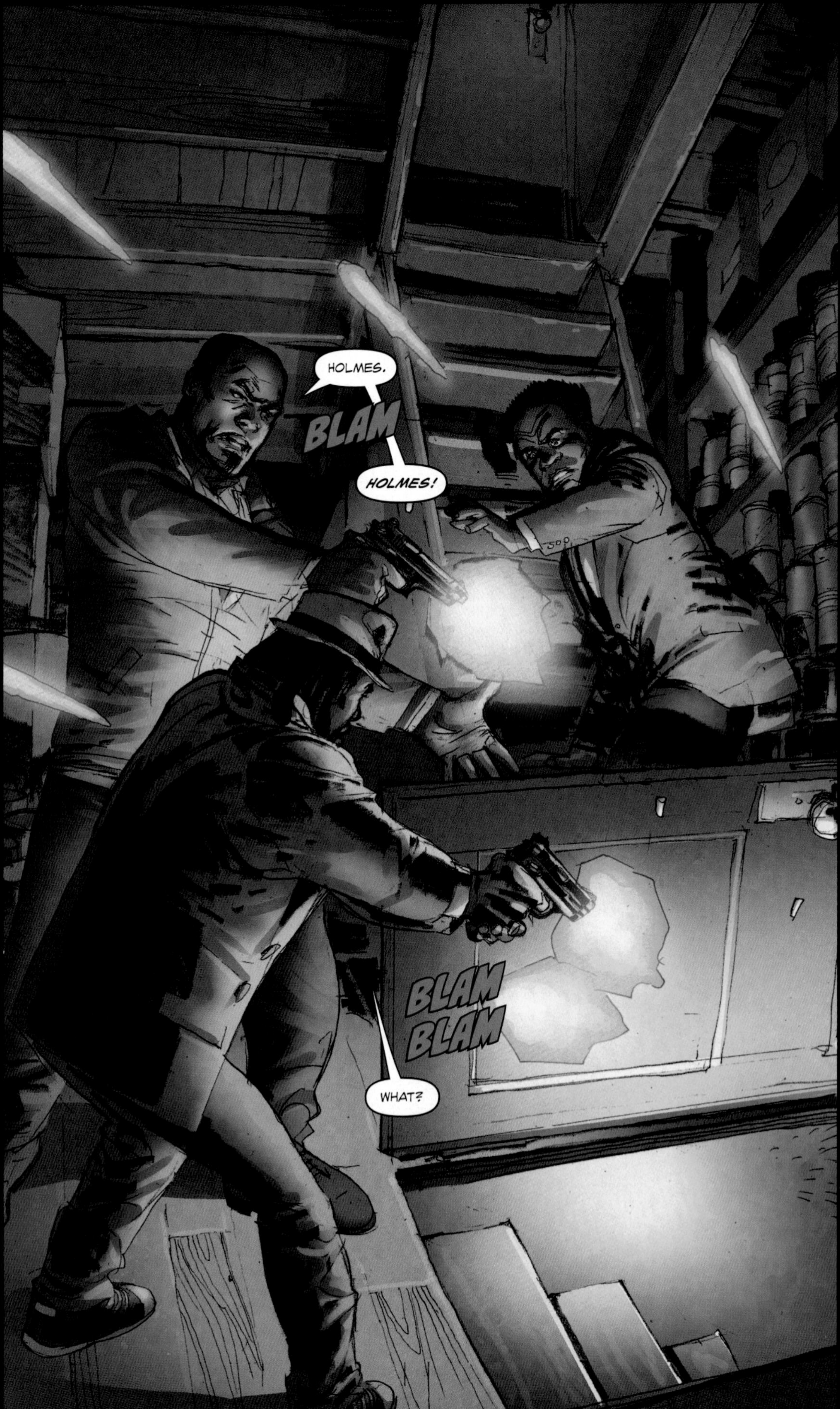
HOLMES.
BLAM
HOLMES!
BLAM
BLAM
WHAT?

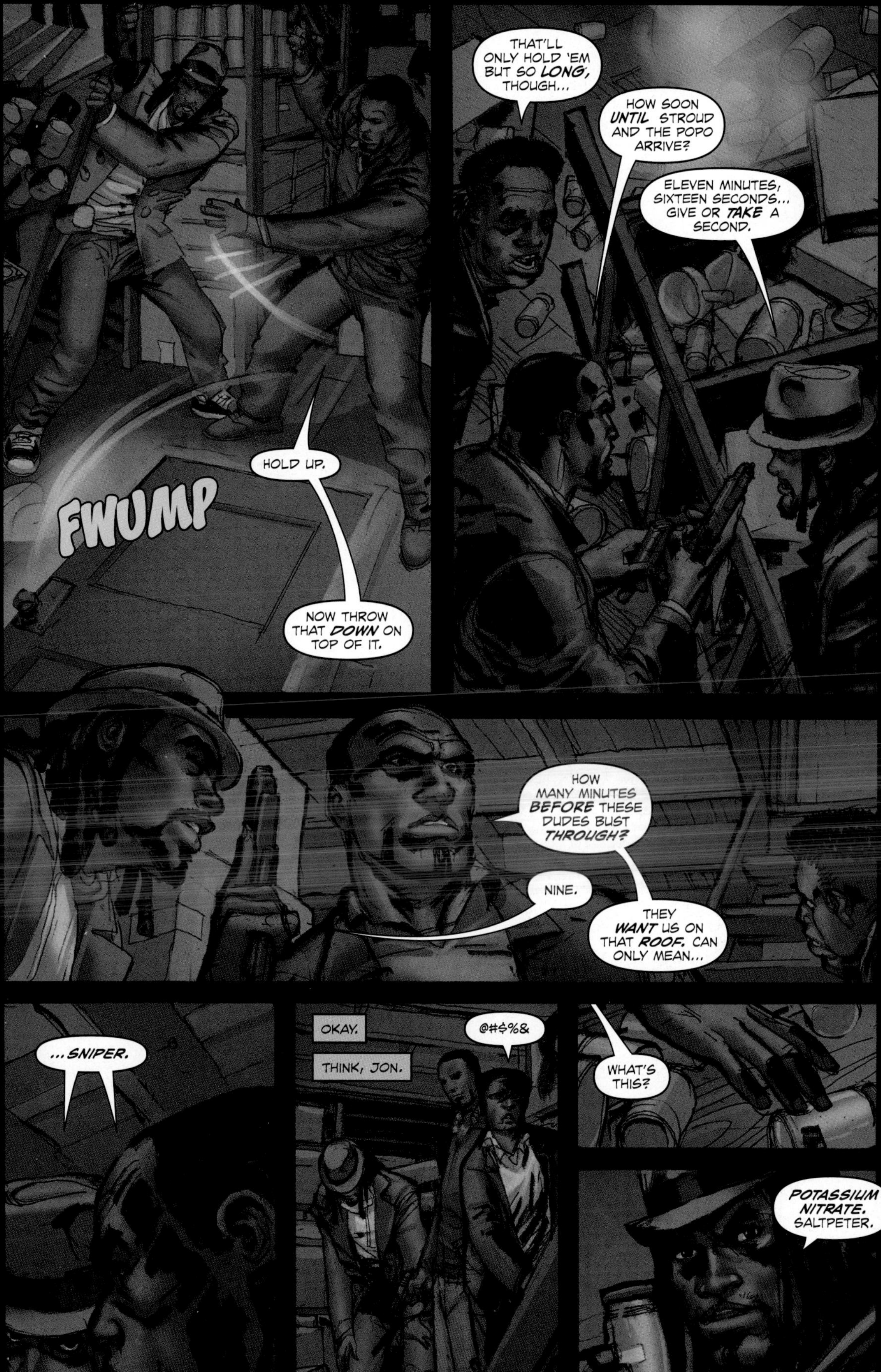

FWUMP
HOLD UP.
NOW THROW THAT DOWN ON TOP OF IT.
THAT'LL ONLY HOLD 'EM BUT SO LONG, THOUGH...
HOW SOON UNTIL STROUD AND THE POPO ARRIVE?
ELEVEN MINUTES, SIXTEEN SECONDS... GIVE OR TAKE A SECOND.
HOW MANY MINUTES BEFORE THESE DUDES BUST THROUGH?
NINE.
THEY WANT US ON THAT ROOF. CAN ONLY MEAN...
...SNIPER.
OKAY.
THINK, JON.
@#$%&
WHAT'S THIS?
POTASSIUM NITRATE. SALTPETER.

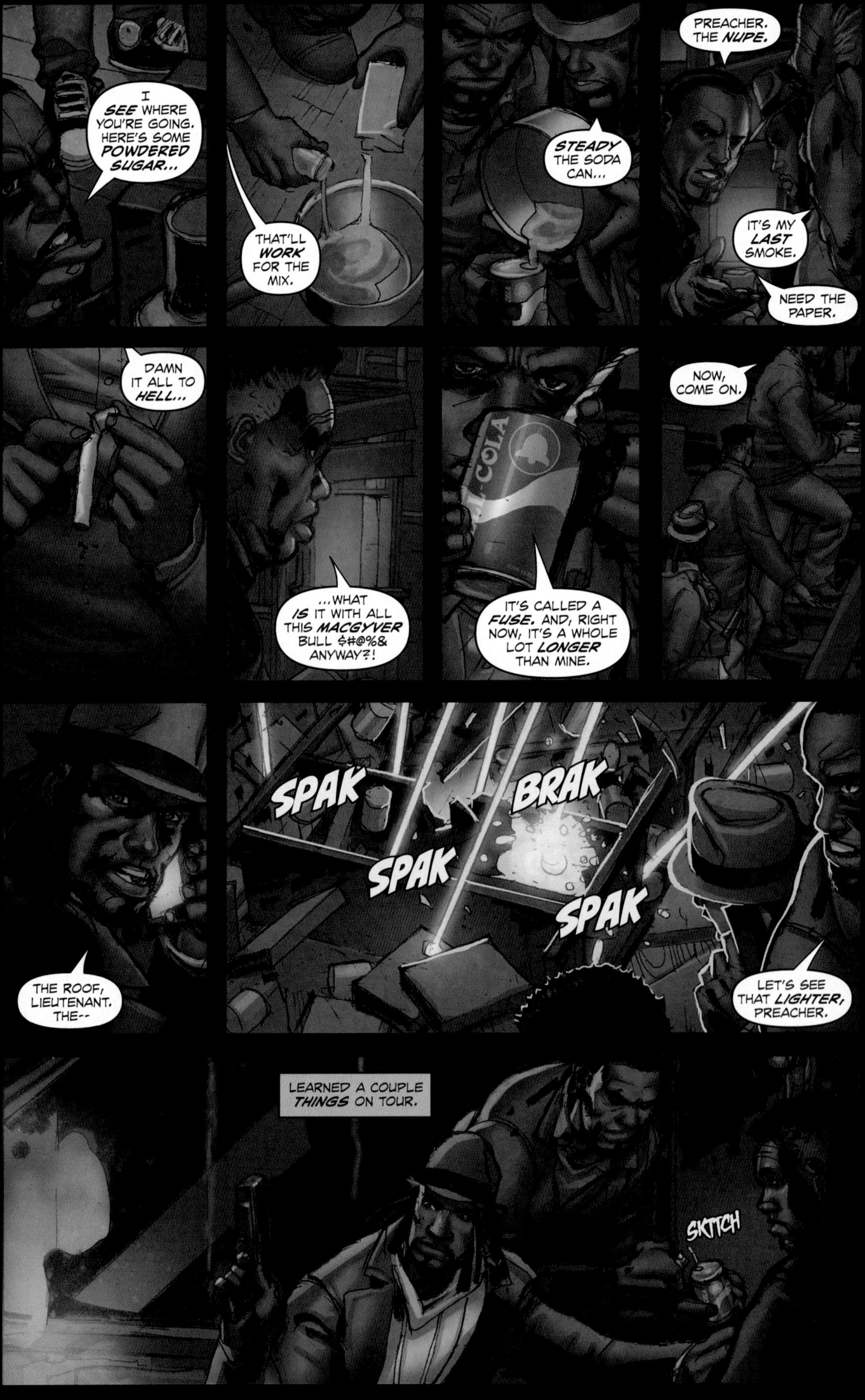
I SEE WHERE YOU'RE GOING. HERE'S SOME POWDERED SUGAR...
THAT'LL WORK FOR THE MIX.
STEADY THE SODA CAN...
PREACHER. THE NUPE.
IT'S MY LAST SMOKE.
NEED THE PAPER.
DAMN IT ALL TO HELL...
...WHAT IS IT WITH ALL THIS MACGYVER BULL $#@%& ANYWAY?!
COLA
IT'S CALLED A FUSE. AND, RIGHT NOW, IT'S A WHOLE LOT LONGER THAN MINE.
NOW, COME ON.
THE ROOF, LIEUTENANT. THE--
SPAK
BRAK
SPAK
SPAK
LET'S SEE THAT LIGHTER, PREACHER.
LEARNED A COUPLE THINGS ON TOUR.
SKTTCH

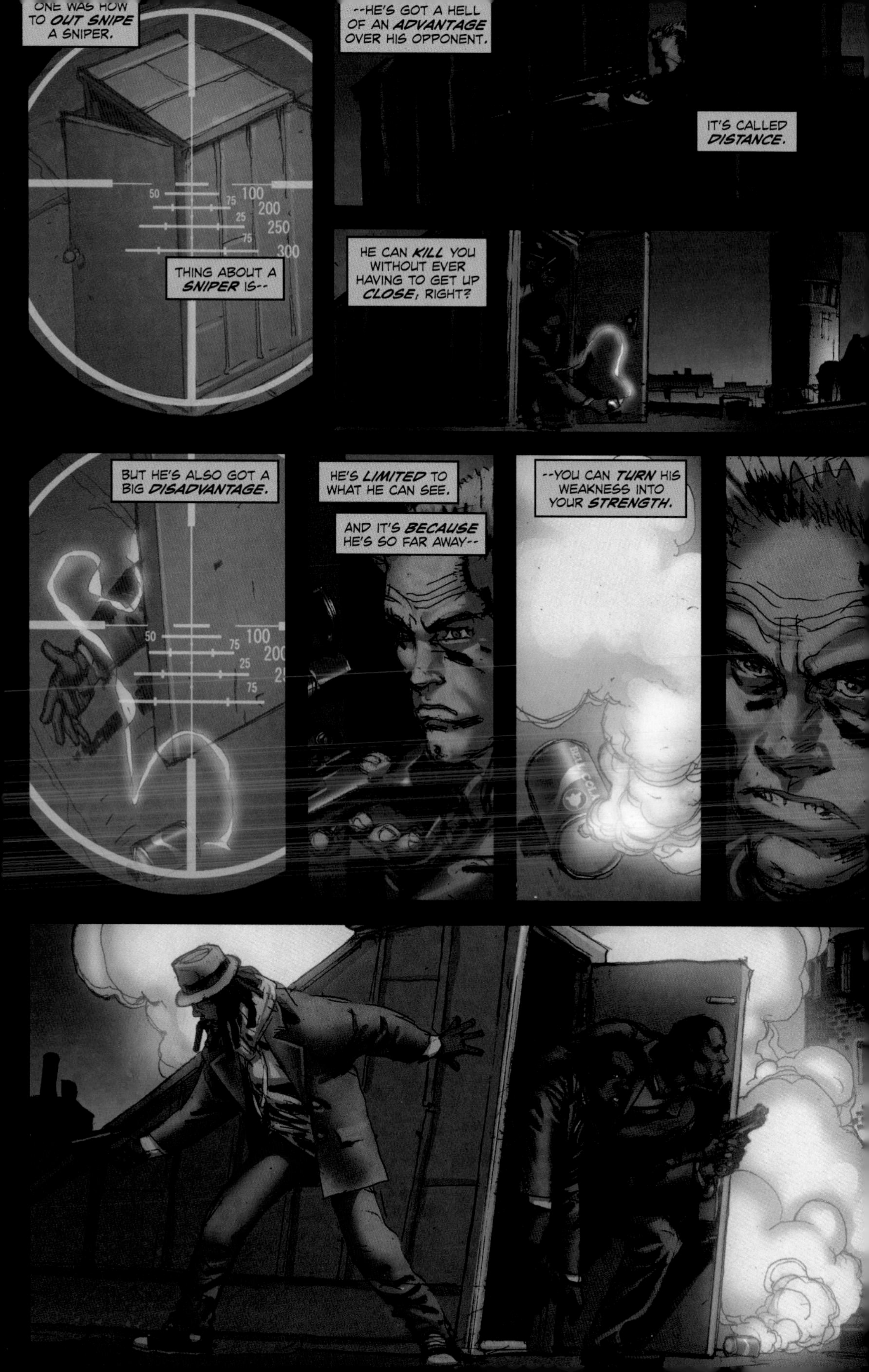

ONE WAS HOW TO OUT SNIPE A SNIPER.
THING ABOUT A SNIPER IS--
--HE'S GOT A HELL OF AN ADVANTAGE OVER HIS OPPONENT.
IT'S CALLED DISTANCE.
HE CAN KILL YOU WITHOUT EVER HAVING TO GET UP CLOSE, RIGHT?
BUT HE'S ALSO GOT A BIG DISADVANTAGE.
HE'S LIMITED TO WHAT HE CAN SEE.
AND IT'S BECAUSE HE'S SO FAR AWAY--
--YOU CAN TURN HIS WEAKNESS INTO YOUR STRENGTH.

WATSON, THE--

ARMORY. I KNOW.

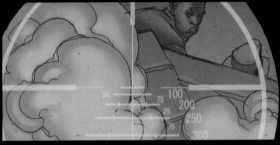

KRAK

AGGHH!!!

RICE!

$#@%&!

$#@%&!

$#@%&!

HOLD ON, PREACHER.

I APPLIED PRESSURE AS BEST AS I COULD--

--BUT RICE NEEDED IMMEDIATE MEDICAL ATTENTION.

DONE DANCING, MAN...

SHUT UP, HUH?

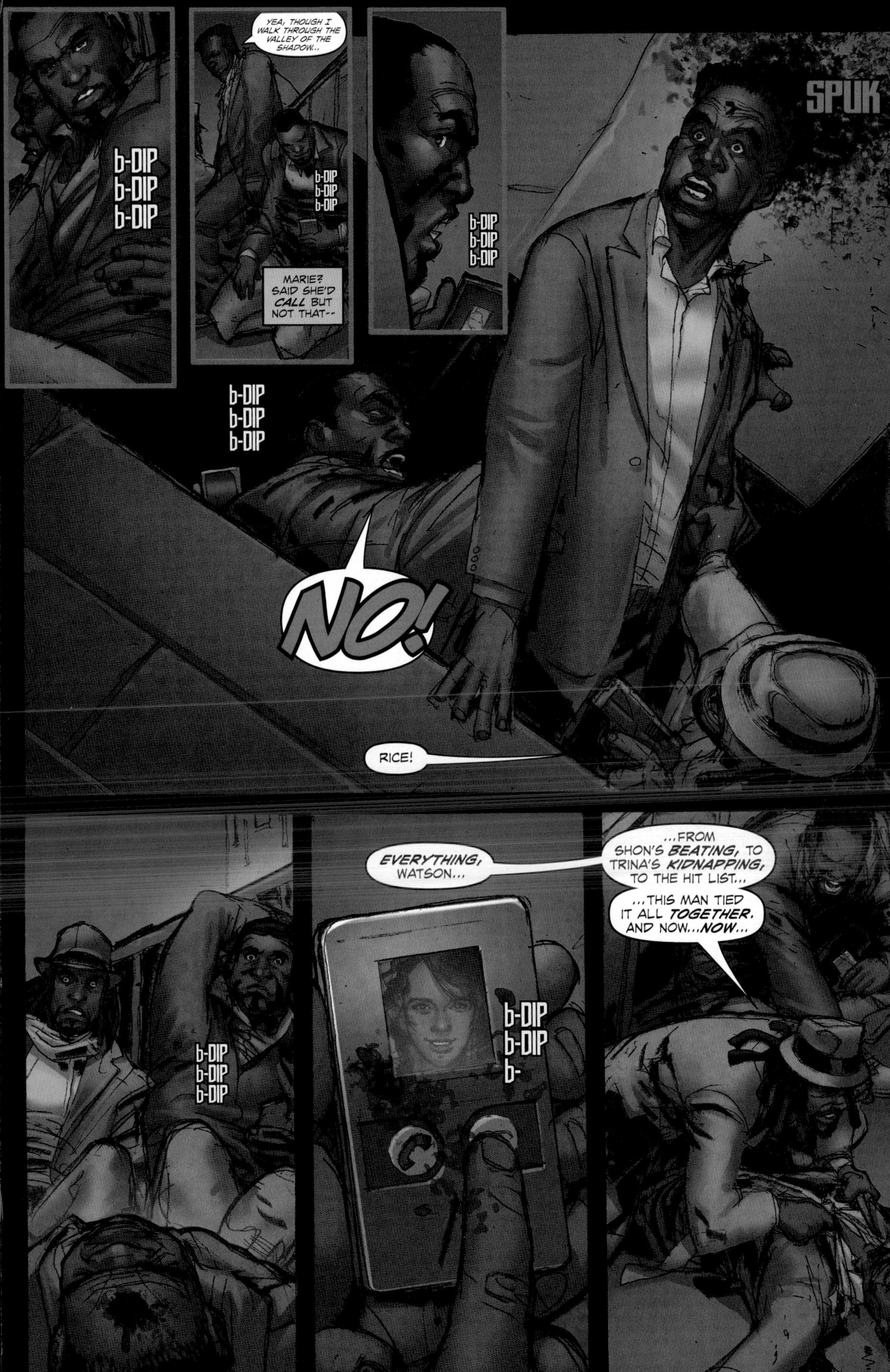
b-DIP
b-DIP
b-DIP
YEA, THOUGH I WALK THROUGH THE VALLEY OF THE SHADOW...
b-DIP
b-DIP
b-DIP
MARIE? SAID SHE'D CALL BUT NOT THAT--
b-DIP
b-DIP
b-DIP
SPUK
b-DIP
b-DIP
b-DIP
NO!
RICE!
b-DIP
b-DIP
b-DIP
EVERYTHING, WATSON...
b-DIP
b-DIP
b-
...FROM SHON'S BEATING, TO TRINA'S KIDNAPPING, TO THE HIT LIST...
...THIS MAN TIED IT ALL TOGETHER. AND NOW...NOW...

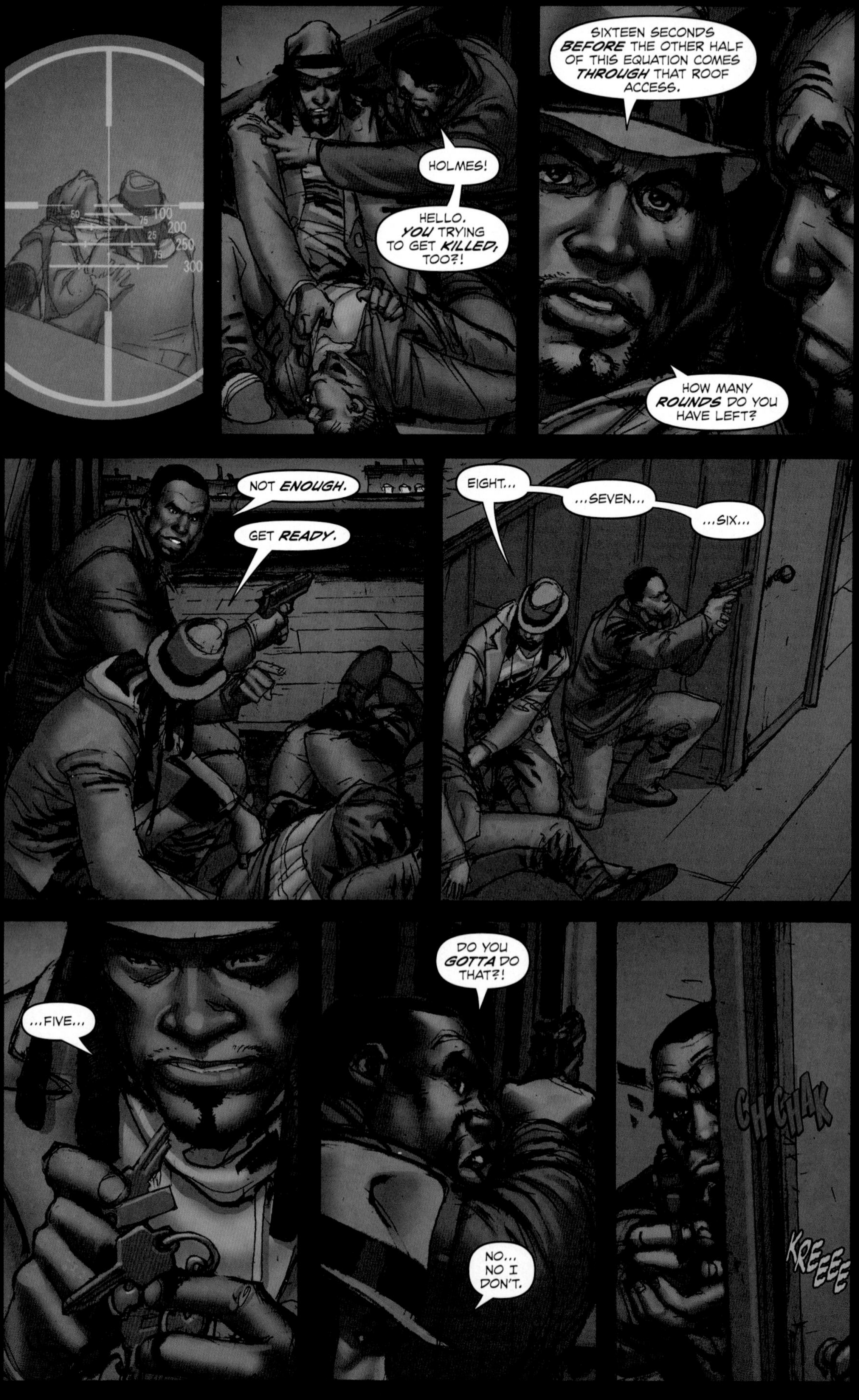

50
75
100
25
200
250
75
300
HOLMES!
HELLO. YOU TRYING TO GET KILLED, TOO?!
SIXTEEN SECONDS BEFORE THE OTHER HALF OF THIS EQUATION COMES THROUGH THAT ROOF ACCESS.
HOW MANY ROUNDS DO YOU HAVE LEFT?
NOT ENOUGH.
GET READY.
EIGHT...
...SEVEN...
...SIX...
...FIVE...
DO YOU GOTTA DO THAT?!
NO... NO I DON'T.
CH-CHAK
KREEEE

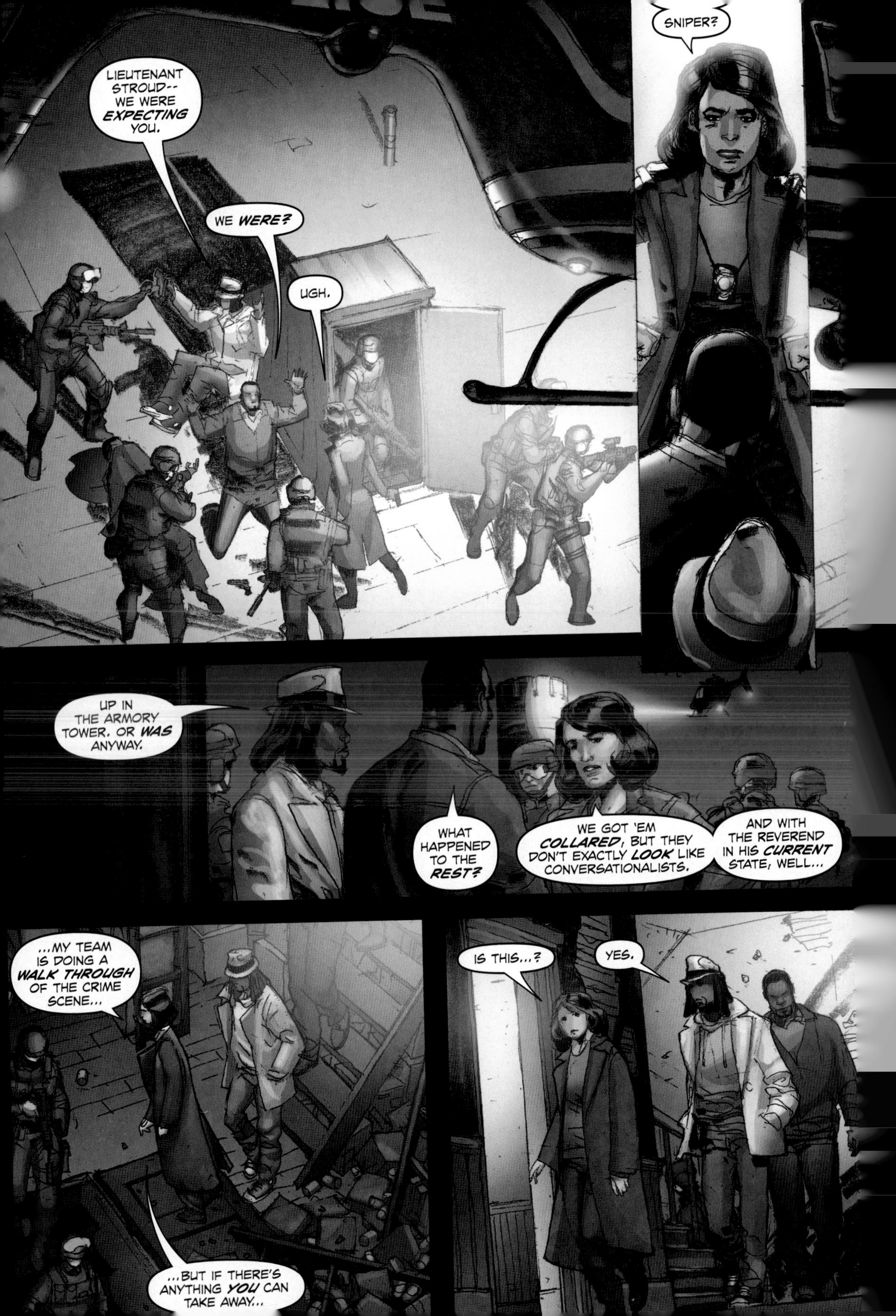
LIEUTENANT STROUD-- WE WERE EXPECTING YOU.
WE WERE?
UGH.
SNIPER?
UP IN THE ARMORY TOWER. OR WAS ANYWAY.
WHAT HAPPENED TO THE REST?
WE GOT 'EM COLLARED, BUT THEY DON'T EXACTLY LOOK LIKE CONVERSATIONALISTS.
AND WITH THE REVEREND IN HIS CURRENT STATE, WELL...
...MY TEAM IS DOING A WALK THROUGH OF THE CRIME SCENE...
...BUT IF THERE'S ANYTHING YOU CAN TAKE AWAY...
IS THIS...?
YES.

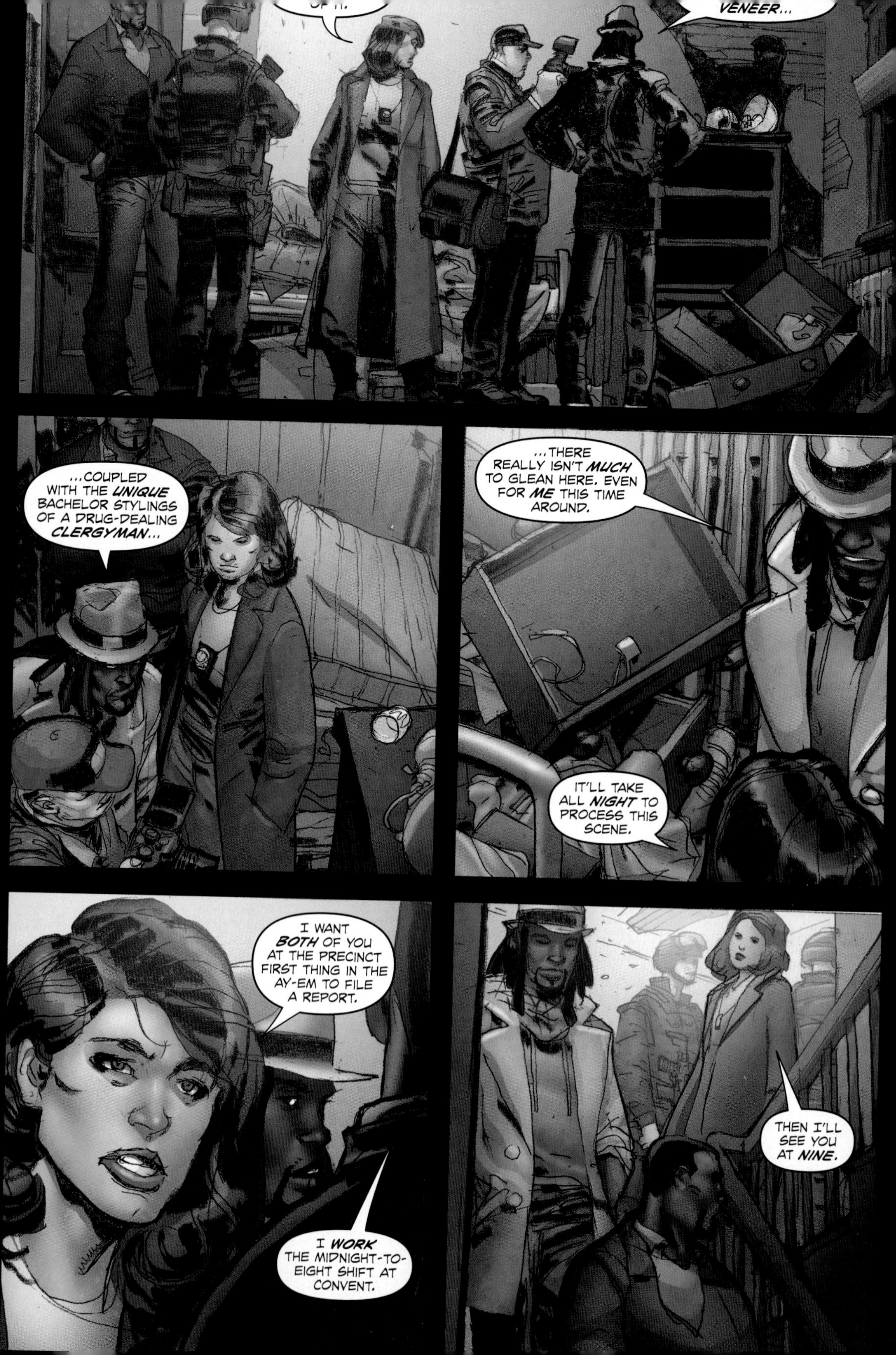
...UP IT.
VENEER...
...COUPLED WITH THE UNIQUE BACHELOR STYLINGS OF A DRUG-DEALING CLERGYMAN...
...THERE REALLY ISN'T MUCH TO GLEAN HERE. EVEN FOR ME THIS TIME AROUND.
IT'LL TAKE ALL NIGHT TO PROCESS THIS SCENE.
I WANT BOTH OF YOU AT THE PRECINCT FIRST THING IN THE AY-EM TO FILE A REPORT.
I WORK THE MIDNIGHT-TO-EIGHT SHIFT AT CONVENT.
THEN I'LL SEE YOU AT NINE.

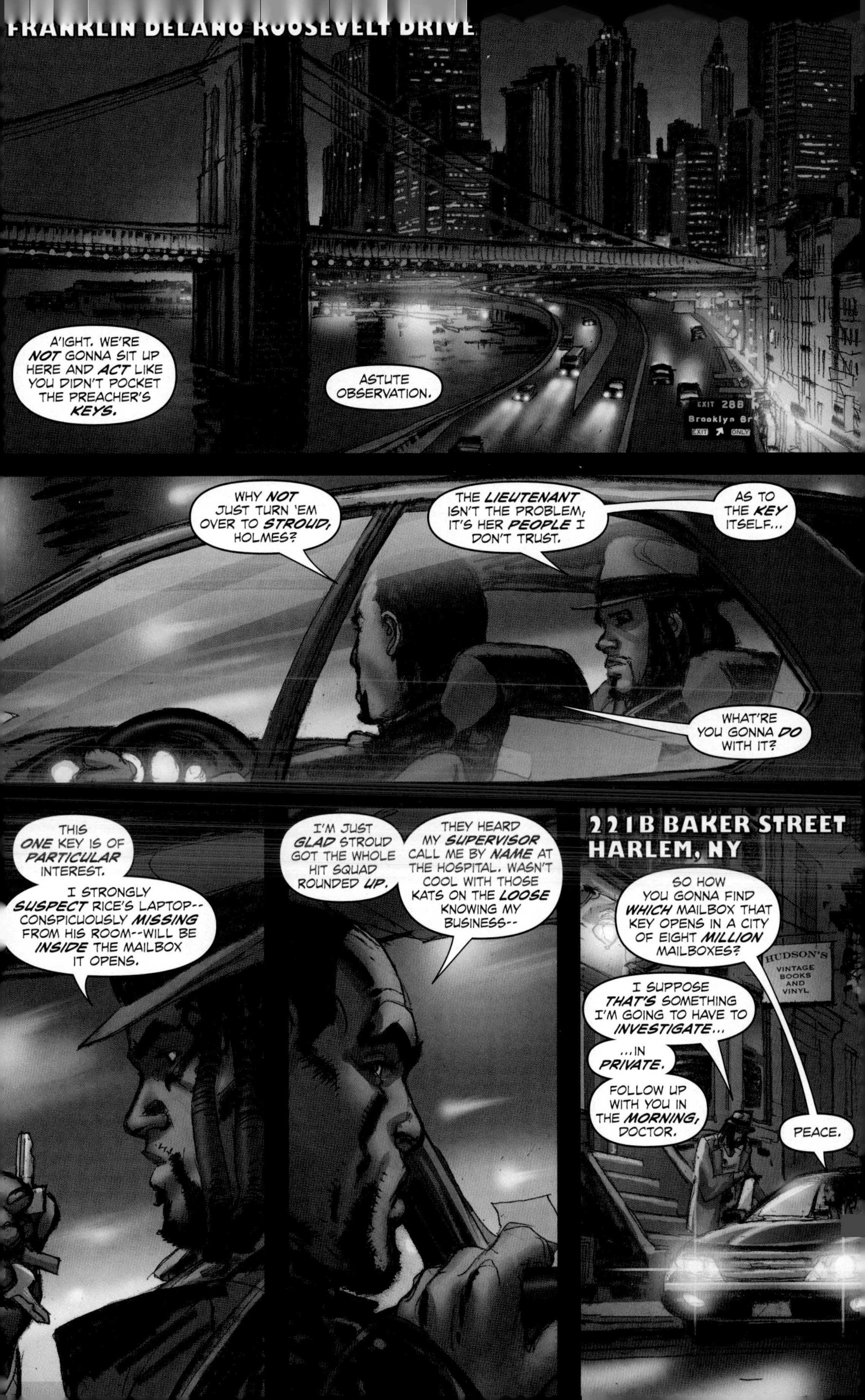
FRANKLIN DELANO ROOSEVELT DRIVE
A'IGHT. WE'RE NOT GONNA SIT UP HERE AND ACT LIKE YOU DIDN'T POCKET THE PREACHER'S KEYS.
ASTUTE OBSERVATION.
EXIT 28B
Brooklyn Br
EXIT ONLY
WHY NOT JUST TURN 'EM OVER TO STROUD, HOLMES?
THE LIEUTENANT ISN'T THE PROBLEM, IT'S HER PEOPLE I DON'T TRUST.
AS TO THE KEY ITSELF...
WHAT'RE YOU GONNA DO WITH IT?
THIS ONE KEY IS OF PARTICULAR INTEREST.
I STRONGLY SUSPECT RICE'S LAPTOP--CONSPICUOUSLY MISSING FROM HIS ROOM--WILL BE INSIDE THE MAILBOX IT OPENS.
I'M JUST GLAD STROUD GOT THE WHOLE HIT SQUAD ROUNDED UP.
THEY HEARD MY SUPERVISOR CALL ME BY NAME AT THE HOSPITAL. WASN'T COOL WITH THOSE KATS ON THE LOOSE KNOWING MY BUSINESS--
221B BAKER STREET HARLEM, NY
SO HOW YOU GONNA FIND WHICH MAILBOX THAT KEY OPENS IN A CITY OF EIGHT MILLION MAILBOXES?
HUDSON'S VINTAGE BOOKS AND VINYL
I SUPPOSE THAT'S SOMETHING I'M GOING TO HAVE TO INVESTIGATE...
...IN PRIVATE.
FOLLOW UP WITH YOU IN THE MORNING, DOCTOR.
PEACE.

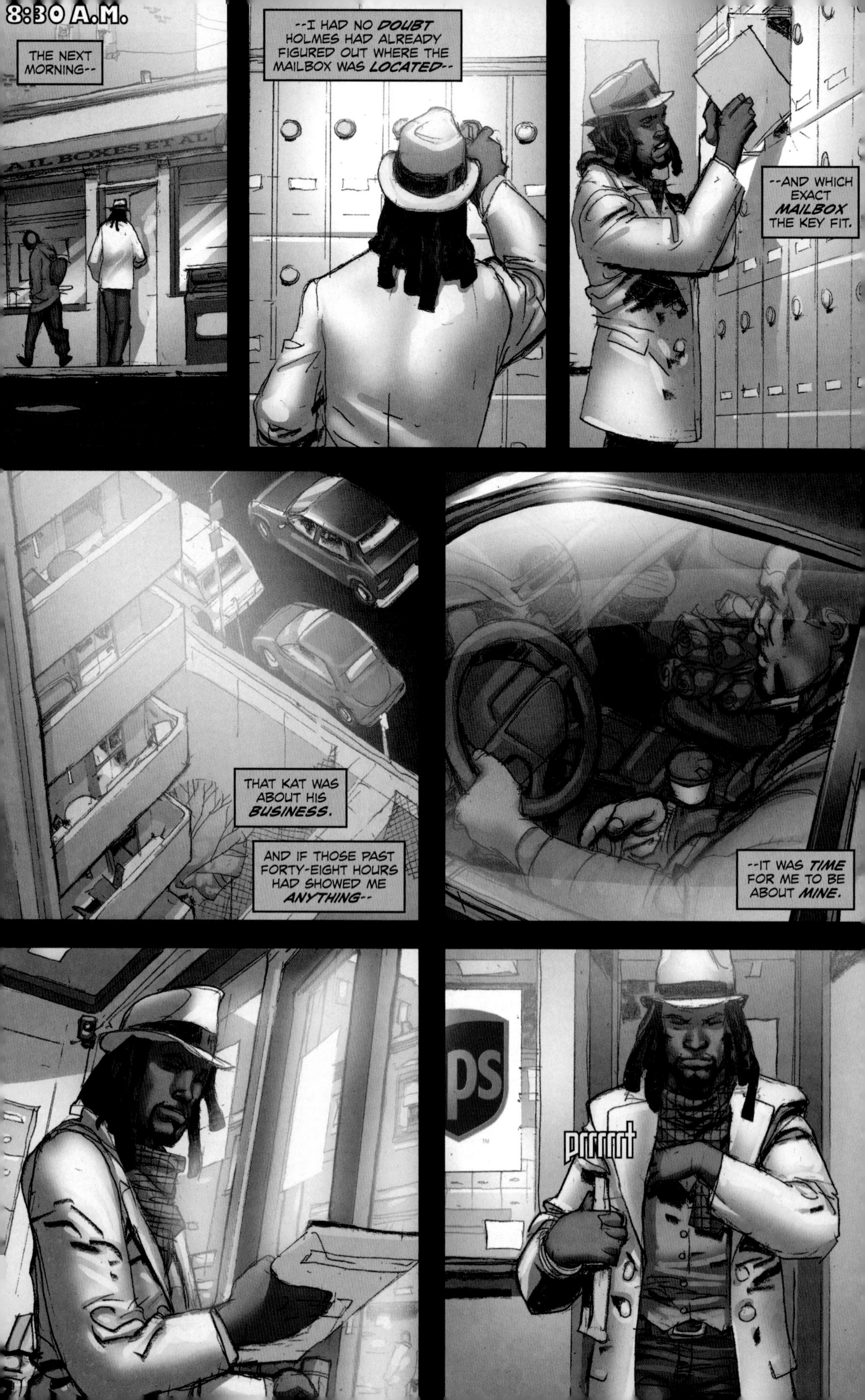
8:30 A.M.
THE NEXT MORNING--
AIL BOXES ET AL
--I HAD NO DOUBT HOLMES HAD ALREADY FIGURED OUT WHERE THE MAILBOX WAS LOCATED--
--AND WHICH EXACT MAILBOX THE KEY FIT.
THAT KAT WAS ABOUT HIS BUSINESS.
AND IF THOSE PAST FORTY-EIGHT HOURS HAD SHOWED ME ANYTHING--
--IT WAS TIME FOR ME TO BE ABOUT MINE.
prrrrrt

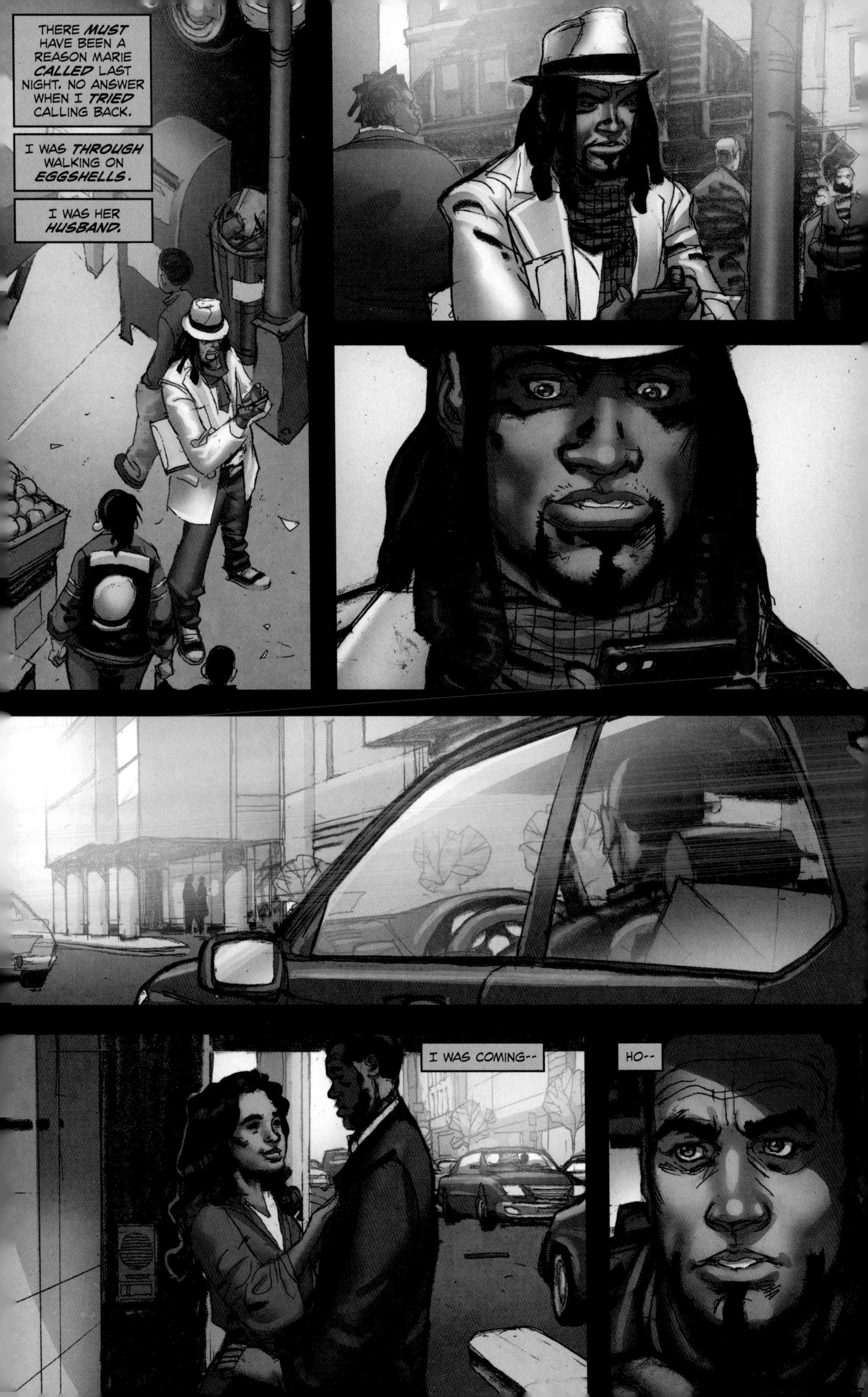
THERE MUST HAVE BEEN A REASON MARIE CALLED LAST NIGHT. NO ANSWER WHEN I TRIED CALLING BACK.
I WAS THROUGH WALKING ON EGGSHELLS.
I WAS HER HUSBAND.
I WAS COMING--
HO--

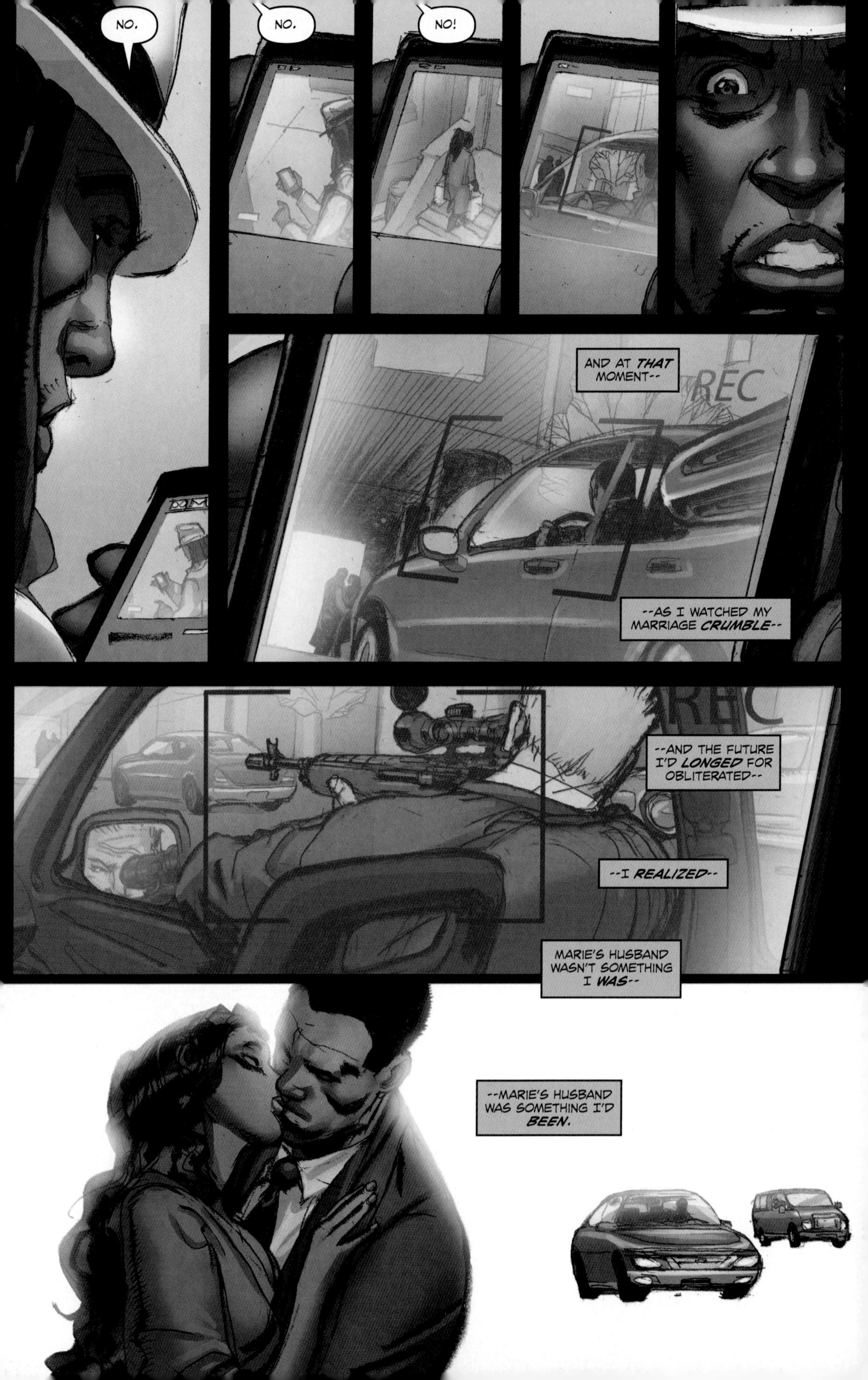
NO.
NO.
NO!
AND AT THAT MOMENT--
REC
--AS I WATCHED MY MARRIAGE CRUMBLE--
REC
--AND THE FUTURE I'D LONGED FOR OBLITERATED--
--I REALIZED--
MARIE'S HUSBAND WASN'T SOMETHING I WAS--
--MARIE'S HUSBAND WAS SOMETHING I'D BEEN.

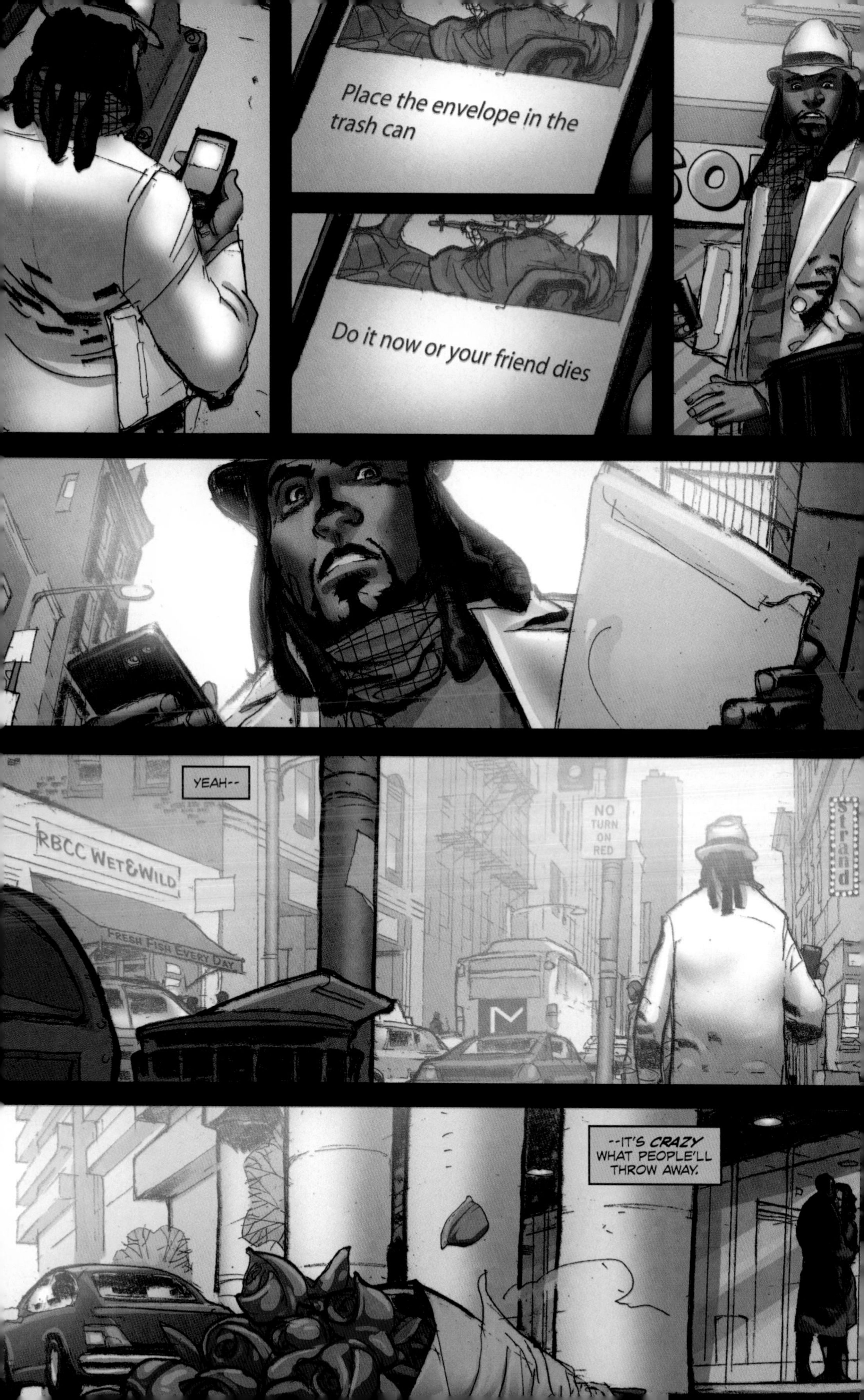
Place the envelope in the trash can
Do it now or your friend dies
YEAH--
RBCC WET&WILD
FRESH FISH EVERY DAY
NO TURN ON RED
Strand
--IT'S *CRAZY* WHAT PEOPLE'LL THROW AWAY.

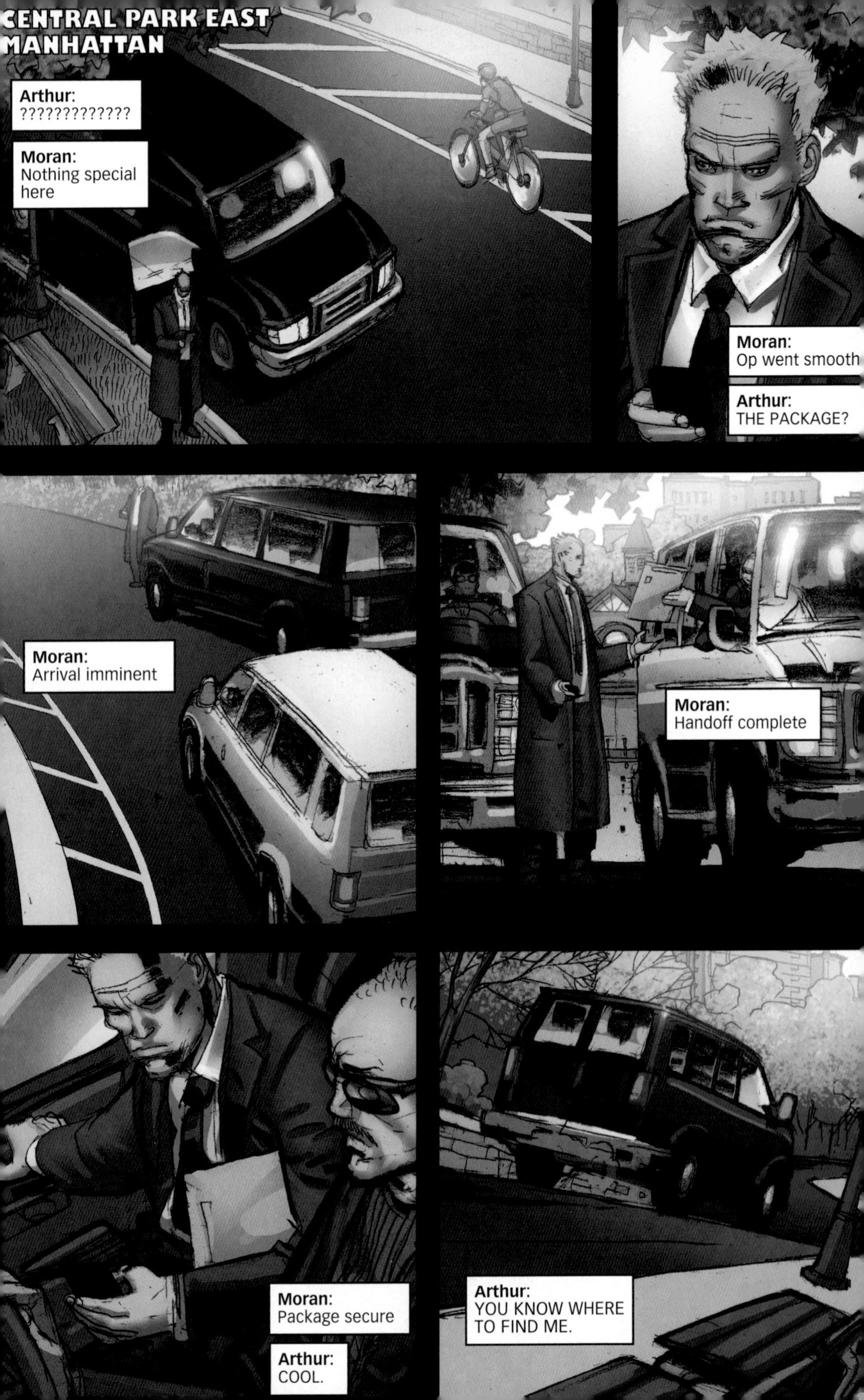
CENTRAL PARK EAST
MANHATTAN
Arthur: ?????????????
Moran: Nothing special here
Moran: Op went smooth
Arthur: THE PACKAGE?
Moran: Arrival imminent
Moran: Handoff complete
Moran: Package secure
Arthur: COOL.
Arthur: YOU KNOW WHERE TO FIND ME.

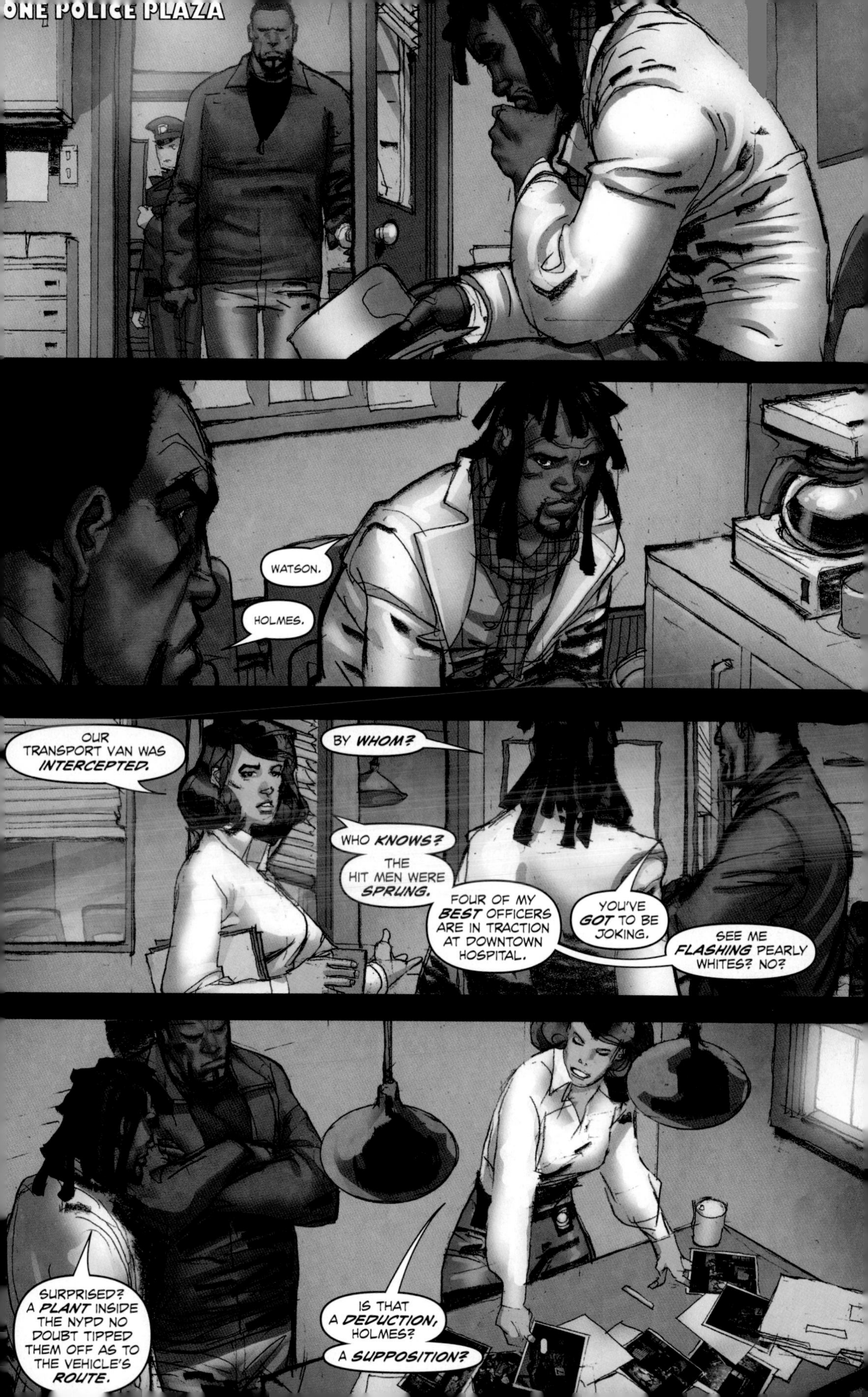
ONE POLICE PLAZA
WATSON.
HOLMES.
OUR TRANSPORT VAN WAS INTERCEPTED.
BY WHOM?
WHO KNOWS?
THE HIT MEN WERE SPRUNG.
FOUR OF MY BEST OFFICERS ARE IN TRACTION AT DOWNTOWN HOSPITAL.
YOU'VE GOT TO BE JOKING.
SEE ME FLASHING PEARLY WHITES? NO?
SURPRISED? A PLANT INSIDE THE NYPD NO DOUBT TIPPED THEM OFF AS TO THE VEHICLE'S ROUTE.
IS THAT A DEDUCTION, HOLMES?
A SUPPOSITION?

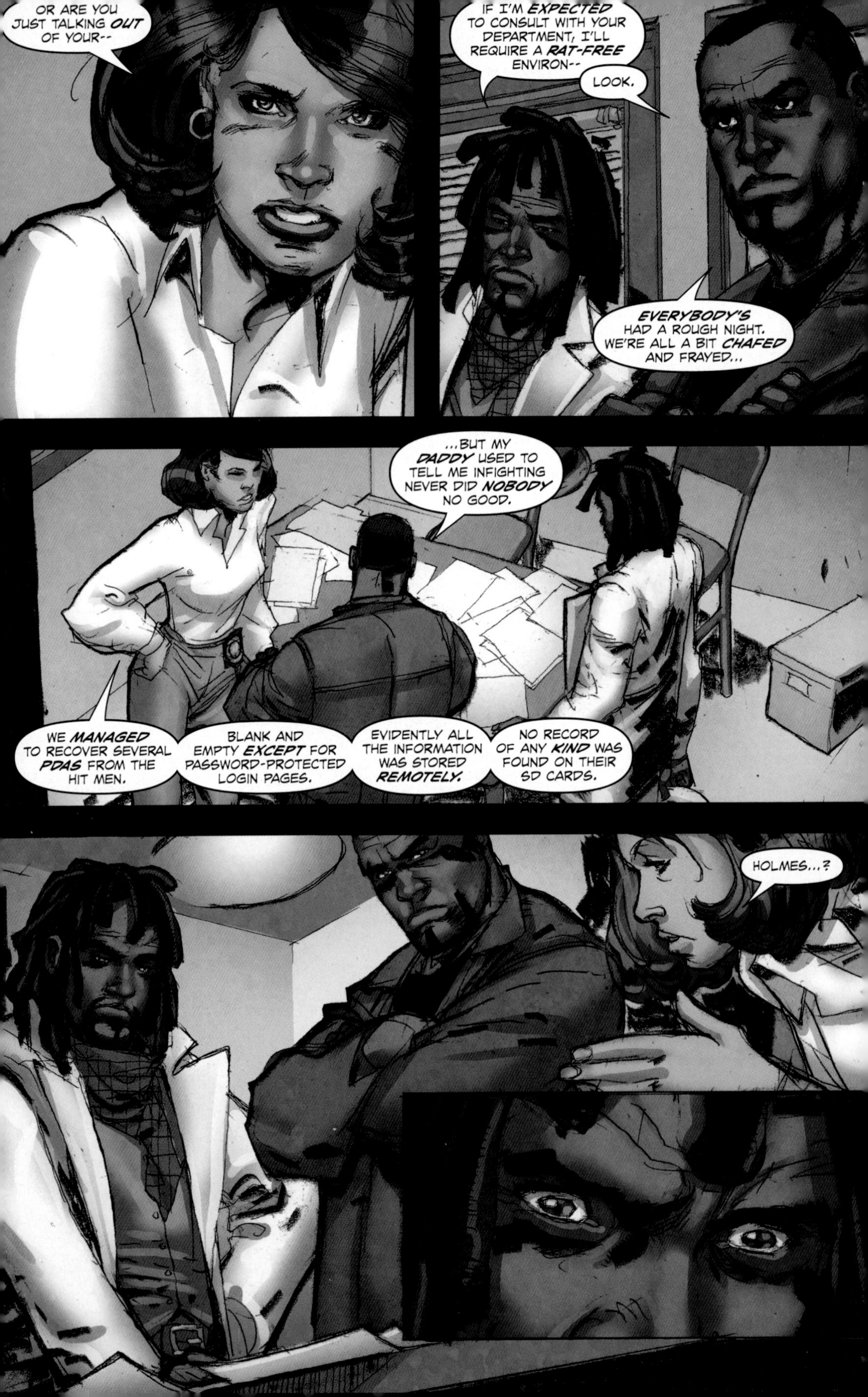

OR ARE YOU JUST TALKING OUT OF YOUR--
IF I'M EXPECTED TO CONSULT WITH YOUR DEPARTMENT, I'LL REQUIRE A RAT-FREE ENVIRON--
LOOK.
EVERYBODY'S HAD A ROUGH NIGHT. WE'RE ALL A BIT CHAFED AND FRAYED...
...BUT MY DADDY USED TO TELL ME INFIGHTING NEVER DID NOBODY NO GOOD.
WE MANAGED TO RECOVER SEVERAL PDAS FROM THE HIT MEN.
BLANK AND EMPTY EXCEPT FOR PASSWORD-PROTECTED LOGIN PAGES.
EVIDENTLY ALL THE INFORMATION WAS STORED REMOTELY.
NO RECORD OF ANY KIND WAS FOUND ON THEIR SD CARDS.
HOLMES...?

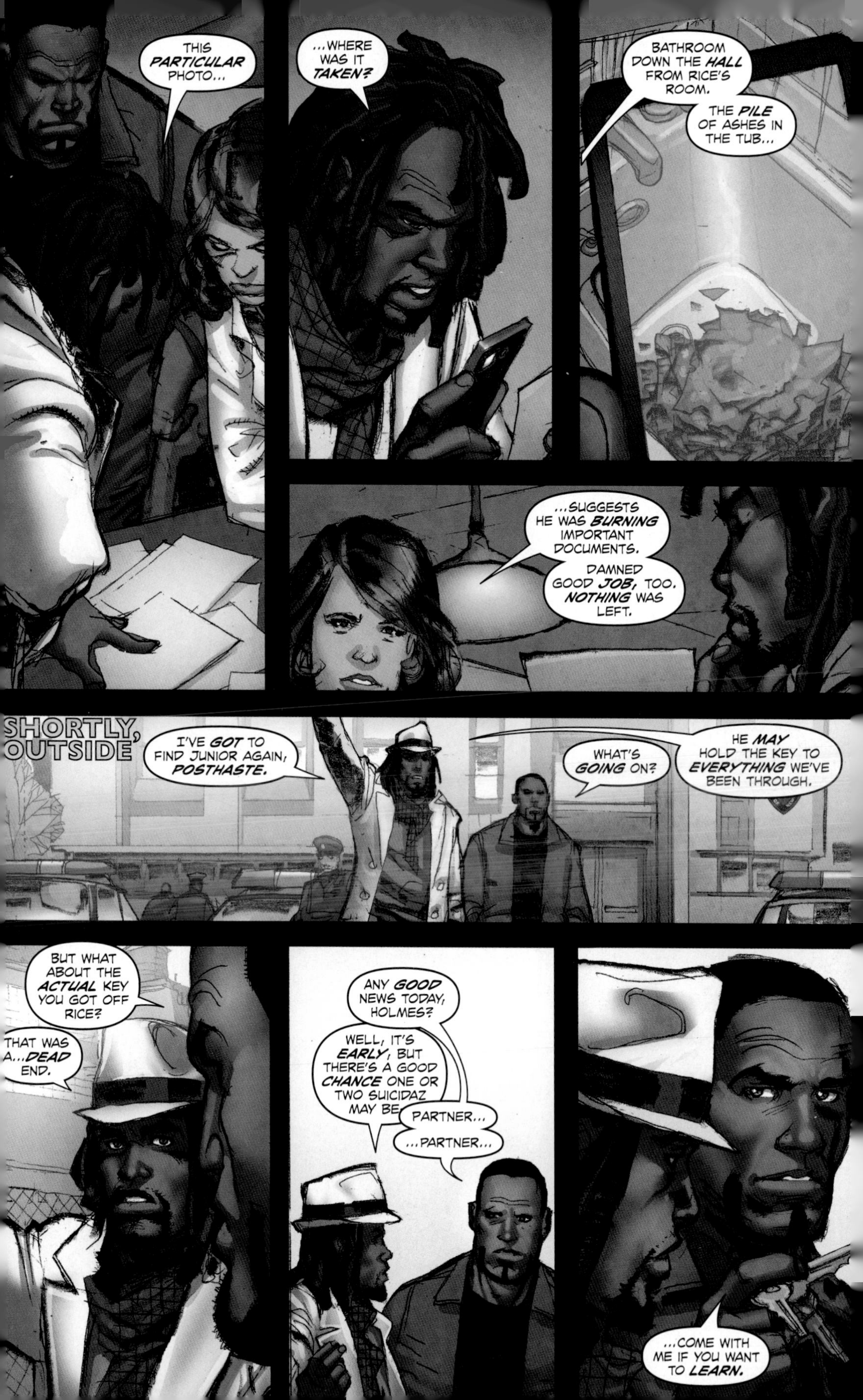

THIS PARTICULAR PHOTO...
...WHERE WAS IT TAKEN?
BATHROOM DOWN THE HALL FROM RICE'S ROOM.
THE PILE OF ASHES IN THE TUB...
...SUGGESTS HE WAS BURNING IMPORTANT DOCUMENTS.
DAMNED GOOD JOB, TOO. NOTHING WAS LEFT.
SHORTLY, OUTSIDE
I'VE GOT TO FIND JUNIOR AGAIN, POSTHASTE.
WHAT'S GOING ON?
HE MAY HOLD THE KEY TO EVERYTHING WE'VE BEEN THROUGH.
BUT WHAT ABOUT THE ACTUAL KEY YOU GOT OFF RICE?
THAT WAS A...DEAD END.
ANY GOOD NEWS TODAY, HOLMES?
WELL, IT'S EARLY, BUT THERE'S A GOOD CHANCE ONE OR TWO SUICIDAZ MAY BE
PARTNER...
...PARTNER...
...COME WITH ME IF YOU WANT TO LEARN.

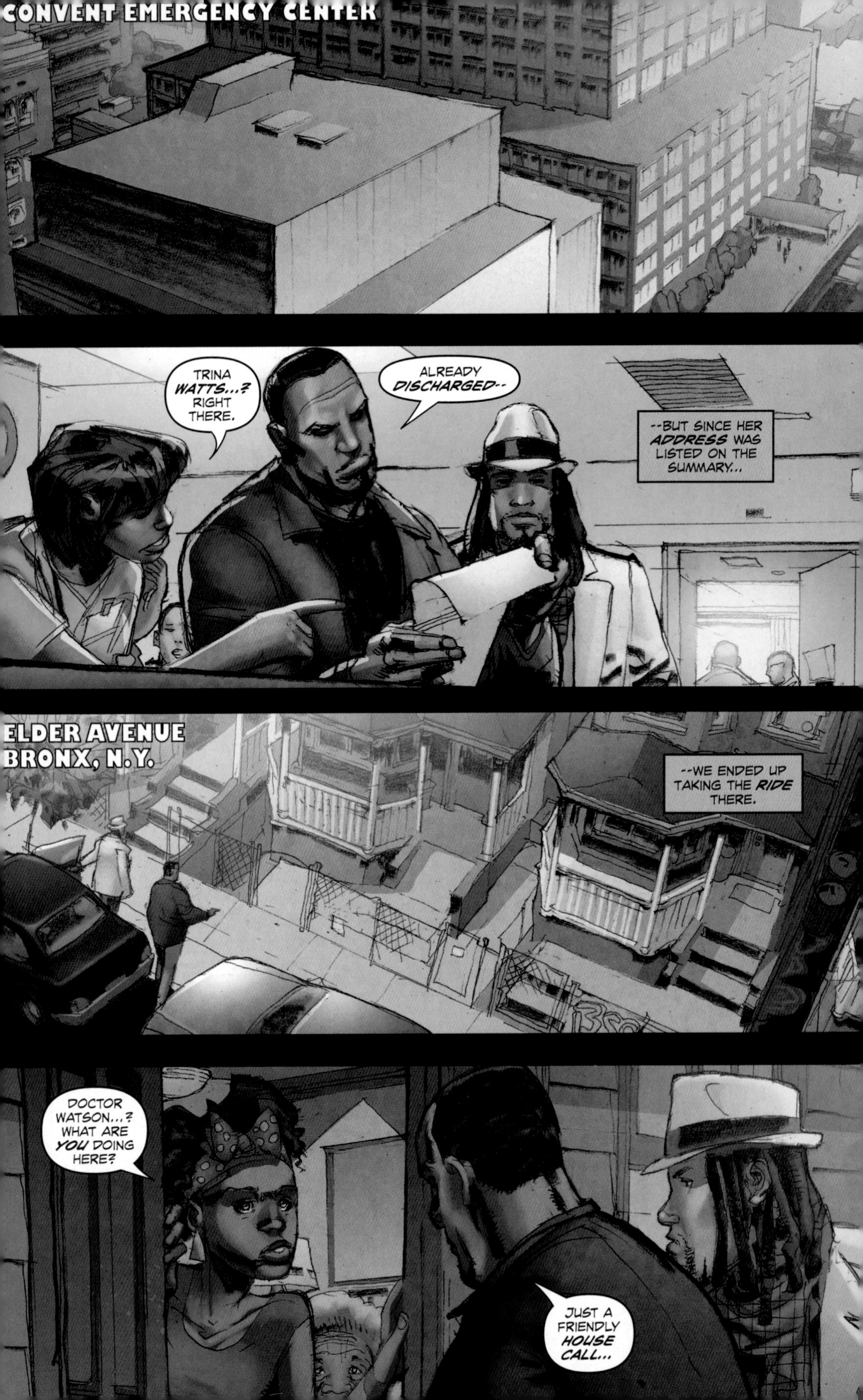
CONVENT EMERGENCY CENTER
TRINA WATTS...? RIGHT THERE.
ALREADY DISCHARGED--
--BUT SINCE HER ADDRESS WAS LISTED ON THE SUMMARY...
ELDER AVENUE BRONX, N.Y.
--WE ENDED UP TAKING THE RIDE THERE.
DOCTOR WATSON...? WHAT ARE YOU DOING HERE?
JUST A FRIENDLY HOUSE CALL...

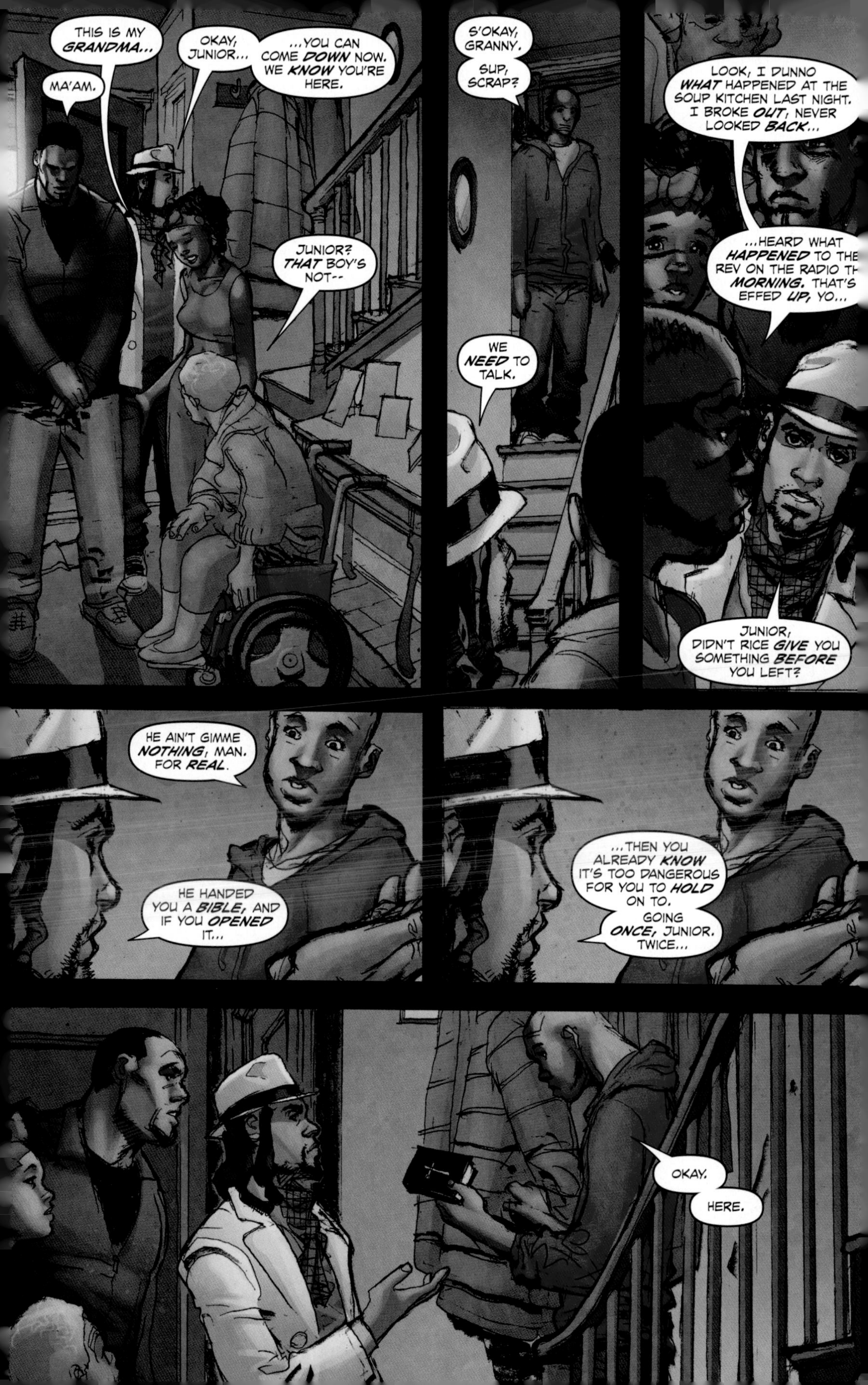
THIS IS MY GRANDMA...
MA'AM.
OKAY, JUNIOR...
...YOU CAN COME DOWN NOW. WE KNOW YOU'RE HERE.
JUNIOR? THAT BOY'S NOT--
S'OKAY, GRANNY.
SUP, SCRAP?
WE NEED TO TALK.
LOOK, I DUNNO WHAT HAPPENED AT THE SOUP KITCHEN LAST NIGHT. I BROKE OUT, NEVER LOOKED BACK...
...HEARD WHAT HAPPENED TO THE REV ON THE RADIO TH MORNING. THAT'S EFFED UP, YO...
JUNIOR, DIDN'T RICE GIVE YOU SOMETHING BEFORE YOU LEFT?
HE AIN'T GIMME NOTHING, MAN. FOR REAL.
HE HANDED YOU A BIBLE, AND IF YOU OPENED IT...
...THEN YOU ALREADY KNOW IT'S TOO DANGEROUS FOR YOU TO HOLD ON TO.
GOING ONCE, JUNIOR. TWICE...
OKAY.
HERE.

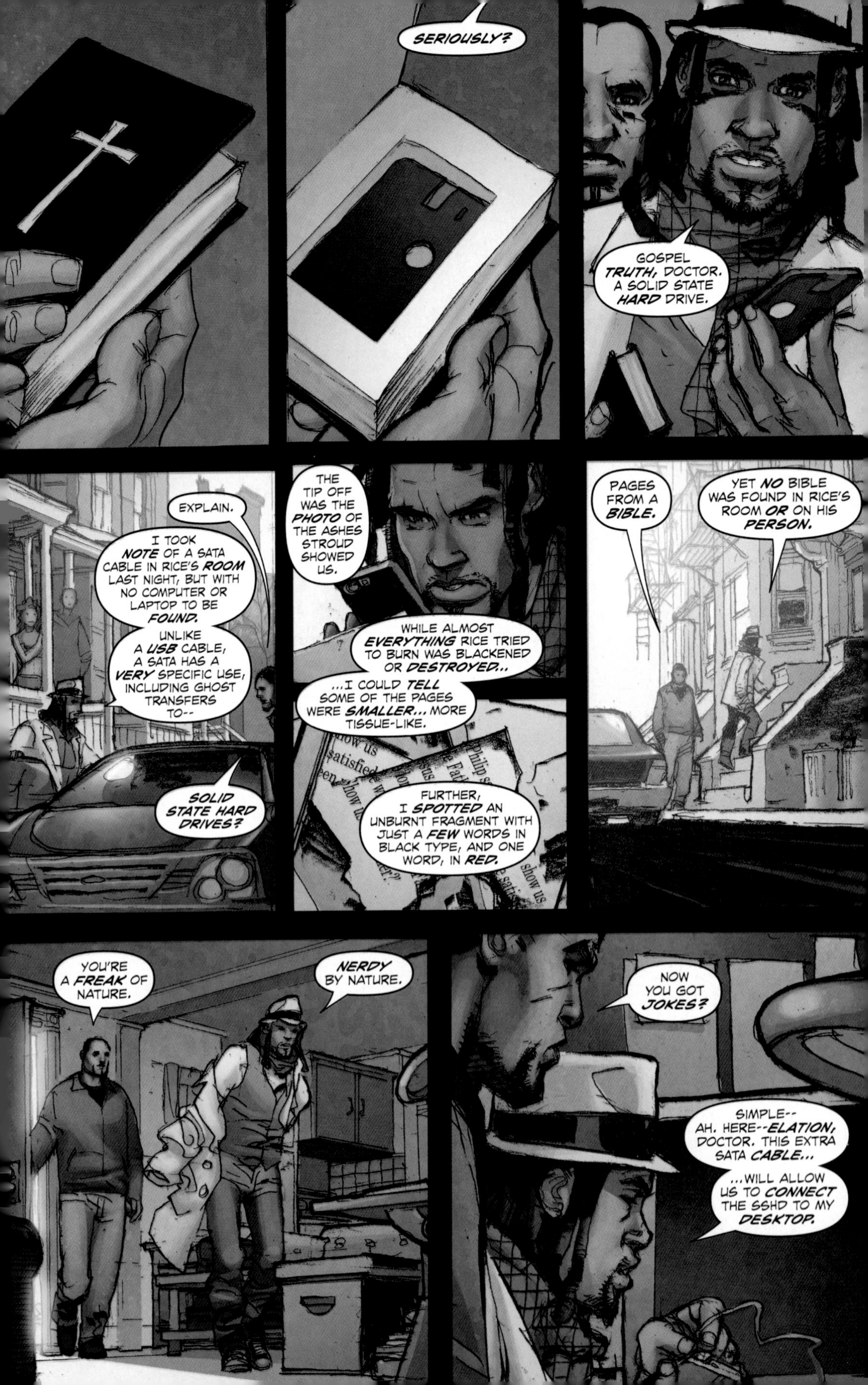
SERIOUSLY?
GOSPEL TRUTH, DOCTOR. A SOLID STATE HARD DRIVE.
EXPLAIN.
I TOOK NOTE OF A SATA CABLE IN RICE'S ROOM LAST NIGHT, BUT WITH NO COMPUTER OR LAPTOP TO BE FOUND.
UNLIKE A USB CABLE, A SATA HAS A VERY SPECIFIC USE, INCLUDING GHOST TRANSFERS TO--
SOLID STATE HARD DRIVES?
THE TIP OFF WAS THE PHOTO OF THE ASHES STROUD SHOWED US.
WHILE ALMOST EVERYTHING RICE TRIED TO BURN WAS BLACKENED OR DESTROYED...
...I COULD TELL SOME OF THE PAGES WERE SMALLER... MORE TISSUE-LIKE.
FURTHER, I SPOTTED AN UNBURNT FRAGMENT WITH JUST A FEW WORDS IN BLACK TYPE, AND ONE WORD, IN RED.
PAGES FROM A BIBLE.
YET NO BIBLE WAS FOUND IN RICE'S ROOM OR ON HIS PERSON.
YOU'RE A FREAK OF NATURE.
NERDY BY NATURE.
NOW YOU GOT JOKES?
SIMPLE-- AH. HERE--ELATION, DOCTOR. THIS EXTRA SATA CABLE...
...WILL ALLOW US TO CONNECT THE SSHD TO MY DESKTOP.

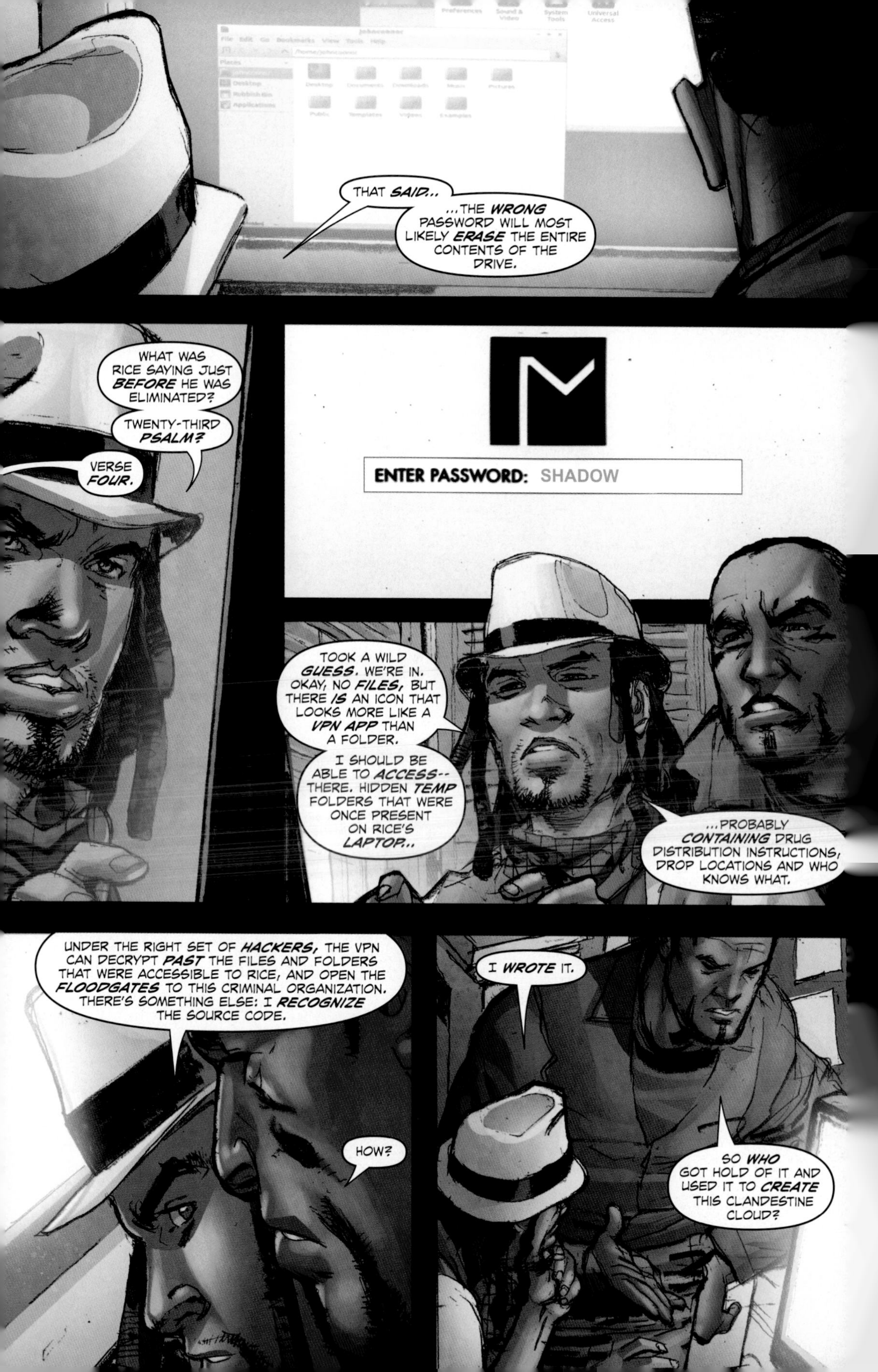
THAT SAID...
...THE WRONG PASSWORD WILL MOST LIKELY ERASE THE ENTIRE CONTENTS OF THE DRIVE.
WHAT WAS RICE SAYING JUST BEFORE HE WAS ELIMINATED?
TWENTY-THIRD PSALM?
VERSE FOUR.
ENTER PASSWORD: SHADOW
TOOK A WILD GUESS. WE'RE IN. OKAY, NO FILES, BUT THERE IS AN ICON THAT LOOKS MORE LIKE A VPN APP THAN A FOLDER.
I SHOULD BE ABLE TO ACCESS-- THERE. HIDDEN TEMP FOLDERS THAT WERE ONCE PRESENT ON RICE'S LAPTOP...
...PROBABLY CONTAINING DRUG DISTRIBUTION INSTRUCTIONS, DROP LOCATIONS AND WHO KNOWS WHAT.
UNDER THE RIGHT SET OF HACKERS, THE VPN CAN DECRYPT PAST THE FILES AND FOLDERS THAT WERE ACCESSIBLE TO RICE, AND OPEN THE FLOODGATES TO THIS CRIMINAL ORGANIZATION. THERE'S SOMETHING ELSE: I RECOGNIZE THE SOURCE CODE.
HOW?
I WROTE IT.
SO WHO GOT HOLD OF IT AND USED IT TO CREATE THIS CLANDESTINE CLOUD?

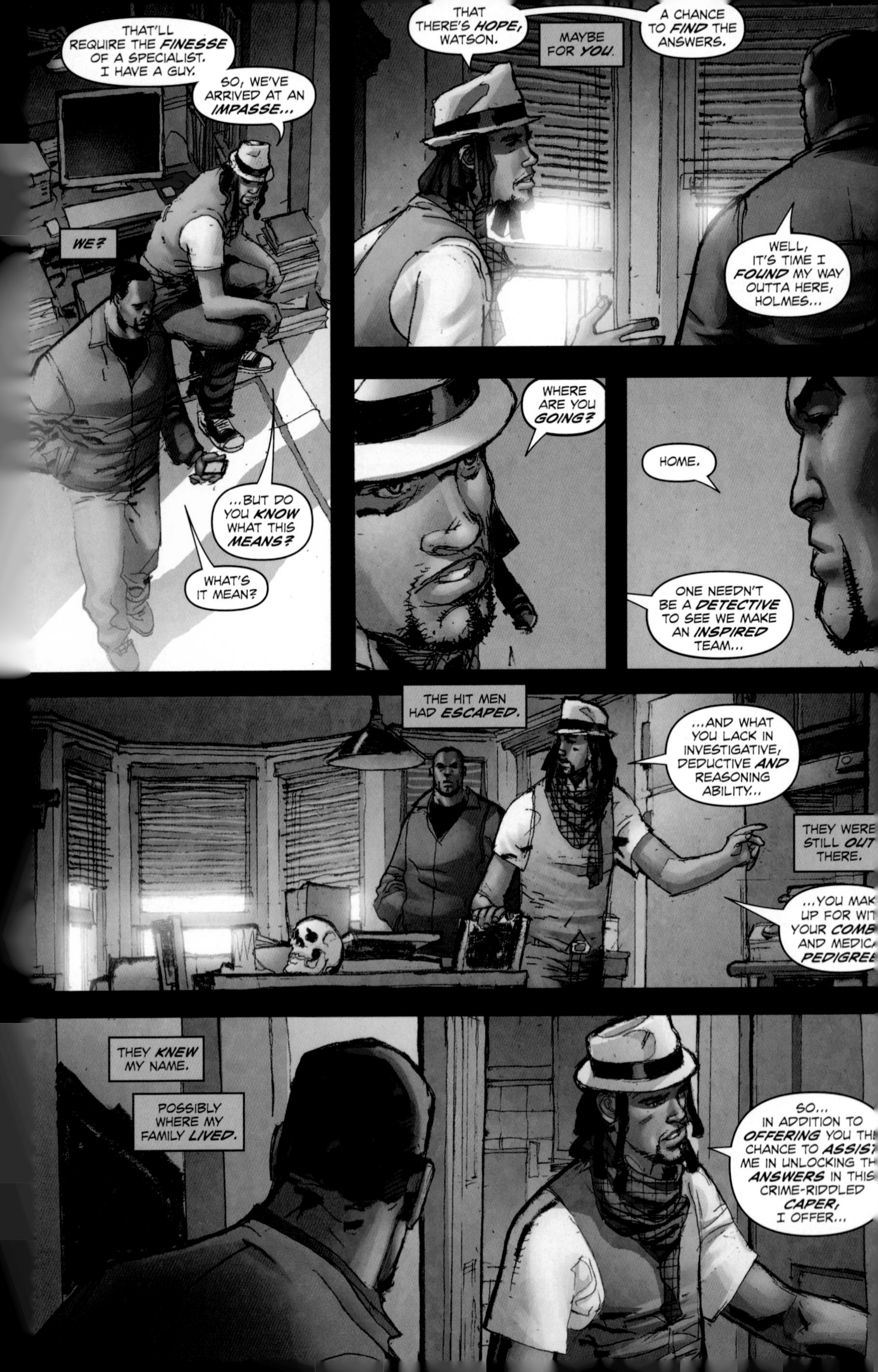
THAT'LL REQUIRE THE FINESSE OF A SPECIALIST. I HAVE A GUY.
SO, WE'VE ARRIVED AT AN IMPASSE...
WE?
...BUT DO YOU KNOW WHAT THIS MEANS?
WHAT'S IT MEAN?
THAT THERE'S HOPE, WATSON.
A CHANCE TO FIND THE ANSWERS.
MAYBE FOR YOU.
WELL, IT'S TIME I FOUND MY WAY OUTTA HERE, HOLMES...
WHERE ARE YOU GOING?
HOME.
ONE NEEDN'T BE A DETECTIVE TO SEE WE MAKE AN INSPIRED TEAM...
THE HIT MEN HAD ESCAPED.
...AND WHAT YOU LACK IN INVESTIGATIVE, DEDUCTIVE AND REASONING ABILITY...
THEY WERE STILL OUT THERE.
...YOU MAK UP FOR WIT YOUR COMB AND MEDICA PEDIGREE
THEY KNEW MY NAME.
POSSIBLY WHERE MY FAMILY LIVED.
SO... IN ADDITION TO OFFERING YOU TH CHANCE TO ASSIST ME IN UNLOCKING TH ANSWERS IN THIS CRIME-RIDDLED CAPER, I OFFER...

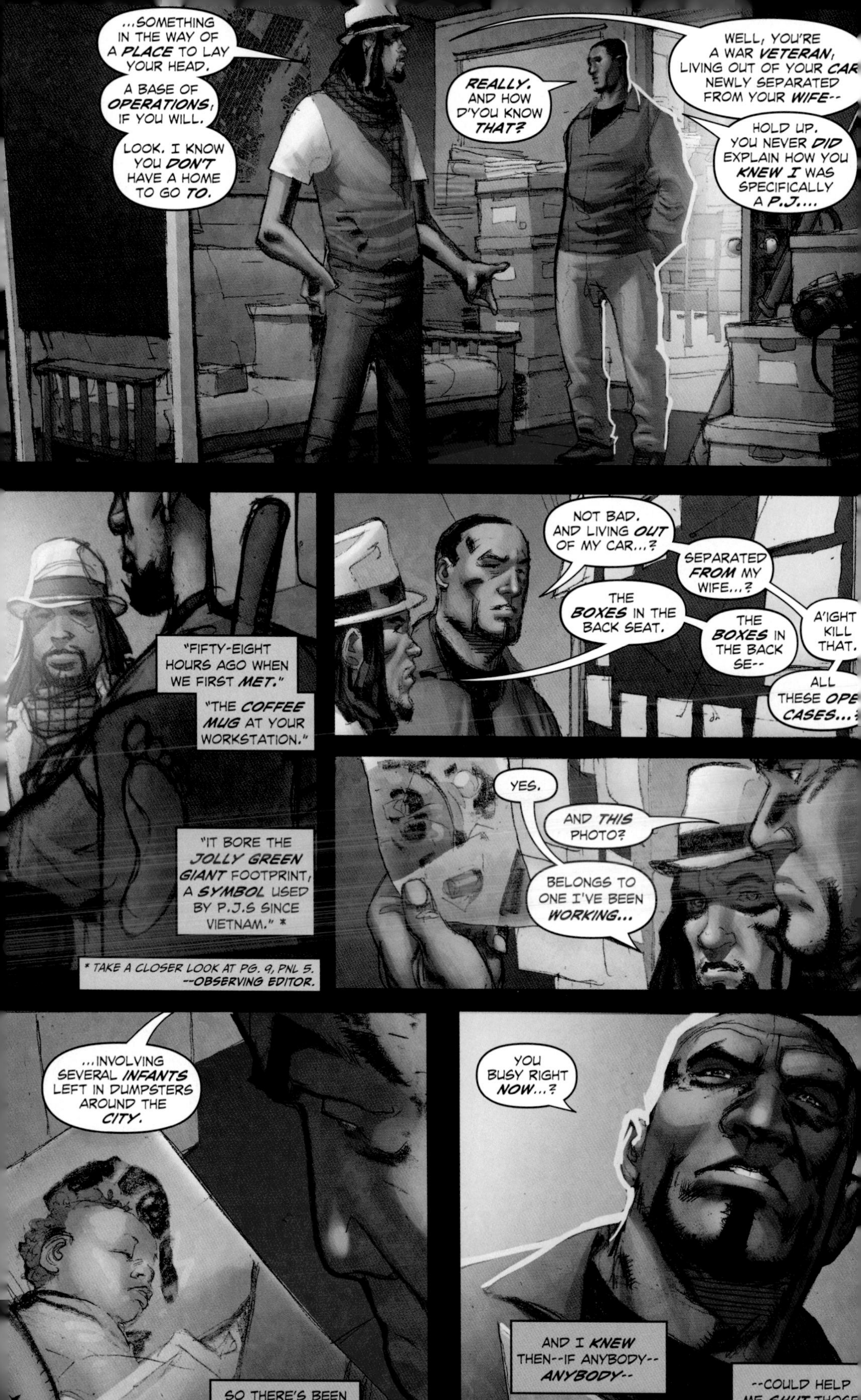
...SOMETHING IN THE WAY OF A PLACE TO LAY YOUR HEAD.
A BASE OF OPERATIONS, IF YOU WILL.
LOOK. I KNOW YOU DON'T HAVE A HOME TO GO TO.
REALLY. AND HOW D'YOU KNOW THAT?
WELL, YOU'RE A WAR VETERAN, LIVING OUT OF YOUR CAR NEWLY SEPARATED FROM YOUR WIFE--
HOLD UP. YOU NEVER DID EXPLAIN HOW YOU KNEW I WAS SPECIFICALLY A P.J....
"FIFTY-EIGHT HOURS AGO WHEN WE FIRST MET."
"THE COFFEE MUG AT YOUR WORKSTATION."
"IT BORE THE JOLLY GREEN GIANT FOOTPRINT, A SYMBOL USED BY P.J.S SINCE VIETNAM." *
* TAKE A CLOSER LOOK AT PG. 9, PNL 5. --OBSERVING EDITOR.
NOT BAD. AND LIVING OUT OF MY CAR...?
THE BOXES IN THE BACK SEAT.
SEPARATED FROM MY WIFE...?
THE BOXES IN THE BACK SE--
A'IGHT KILL THAT.
ALL THESE OPE CASES...?
YES.
AND THIS PHOTO?
BELONGS TO ONE I'VE BEEN WORKING...
...INVOLVING SEVERAL INFANTS LEFT IN DUMPSTERS AROUND THE CITY.
SO THERE'S BEEN MORE THAN ONE?
YOU BUSY RIGHT NOW...?
AND I KNEW THEN--IF ANYBODY-- ANYBODY--
--COULD HELP ME SHUT THOSE GUYS DOWN--

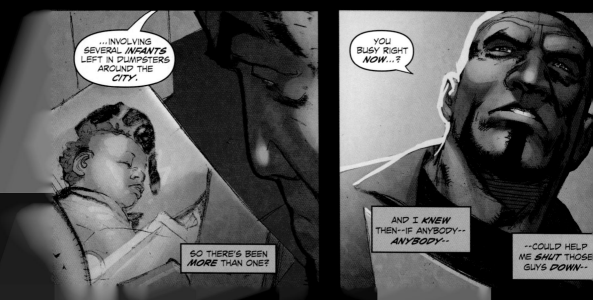

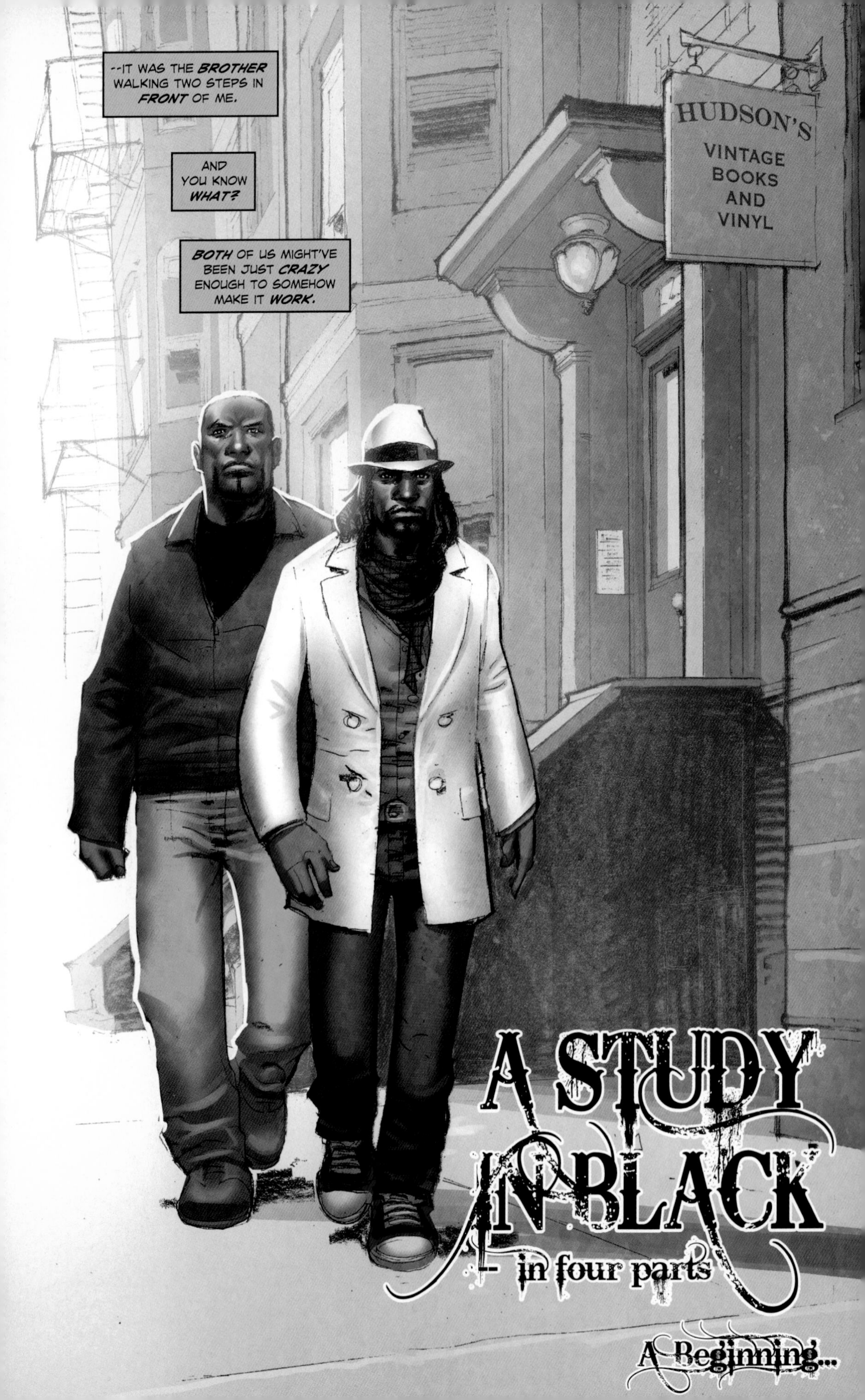
--IT WAS THE BROTHER WALKING TWO STEPS IN FRONT OF ME.
AND YOU KNOW WHAT?
BOTH OF US MIGHT'VE BEEN JUST CRAZY ENOUGH TO SOMEHOW MAKE IT WORK.
HUDSON'S
VINTAGE BOOKS AND VINYL
A STUDY IN BLACK
- in four parts
A Beginning...

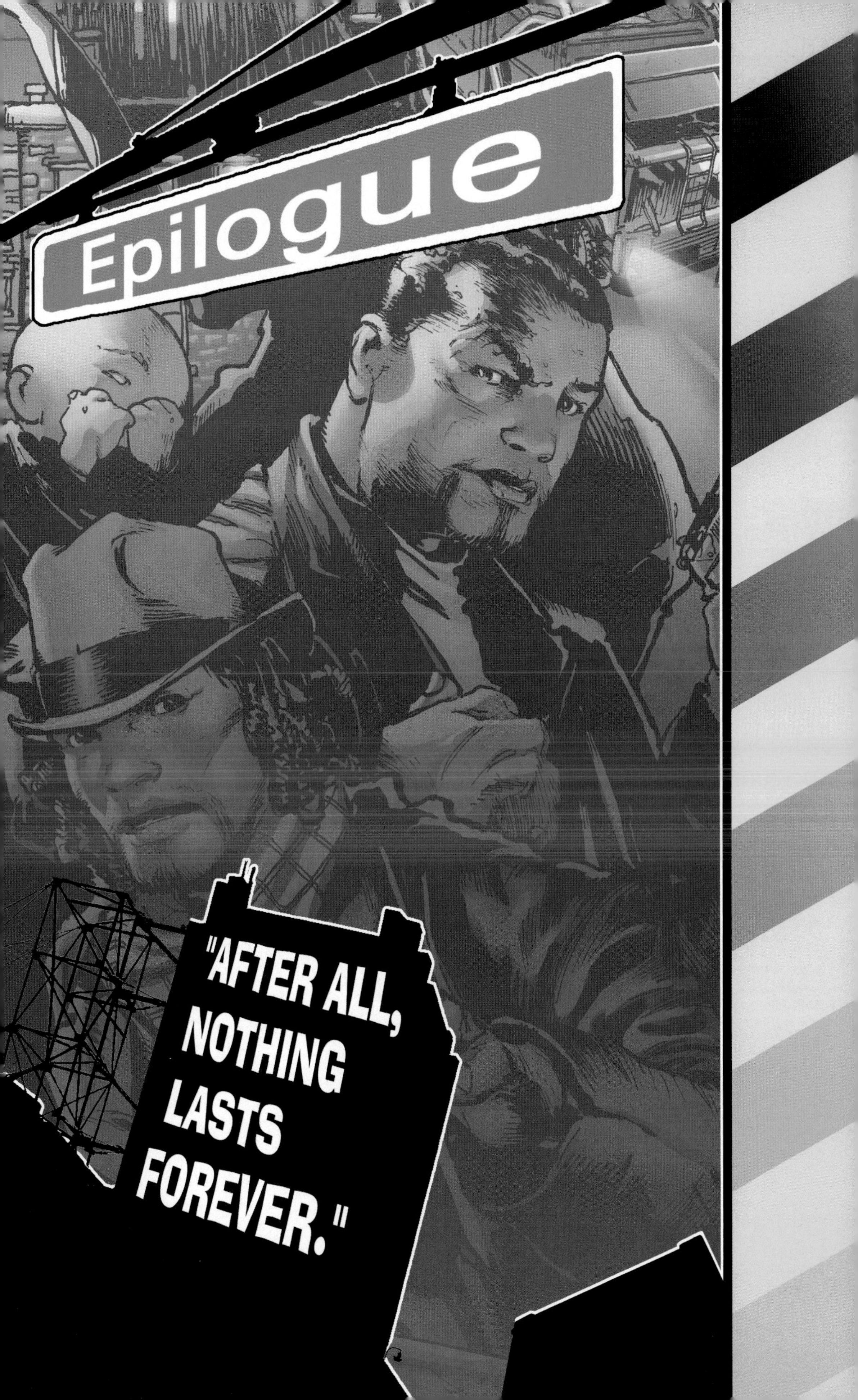
Epilogue
"AFTER ALL, NOTHING LASTS FOREVER."

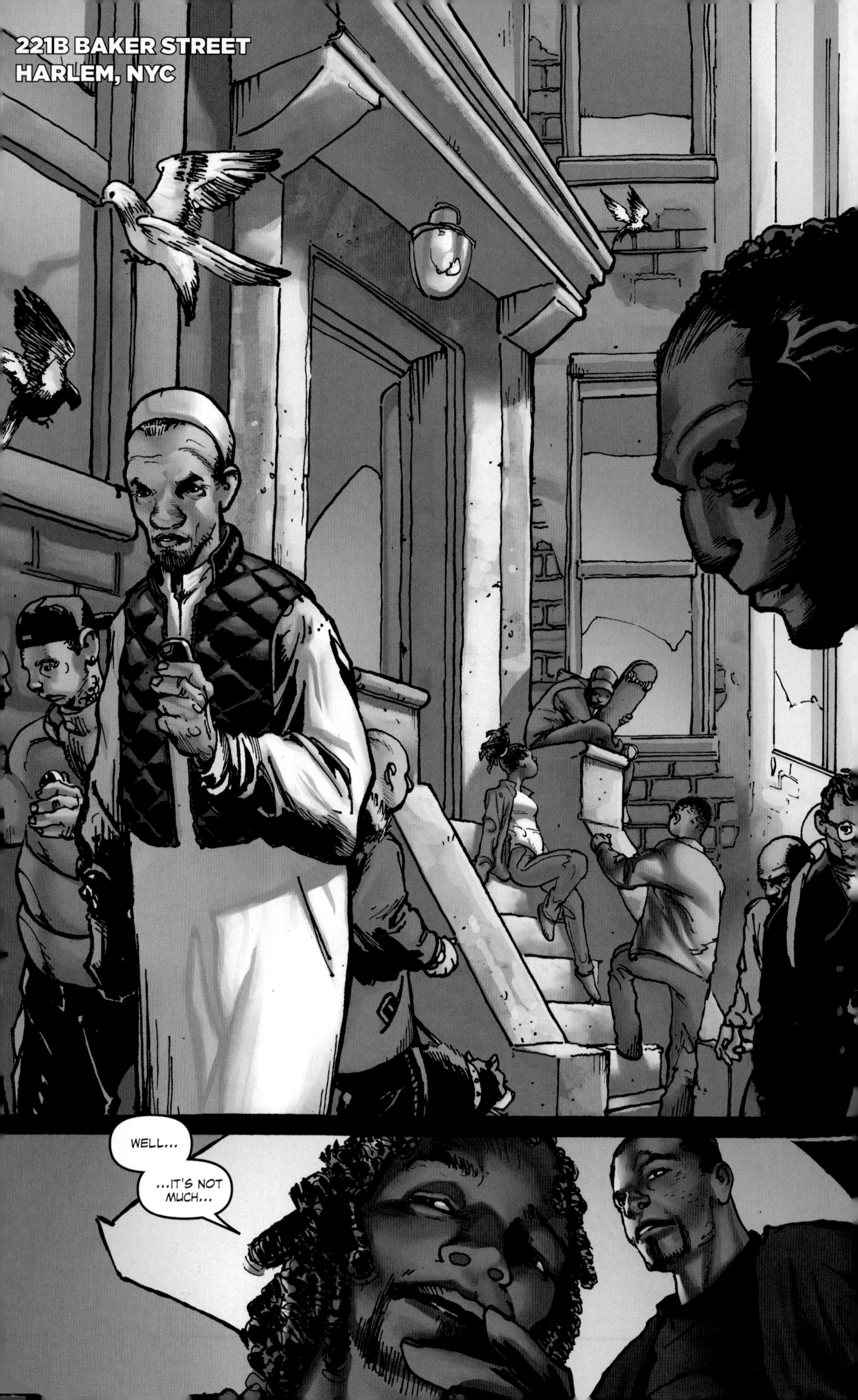
221B BAKER STREET
HARLEM, NYC
WELL...
...IT'S NOT MUCH...

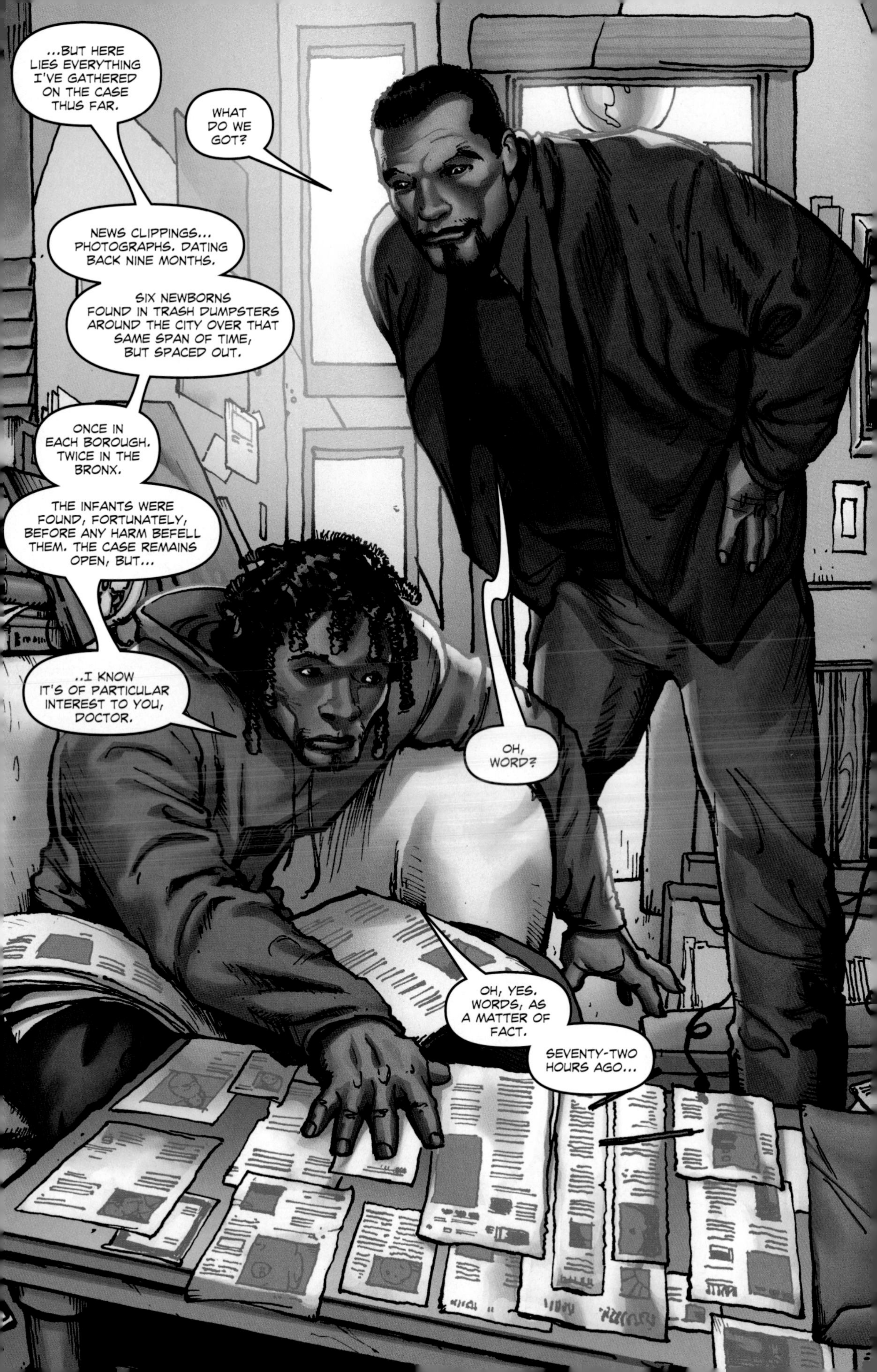

...BUT HERE LIES EVERYTHING I'VE GATHERED ON THE CASE THUS FAR.
WHAT DO WE GOT?
NEWS CLIPPINGS... PHOTOGRAPHS. DATING BACK NINE MONTHS.
SIX NEWBORNS FOUND IN TRASH DUMPSTERS AROUND THE CITY OVER THAT SAME SPAN OF TIME, BUT SPACED OUT.
ONCE IN EACH BOROUGH. TWICE IN THE BRONX.
THE INFANTS WERE FOUND, FORTUNATELY, BEFORE ANY HARM BEFELL THEM. THE CASE REMAINS OPEN, BUT...
..I KNOW IT'S OF PARTICULAR INTEREST TO YOU, DOCTOR.
OH, WORD?
OH, YES. WORDS, AS A MATTER OF FACT.
SEVENTY-TWO HOURS AGO...

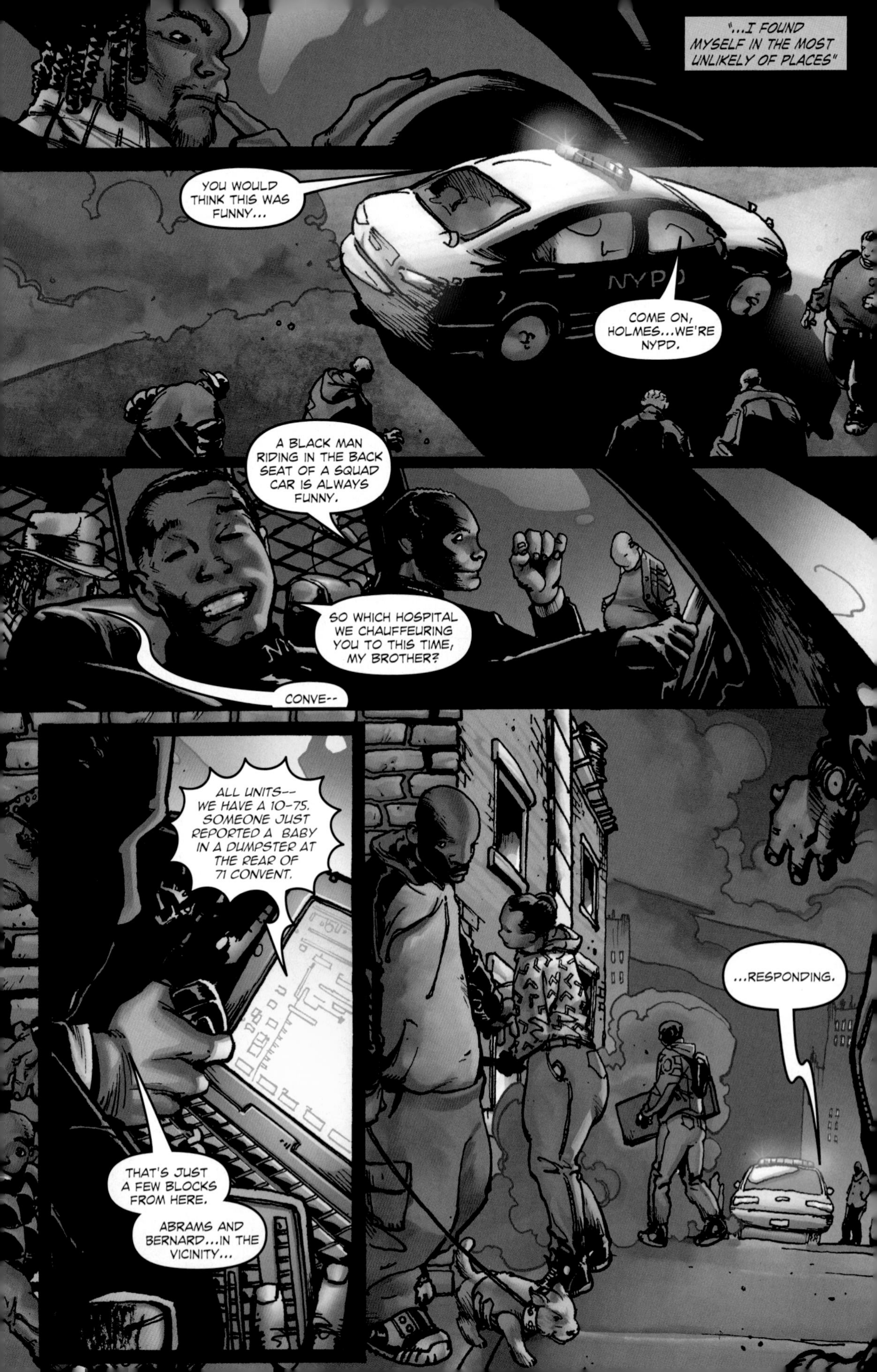
"...I FOUND MYSELF IN THE MOST UNLIKELY OF PLACES"
YOU WOULD THINK THIS WAS FUNNY...
COME ON, HOLMES...WE'RE NYPD.
NYPD
A BLACK MAN RIDING IN THE BACK SEAT OF A SQUAD CAR IS ALWAYS FUNNY.
SO WHICH HOSPITAL WE CHAUFFEURING YOU TO THIS TIME, MY BROTHER?
CONVE--
ALL UNITS-- WE HAVE A 10-75. SOMEONE JUST REPORTED A BABY IN A DUMPSTER AT THE REAR OF 71 CONVENT.
THAT'S JUST A FEW BLOCKS FROM HERE.
ABRAMS AND BERNARD...IN THE VICINITY...
...RESPONDING.

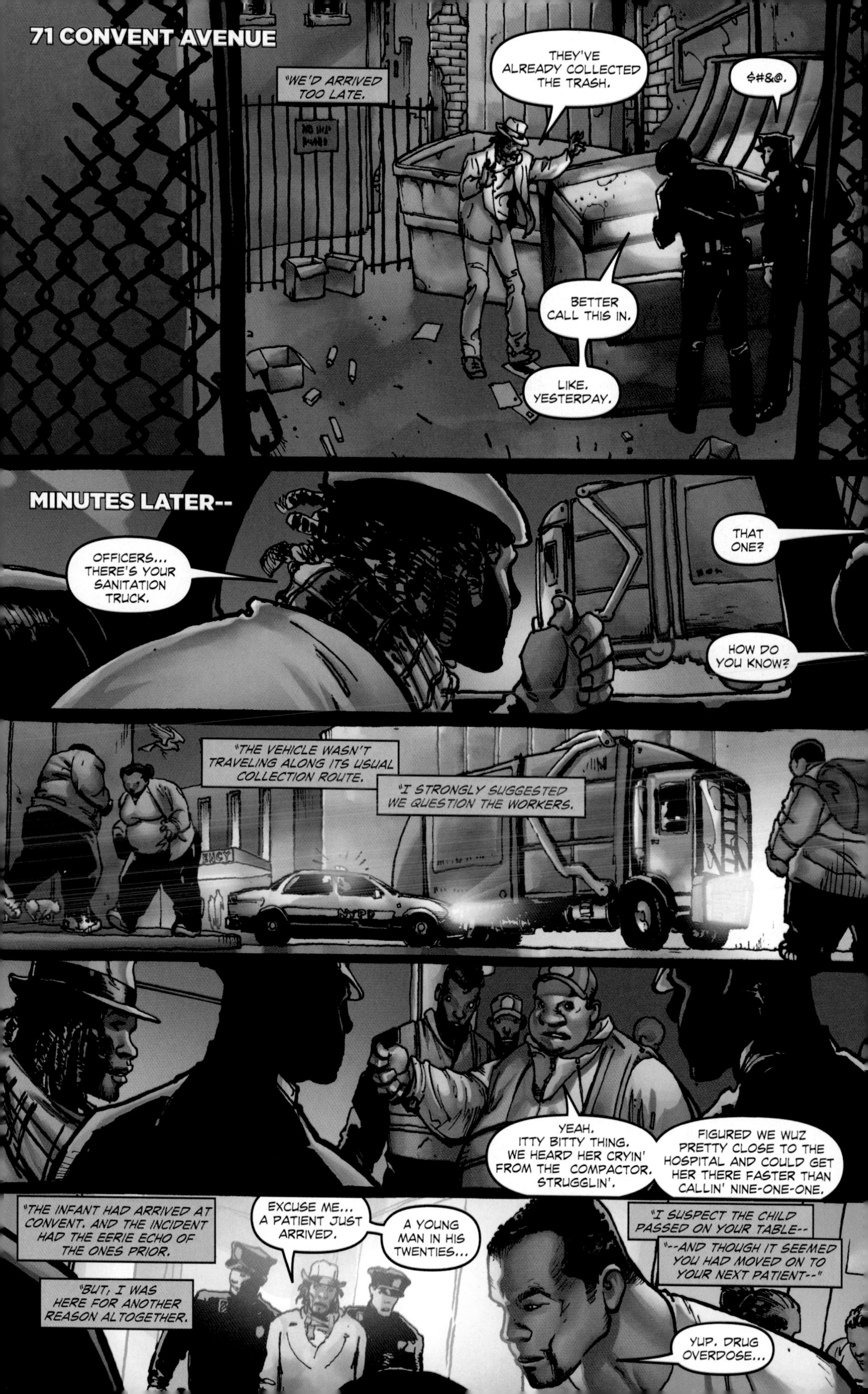
71 CONVENT AVENUE
"WE'D ARRIVED TOO LATE.
THEY'VE ALREADY COLLECTED THE TRASH.
$#&@.
BETTER CALL THIS IN.
LIKE. YESTERDAY.
MINUTES LATER--
OFFICERS... THERE'S YOUR SANITATION TRUCK.
THAT ONE?
HOW DO YOU KNOW?
"THE VEHICLE WASN'T TRAVELING ALONG ITS USUAL COLLECTION ROUTE.
"I STRONGLY SUGGESTED WE QUESTION THE WORKERS.
YEAH. ITTY BITTY THING. WE HEARD HER CRYIN' FROM THE COMPACTOR. STRUGGLIN'.
FIGURED WE WUZ PRETTY CLOSE TO THE HOSPITAL AND COULD GET HER THERE FASTER THAN CALLIN' NINE-ONE-ONE.
"THE INFANT HAD ARRIVED AT CONVENT. AND THE INCIDENT HAD THE EERIE ECHO OF THE ONES PRIOR.
"BUT, I WAS HERE FOR ANOTHER REASON ALTOGETHER.
EXCUSE ME... A PATIENT JUST ARRIVED.
A YOUNG MAN IN HIS TWENTIES...
"I SUSPECT THE CHILD PASSED ON YOUR TABLE--
"--AND THOUGH IT SEEMED YOU HAD MOVED ON TO YOUR NEXT PATIENT--"
YUP. DRUG OVERDOSE...

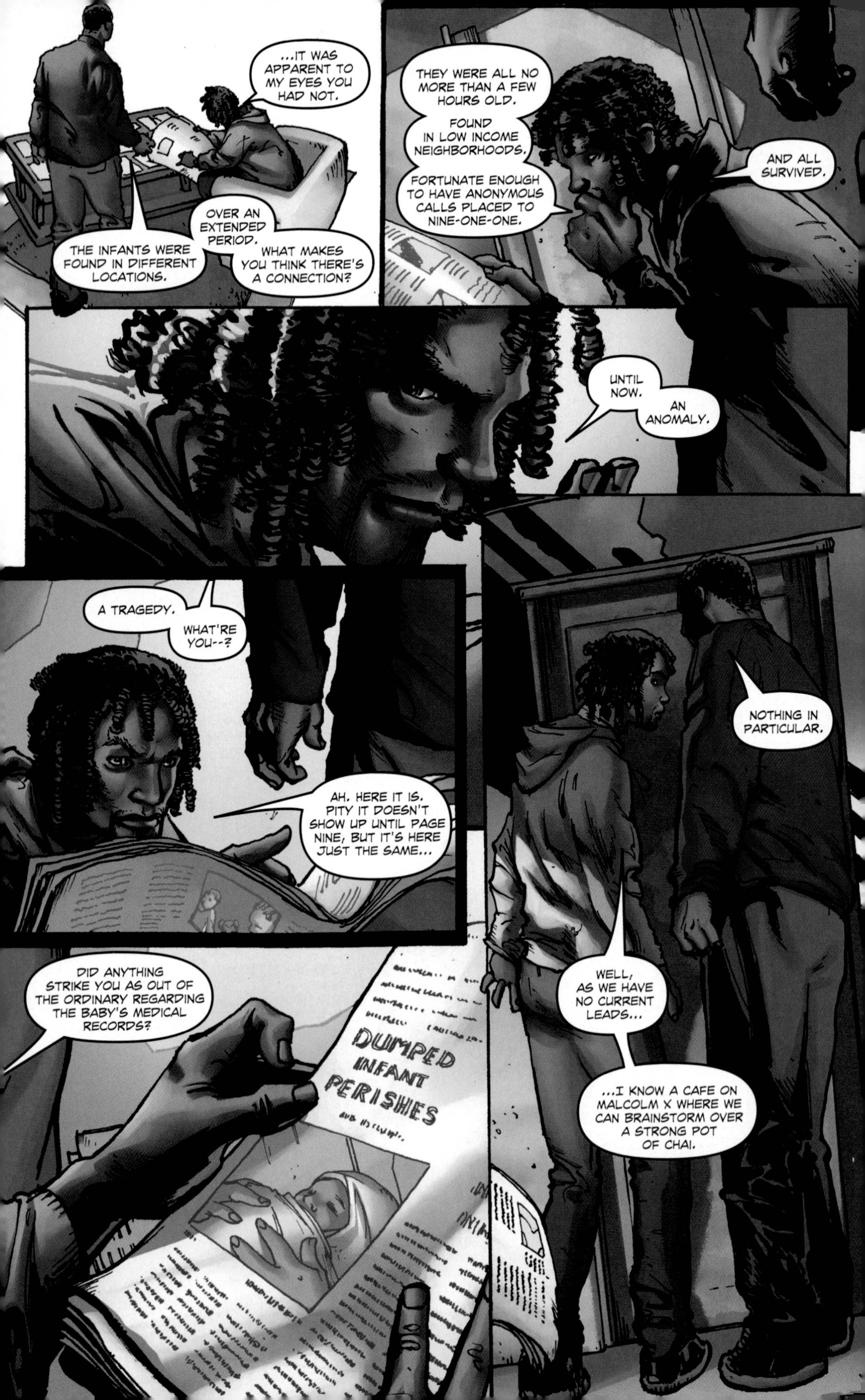

...IT WAS APPARENT TO MY EYES YOU HAD NOT.
THE INFANTS WERE FOUND IN DIFFERENT LOCATIONS.
OVER AN EXTENDED PERIOD.
WHAT MAKES YOU THINK THERE'S A CONNECTION?
THEY WERE ALL NO MORE THAN A FEW HOURS OLD.
FOUND IN LOW INCOME NEIGHBORHOODS.
FORTUNATE ENOUGH TO HAVE ANONYMOUS CALLS PLACED TO NINE-ONE-ONE.
AND ALL SURVIVED.
UNTIL NOW.
AN ANOMALY.
A TRAGEDY.
WHAT'RE YOU--?
AH. HERE IT IS. PITY IT DOESN'T SHOW UP UNTIL PAGE NINE, BUT IT'S HERE JUST THE SAME...
NOTHING IN PARTICULAR.
DID ANYTHING STRIKE YOU AS OUT OF THE ORDINARY REGARDING THE BABY'S MEDICAL RECORDS?
DUMPED INFANT PERISHES
WELL, AS WE HAVE NO CURRENT LEADS...
...I KNOW A CAFE ON MALCOLM X WHERE WE CAN BRAINSTORM OVER A STRONG POT OF CHAI.

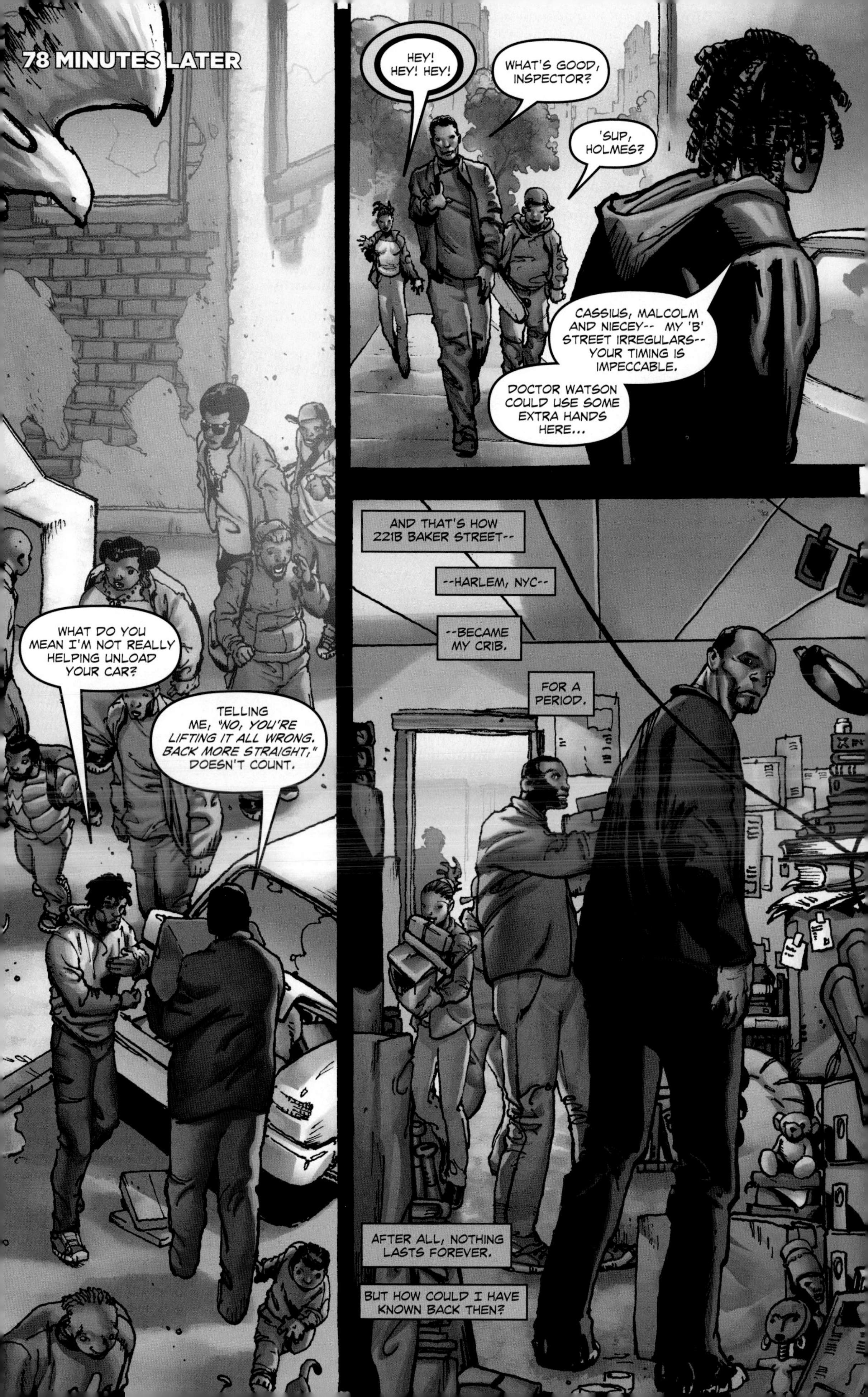
78 MINUTES LATER
WHAT DO YOU MEAN I'M NOT REALLY HELPING UNLOAD YOUR CAR?
TELLING ME, "NO, YOU'RE LIFTING IT ALL WRONG. BACK MORE STRAIGHT," DOESN'T COUNT.
HEY! HEY! HEY!
WHAT'S GOOD, INSPECTOR?
'SUP, HOLMES?
CASSIUS, MALCOLM AND NIECEY-- MY 'B' STREET IRREGULARS-- YOUR TIMING IS IMPECCABLE.
DOCTOR WATSON COULD USE SOME EXTRA HANDS HERE...
AND THAT'S HOW 221B BAKER STREET--
--HARLEM, NYC--
--BECAME MY CRIB.
FOR A PERIOD.
AFTER ALL, NOTHING LASTS FOREVER.
BUT HOW COULD I HAVE KNOWN BACK THEN?

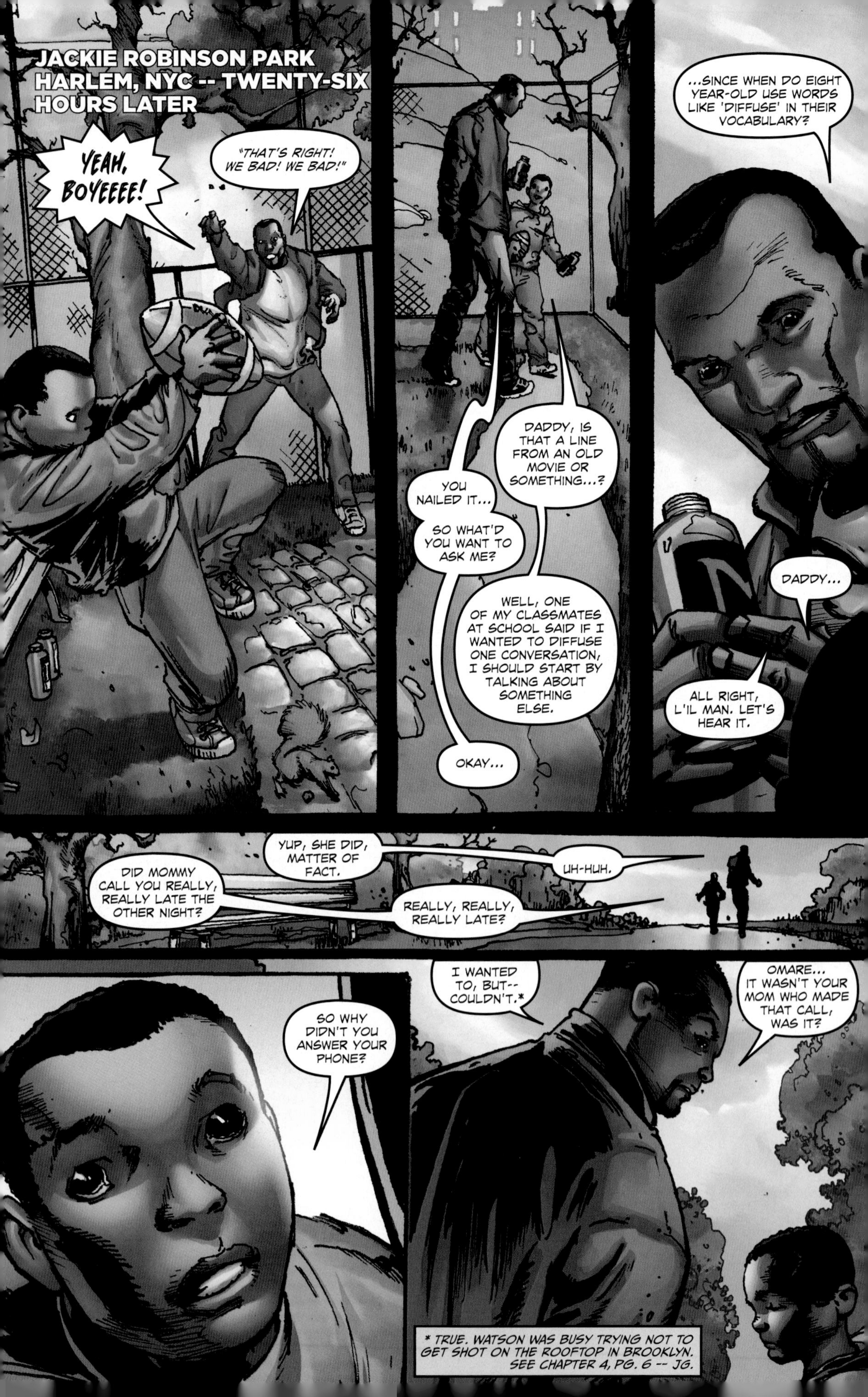
JACKIE ROBINSON PARK HARLEM, NYC -- TWENTY-SIX HOURS LATER
YEAH, BOYEEEE!
"THAT'S RIGHT! WE BAD! WE BAD!"
DADDY, IS THAT A LINE FROM AN OLD MOVIE OR SOMETHING...?
YOU NAILED IT...
SO WHAT'D YOU WANT TO ASK ME?
WELL, ONE OF MY CLASSMATES AT SCHOOL SAID IF I WANTED TO DIFFUSE ONE CONVERSATION, I SHOULD START BY TALKING ABOUT SOMETHING ELSE.
OKAY...
...SINCE WHEN DO EIGHT YEAR-OLD USE WORDS LIKE 'DIFFUSE' IN THEIR VOCABULARY?
DADDY...
ALL RIGHT, L'IL MAN. LET'S HEAR IT.
DID MOMMY CALL YOU REALLY, REALLY LATE THE OTHER NIGHT?
YUP, SHE DID, MATTER OF FACT.
REALLY, REALLY, REALLY LATE?
UH-HUH.
SO WHY DIDN'T YOU ANSWER YOUR PHONE?
I WANTED TO, BUT-- COULDN'T.*
OMARE... IT WASN'T YOUR MOM WHO MADE THAT CALL, WAS IT?
* TRUE. WATSON WAS BUSY TRYING NOT TO GET SHOT ON THE ROOFTOP IN BROOKLYN. SEE CHAPTER 4, PG. 6 -- JG.

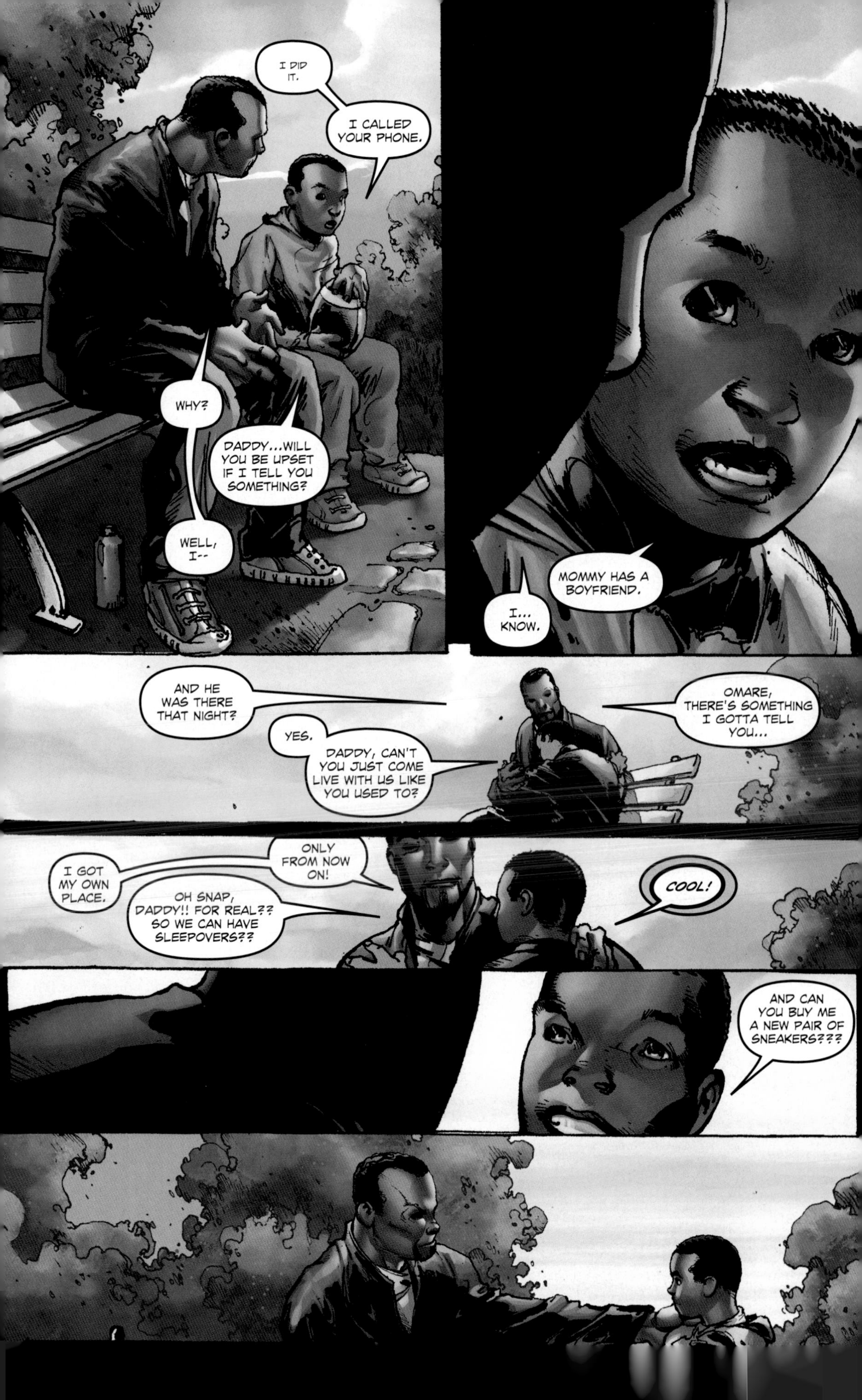
I DID IT.
I CALLED YOUR PHONE.
WHY?
DADDY...WILL YOU BE UPSET IF I TELL YOU SOMETHING?
WELL, I--
MOMMY HAS A BOYFRIEND.
I... KNOW.
AND HE WAS THERE THAT NIGHT?
YES.
DADDY, CAN'T YOU JUST COME LIVE WITH US LIKE YOU USED TO?
OMARE, THERE'S SOMETHING I GOTTA TELL YOU...
I GOT MY OWN PLACE.
ONLY FROM NOW ON!
OH SNAP, DADDY!! FOR REAL?? SO WE CAN HAVE SLEEPOVERS??
COOL!
AND CAN YOU BUY ME A NEW PAIR OF SNEAKERS???

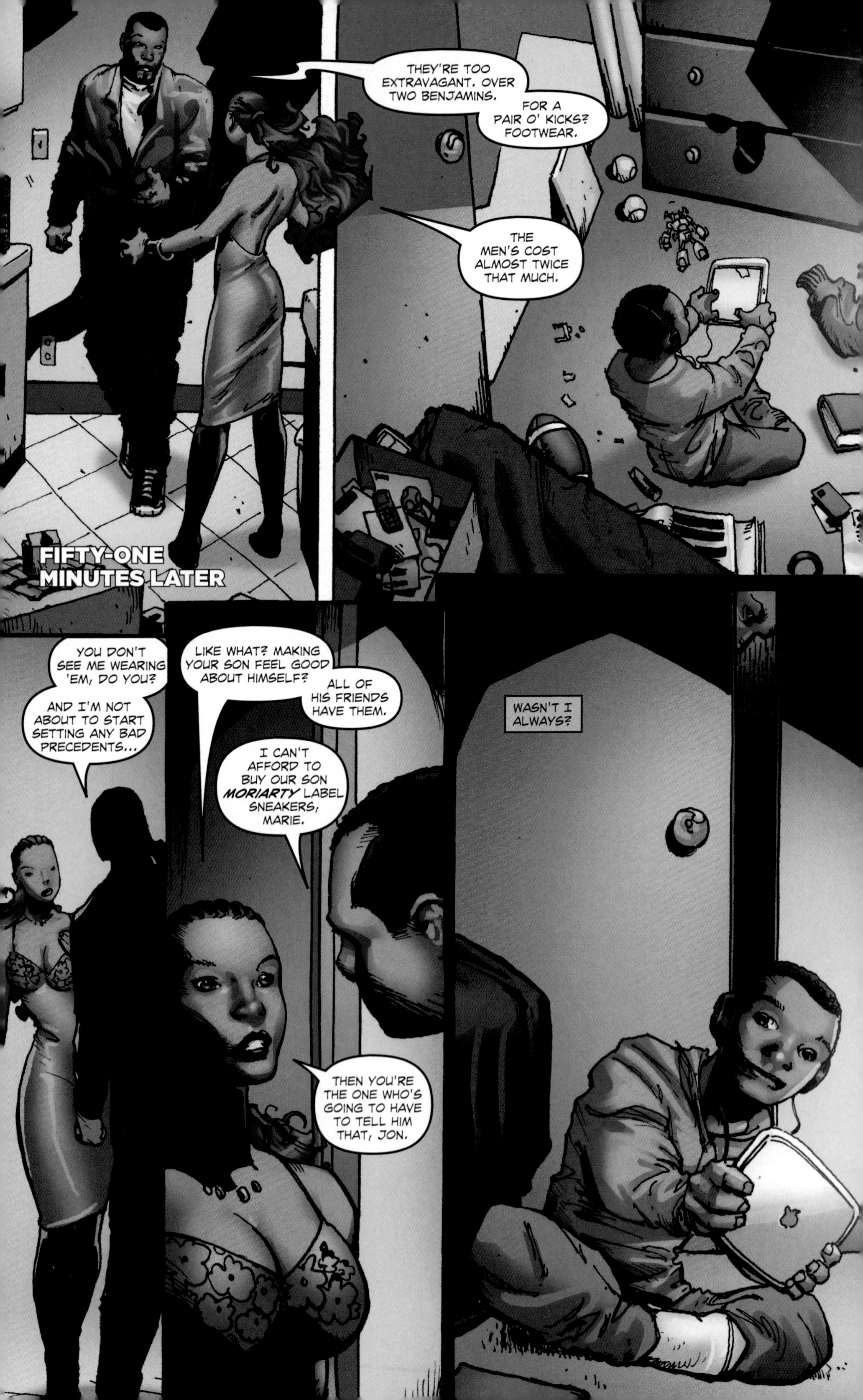

THEY'RE TOO EXTRAVAGANT. OVER TWO BENJAMINS.
FOR A PAIR O' KICKS? FOOTWEAR.
THE MEN'S COST ALMOST TWICE THAT MUCH.
FIFTY-ONE MINUTES LATER
YOU DON'T SEE ME WEARING 'EM, DO YOU?
AND I'M NOT ABOUT TO START SETTING ANY BAD PRECEDENTS...
LIKE WHAT? MAKING YOUR SON FEEL GOOD ABOUT HIMSELF?
ALL OF HIS FRIENDS HAVE THEM.
I CAN'T AFFORD TO BUY OUR SON MORIARTY LABEL SNEAKERS, MARIE.
THEN YOU'RE THE ONE WHO'S GOING TO HAVE TO TELL HIM THAT, JON.
WASN'T I ALWAYS?

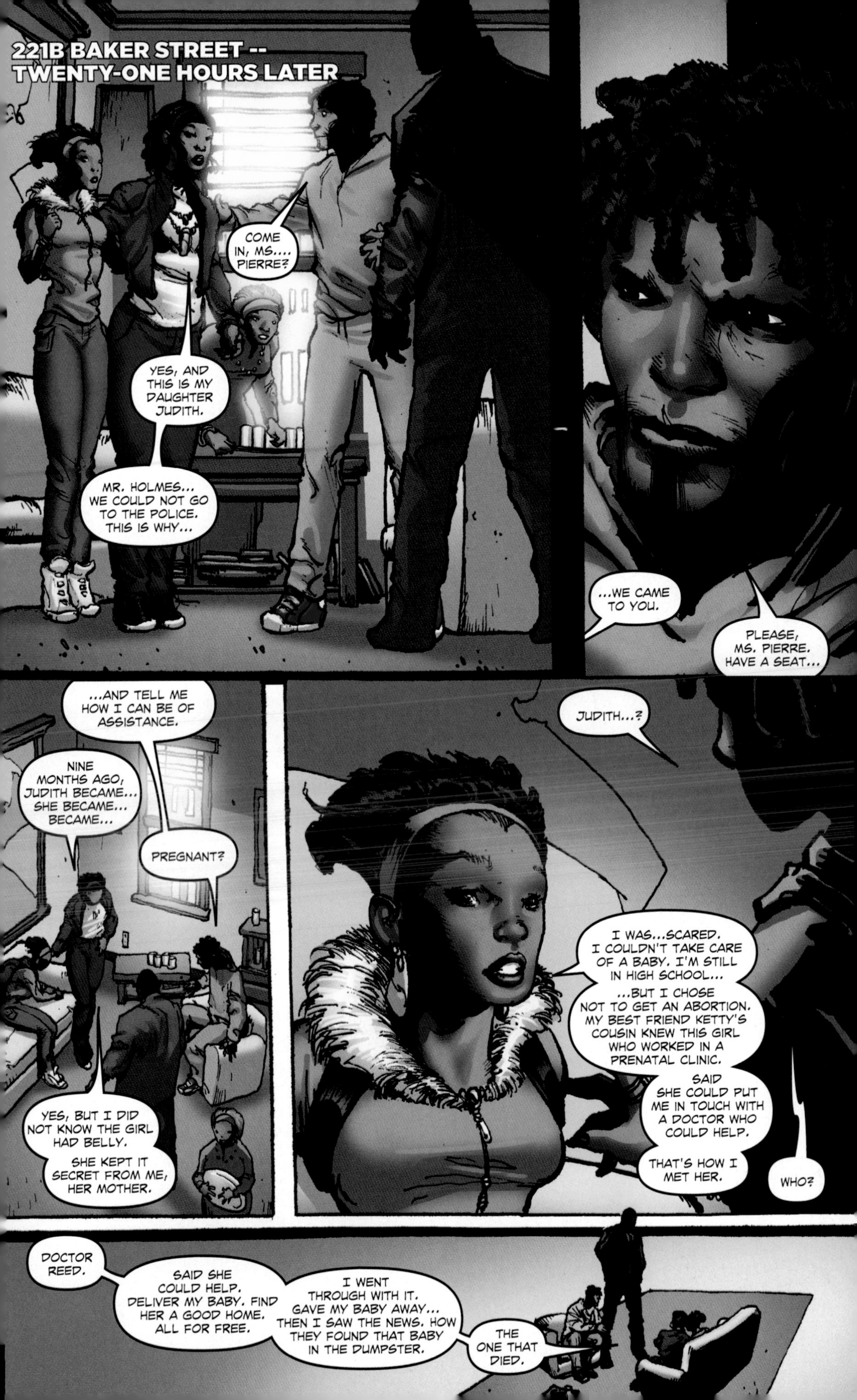

221B BAKER STREET -- TWENTY-ONE HOURS LATER
COME IN, MS.... PIERRE?
YES, AND THIS IS MY DAUGHTER JUDITH.
MR. HOLMES... WE COULD NOT GO TO THE POLICE. THIS IS WHY...
...WE CAME TO YOU.
PLEASE, MS. PIERRE. HAVE A SEAT...
...AND TELL ME HOW I CAN BE OF ASSISTANCE.
NINE MONTHS AGO, JUDITH BECAME... SHE BECAME... BECAME...
PREGNANT?
YES, BUT I DID NOT KNOW THE GIRL HAD BELLY.
SHE KEPT IT SECRET FROM ME, HER MOTHER.
JUDITH...?
I WAS...SCARED. I COULDN'T TAKE CARE OF A BABY. I'M STILL IN HIGH SCHOOL...
...BUT I CHOSE NOT TO GET AN ABORTION. MY BEST FRIEND KETTY'S COUSIN KNEW THIS GIRL WHO WORKED IN A PRENATAL CLINIC.
SAID SHE COULD PUT ME IN TOUCH WITH A DOCTOR WHO COULD HELP.
THAT'S HOW I MET HER.
WHO?
DOCTOR REED.
SAID SHE COULD HELP. DELIVER MY BABY. FIND HER A GOOD HOME. ALL FOR FREE.
I WENT THROUGH WITH IT. GAVE MY BABY AWAY... THEN I SAW THE NEWS. HOW THEY FOUND THAT BABY IN THE DUMPSTER.
THE ONE THAT DIED.

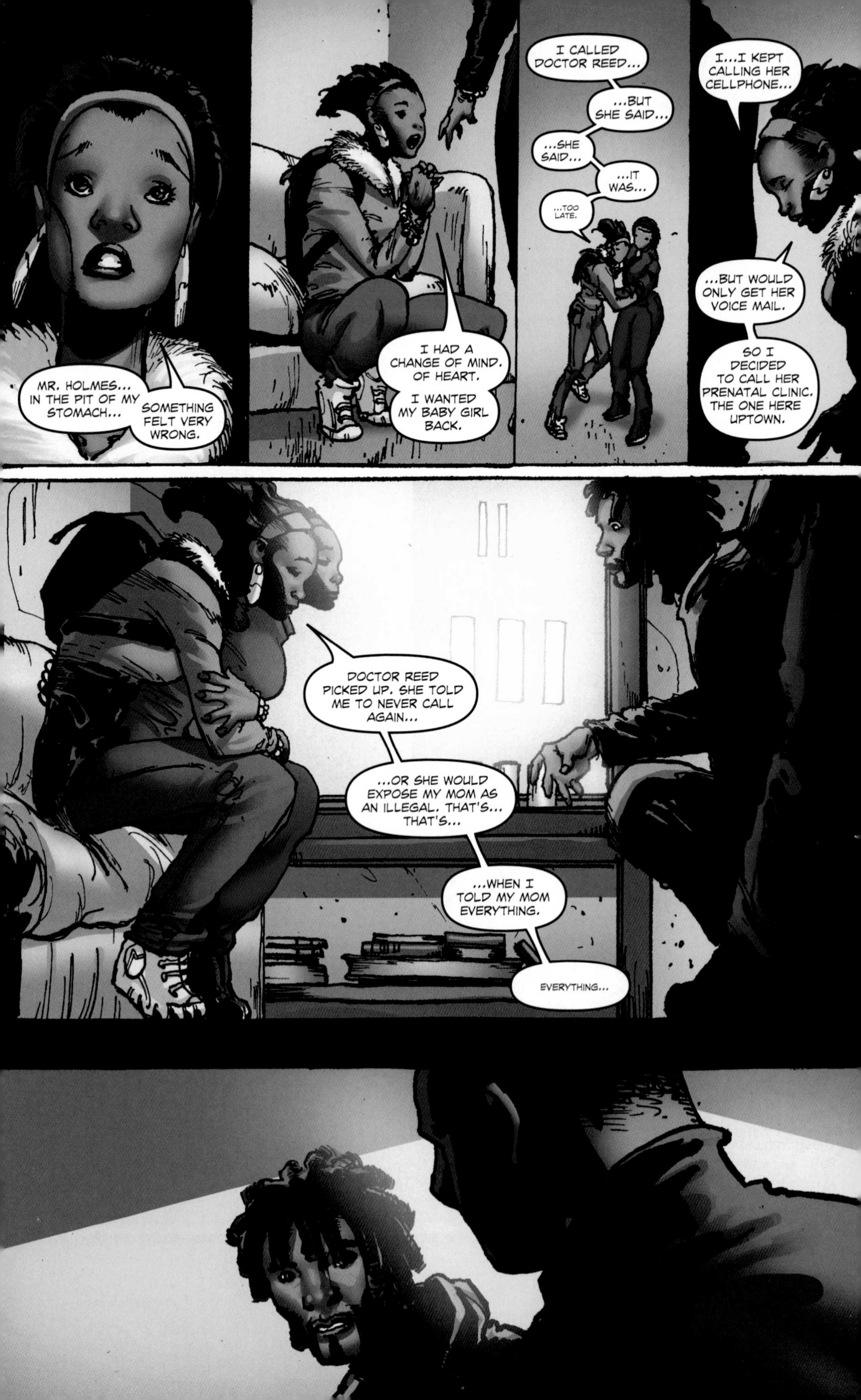
MR. HOLMES... IN THE PIT OF MY STOMACH...
SOMETHING FELT VERY WRONG.
I HAD A CHANGE OF MIND. OF HEART.
I WANTED MY BABY GIRL BACK.
I CALLED DOCTOR REED...
...BUT SHE SAID...
...SHE SAID...
...IT WAS...
...TOO LATE.
I...I KEPT CALLING HER CELLPHONE...
...BUT WOULD ONLY GET HER VOICE MAIL.
SO I DECIDED TO CALL HER PRENATAL CLINIC. THE ONE HERE UPTOWN.
DOCTOR REED PICKED UP. SHE TOLD ME TO NEVER CALL AGAIN...
...OR SHE WOULD EXPOSE MY MOM AS AN ILLEGAL. THAT'S... THAT'S...
...WHEN I TOLD MY MOM EVERYTHING.
EVERYTHING...

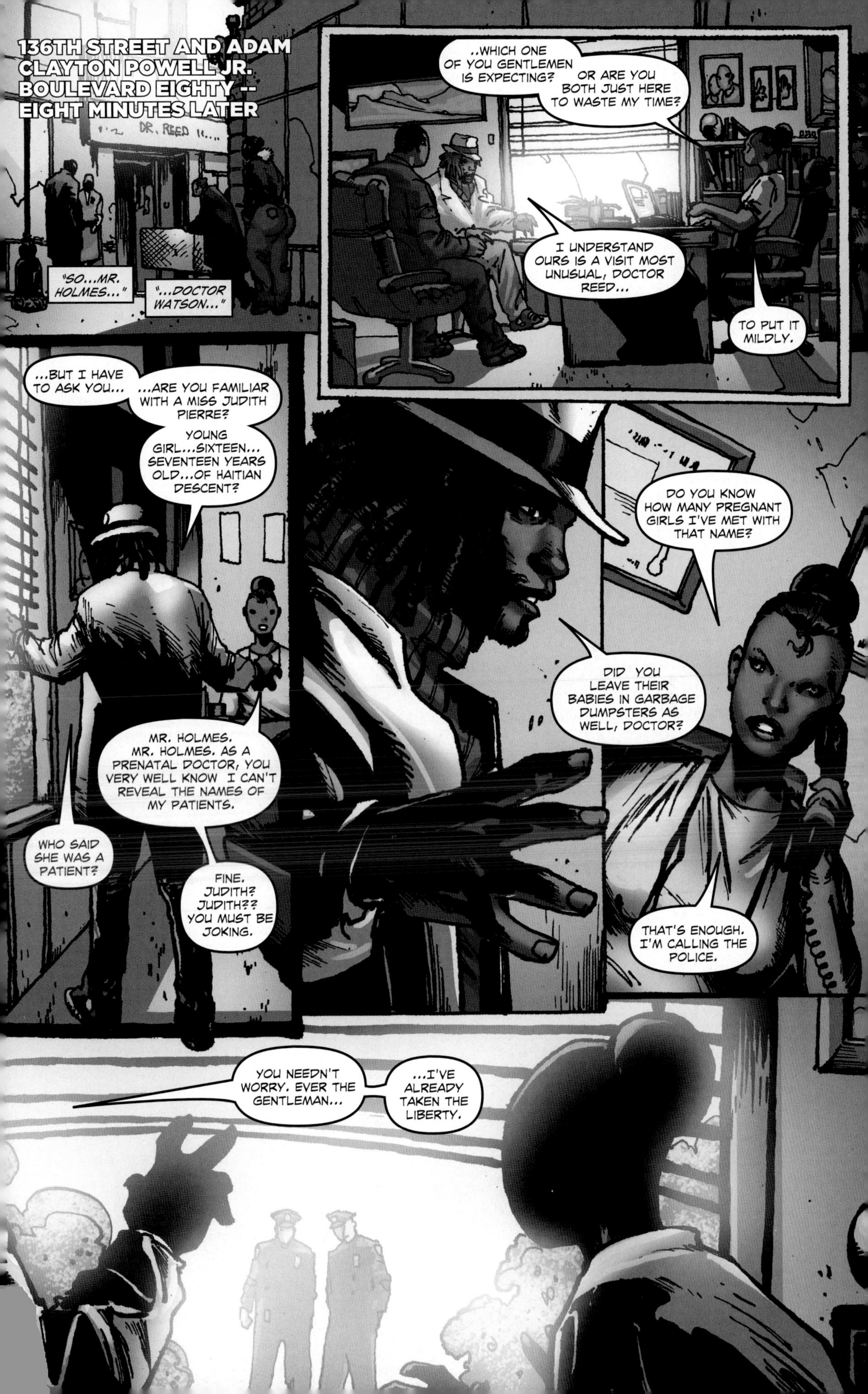

136TH STREET AND ADAM CLAYTON POWELL JR. BOULEVARD EIGHTY -- EIGHT MINUTES LATER
DR. REED
"SO...MR. HOLMES..."
"...DOCTOR WATSON..."
..WHICH ONE OF YOU GENTLEMEN IS EXPECTING?
OR ARE YOU BOTH JUST HERE TO WASTE MY TIME?
I UNDERSTAND OURS IS A VISIT MOST UNUSUAL, DOCTOR REED...
TO PUT IT MILDLY.
...BUT I HAVE TO ASK YOU...
...ARE YOU FAMILIAR WITH A MISS JUDITH PIERRE?
YOUNG GIRL...SIXTEEN... SEVENTEEN YEARS OLD...OF HAITIAN DESCENT?
MR. HOLMES. MR. HOLMES. AS A PRENATAL DOCTOR, YOU VERY WELL KNOW I CAN'T REVEAL THE NAMES OF MY PATIENTS.
WHO SAID SHE WAS A PATIENT?
FINE. JUDITH? JUDITH?? YOU MUST BE JOKING.
DO YOU KNOW HOW MANY PREGNANT GIRLS I'VE MET WITH THAT NAME?
DID YOU LEAVE THEIR BABIES IN GARBAGE DUMPSTERS AS WELL, DOCTOR?
THAT'S ENOUGH. I'M CALLING THE POLICE.
YOU NEEDN'T WORRY. EVER THE GENTLEMAN...
...I'VE ALREADY TAKEN THE LIBERTY.

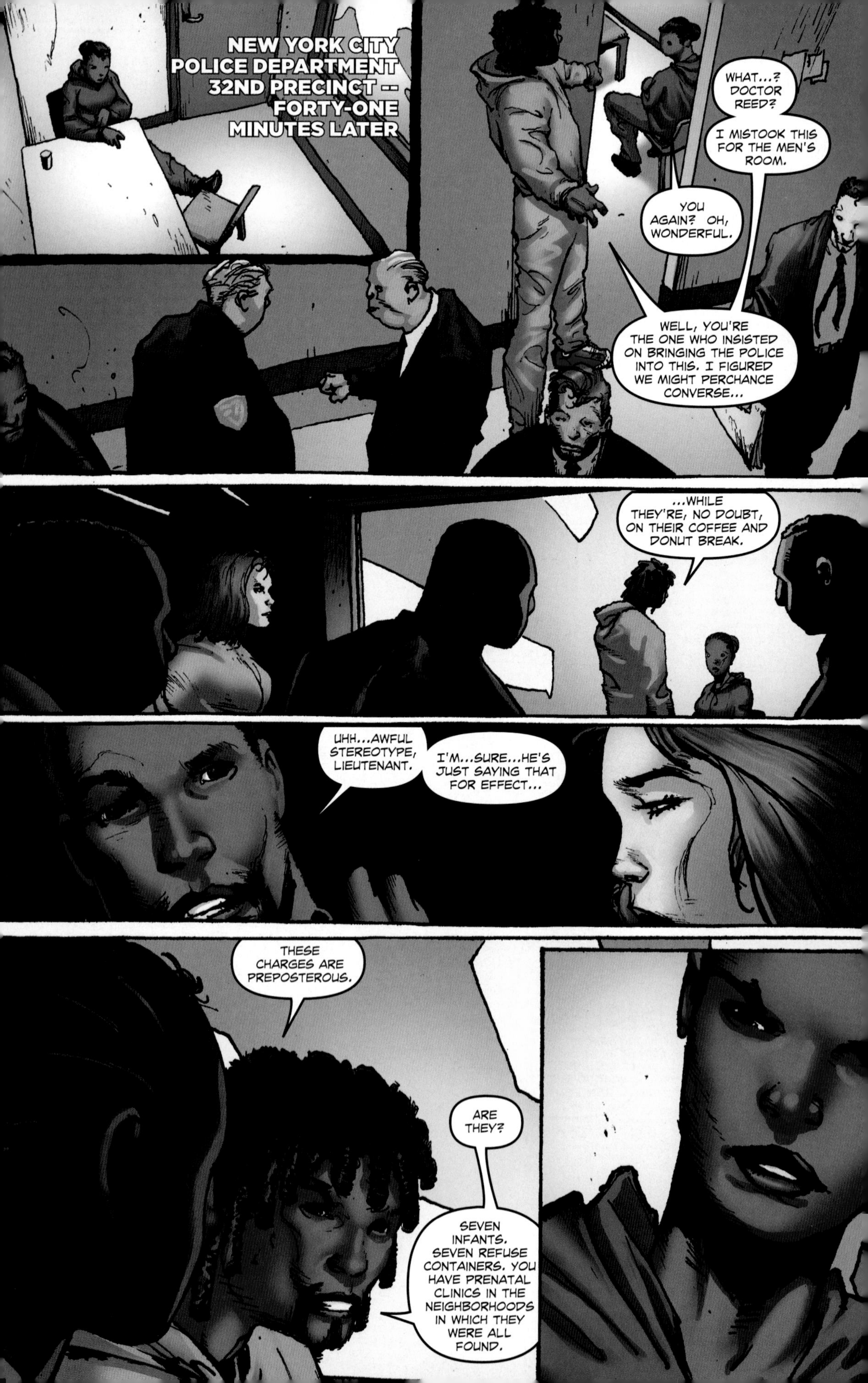
NEW YORK CITY POLICE DEPARTMENT 32ND PRECINCT -- FORTY-ONE MINUTES LATER
WHAT...? DOCTOR REED?
I MISTOOK THIS FOR THE MEN'S ROOM.
YOU AGAIN? OH, WONDERFUL.
WELL, YOU'RE THE ONE WHO INSISTED ON BRINGING THE POLICE INTO THIS. I FIGURED WE MIGHT PERCHANCE CONVERSE...
...WHILE THEY'RE, NO DOUBT, ON THEIR COFFEE AND DONUT BREAK.
UHH...AWFUL STEREOTYPE, LIEUTENANT.
I'M...SURE...HE'S JUST SAYING THAT FOR EFFECT...
THESE CHARGES ARE PREPOSTEROUS.
ARE THEY?
SEVEN INFANTS. SEVEN REFUSE CONTAINERS. YOU HAVE PRENATAL CLINICS IN THE NEIGHBORHOODS IN WHICH THEY WERE ALL FOUND.

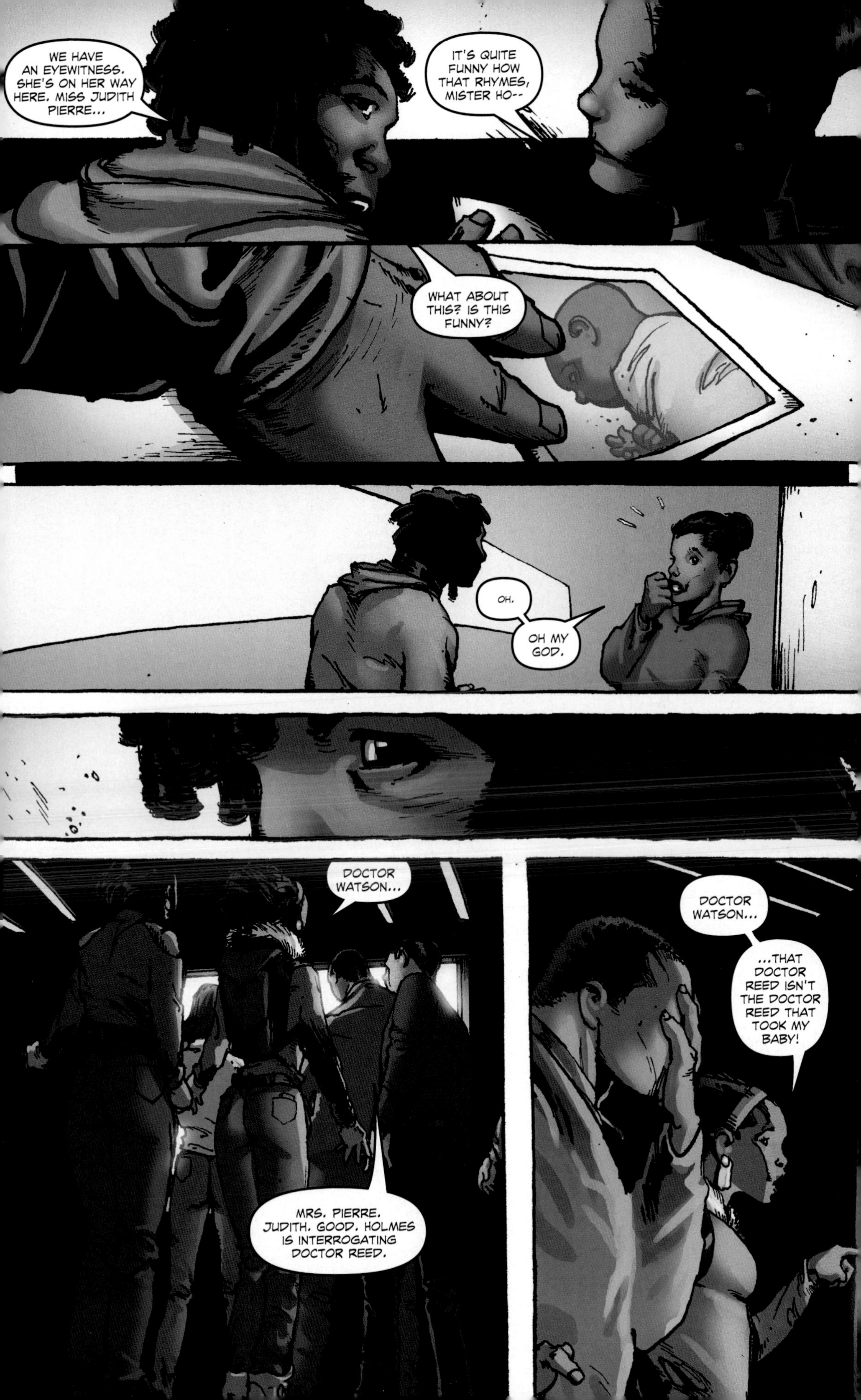
WE HAVE AN EYEWITNESS. SHE'S ON HER WAY HERE. MISS JUDITH PIERRE...
IT'S QUITE FUNNY HOW THAT RHYMES, MISTER HO--
WHAT ABOUT THIS? IS THIS FUNNY?
OH.
OH MY GOD.
DOCTOR WATSON...
MRS. PIERRE. JUDITH. GOOD. HOLMES IS INTERROGATING DOCTOR REED.
DOCTOR WATSON...
...THAT DOCTOR REED ISN'T THE DOCTOR REED THAT TOOK MY BABY!

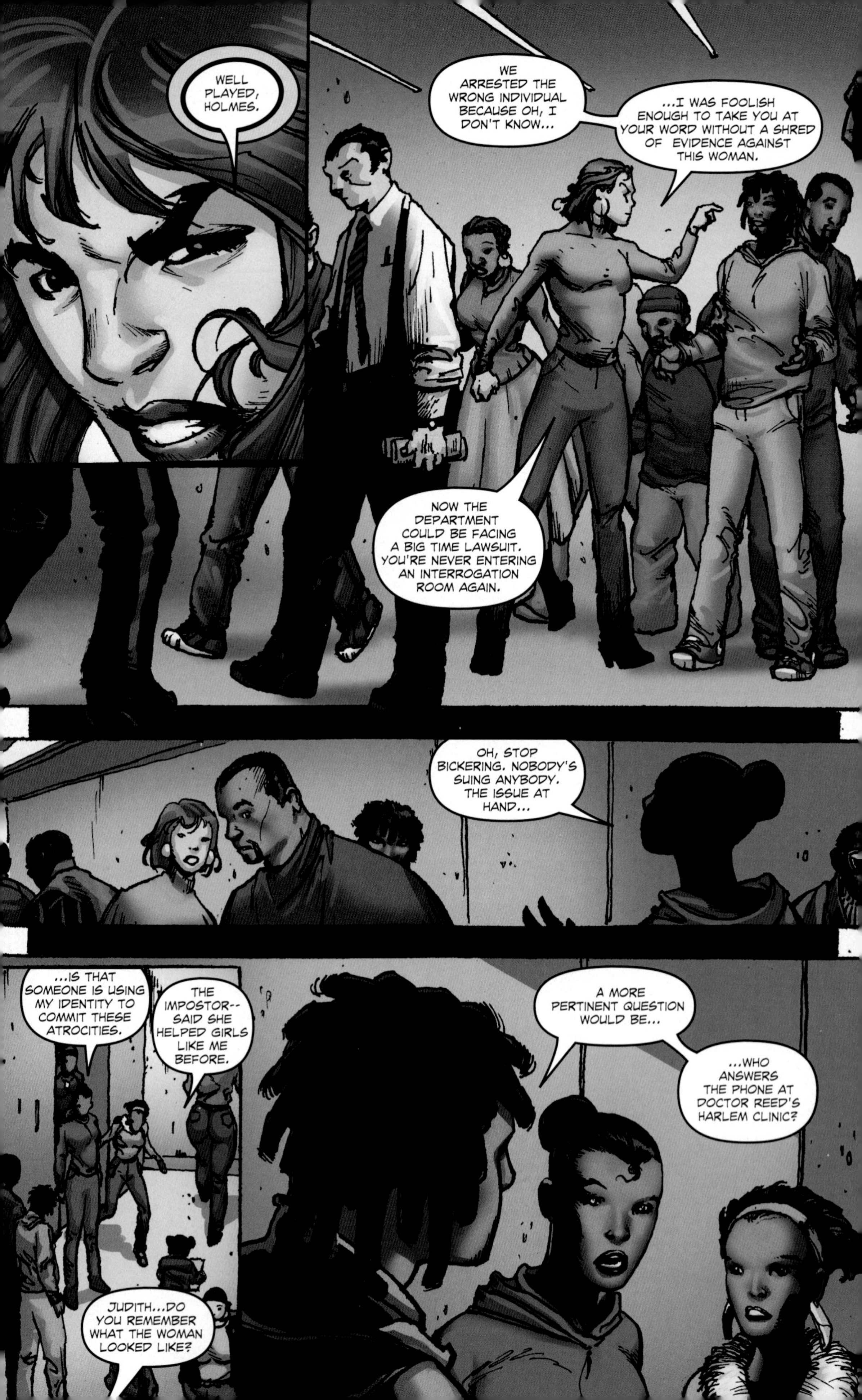
WELL PLAYED, HOLMES.
WE ARRESTED THE WRONG INDIVIDUAL BECAUSE OH, I DON'T KNOW...
...I WAS FOOLISH ENOUGH TO TAKE YOU AT YOUR WORD WITHOUT A SHRED OF EVIDENCE AGAINST THIS WOMAN.
NOW THE DEPARTMENT COULD BE FACING A BIG TIME LAWSUIT. YOU'RE NEVER ENTERING AN INTERROGATION ROOM AGAIN.
OH, STOP BICKERING. NOBODY'S SUING ANYBODY. THE ISSUE AT HAND...
...IS THAT SOMEONE IS USING MY IDENTITY TO COMMIT THESE ATROCITIES.
THE IMPOSTOR--SAID SHE HELPED GIRLS LIKE ME BEFORE.
A MORE PERTINENT QUESTION WOULD BE...
...WHO ANSWERS THE PHONE AT DOCTOR REED'S HARLEM CLINIC?
JUDITH...DO YOU REMEMBER WHAT THE WOMAN LOOKED LIKE?

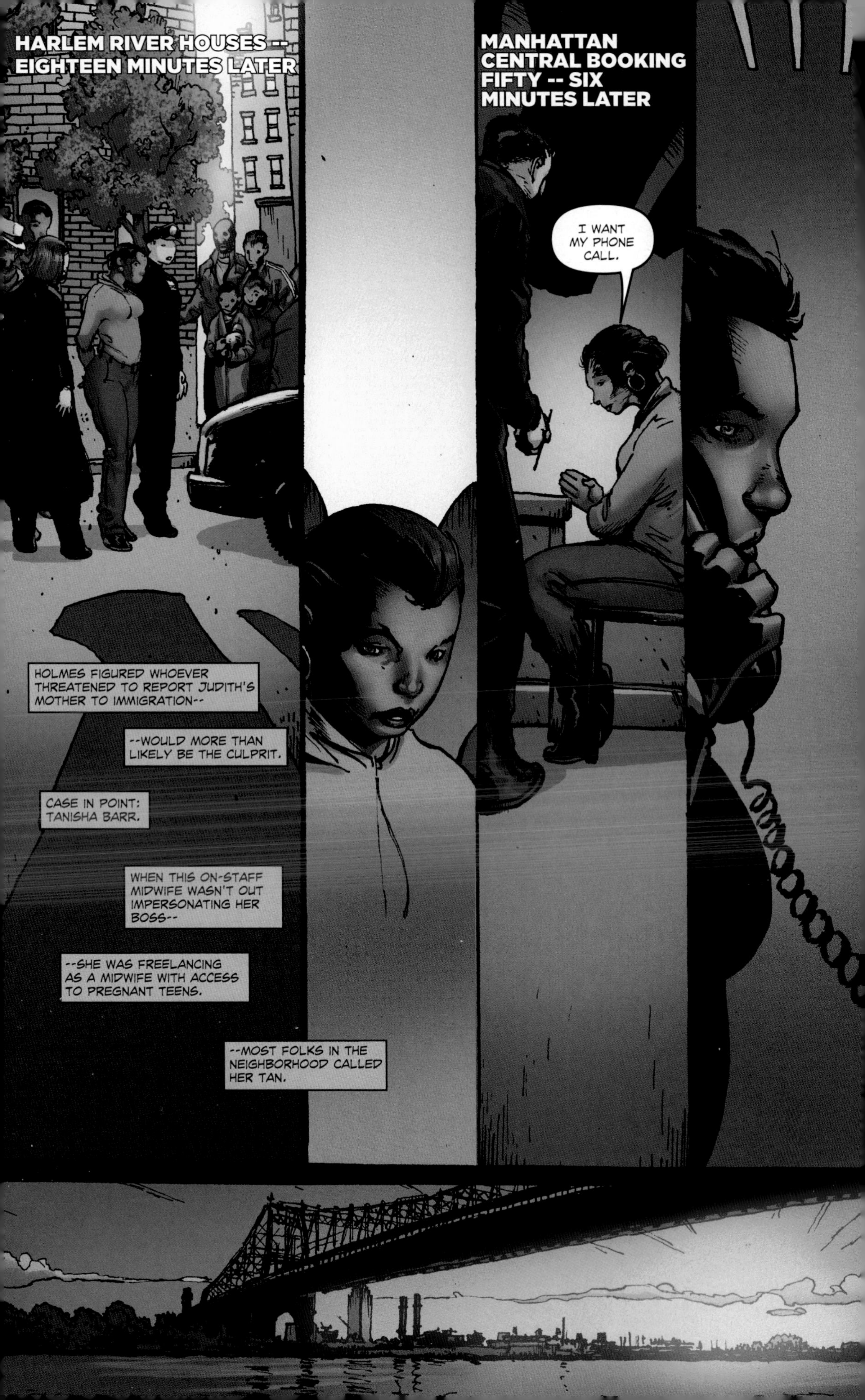
HARLEM RIVER HOUSES -- EIGHTEEN MINUTES LATER
HOLMES FIGURED WHOEVER THREATENED TO REPORT JUDITH'S MOTHER TO IMMIGRATION--
--WOULD MORE THAN LIKELY BE THE CULPRIT.
CASE IN POINT: TANISHA BARR.
WHEN THIS ON-STAFF MIDWIFE WASN'T OUT IMPERSONATING HER BOSS--
--SHE WAS FREELANCING AS A MIDWIFE WITH ACCESS TO PREGNANT TEENS.
--MOST FOLKS IN THE NEIGHBORHOOD CALLED HER TAN.
MANHATTAN CENTRAL BOOKING FIFTY -- SIX MINUTES LATER
I WANT MY PHONE CALL.

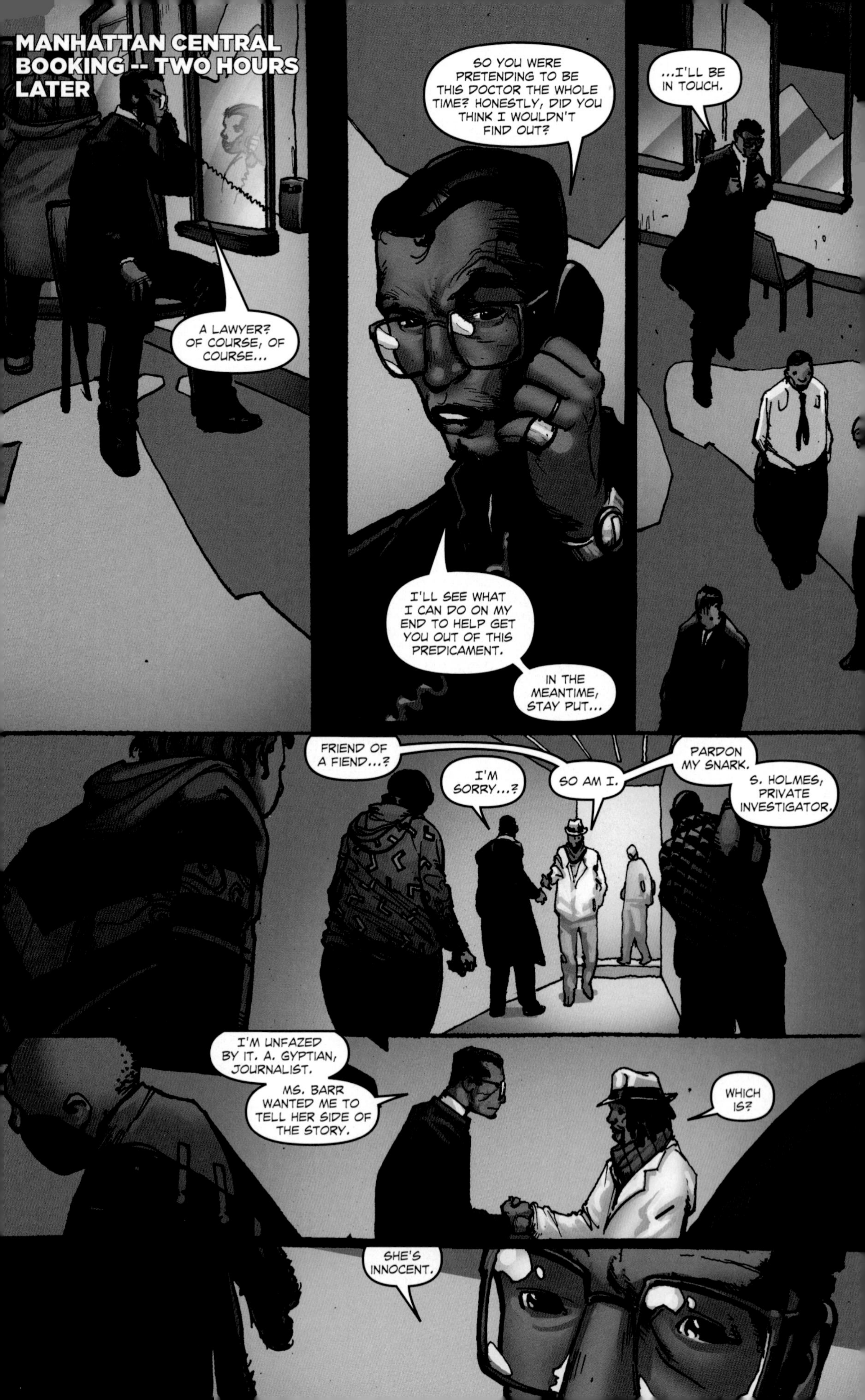
MANHATTAN CENTRAL BOOKING -- TWO HOURS LATER
A LAWYER? OF COURSE, OF COURSE...
SO YOU WERE PRETENDING TO BE THIS DOCTOR THE WHOLE TIME? HONESTLY, DID YOU THINK I WOULDN'T FIND OUT?
I'LL SEE WHAT I CAN DO ON MY END TO HELP GET YOU OUT OF THIS PREDICAMENT.
IN THE MEANTIME, STAY PUT...
...I'LL BE IN TOUCH.
FRIEND OF A FIEND...?
I'M SORRY...?
SO AM I.
PARDON MY SNARK.
S. HOLMES, PRIVATE INVESTIGATOR.
I'M UNFAZED BY IT. A. GYPTIAN, JOURNALIST.
MS. BARR WANTED ME TO TELL HER SIDE OF THE STORY.
WHICH IS?
SHE'S INNOCENT.

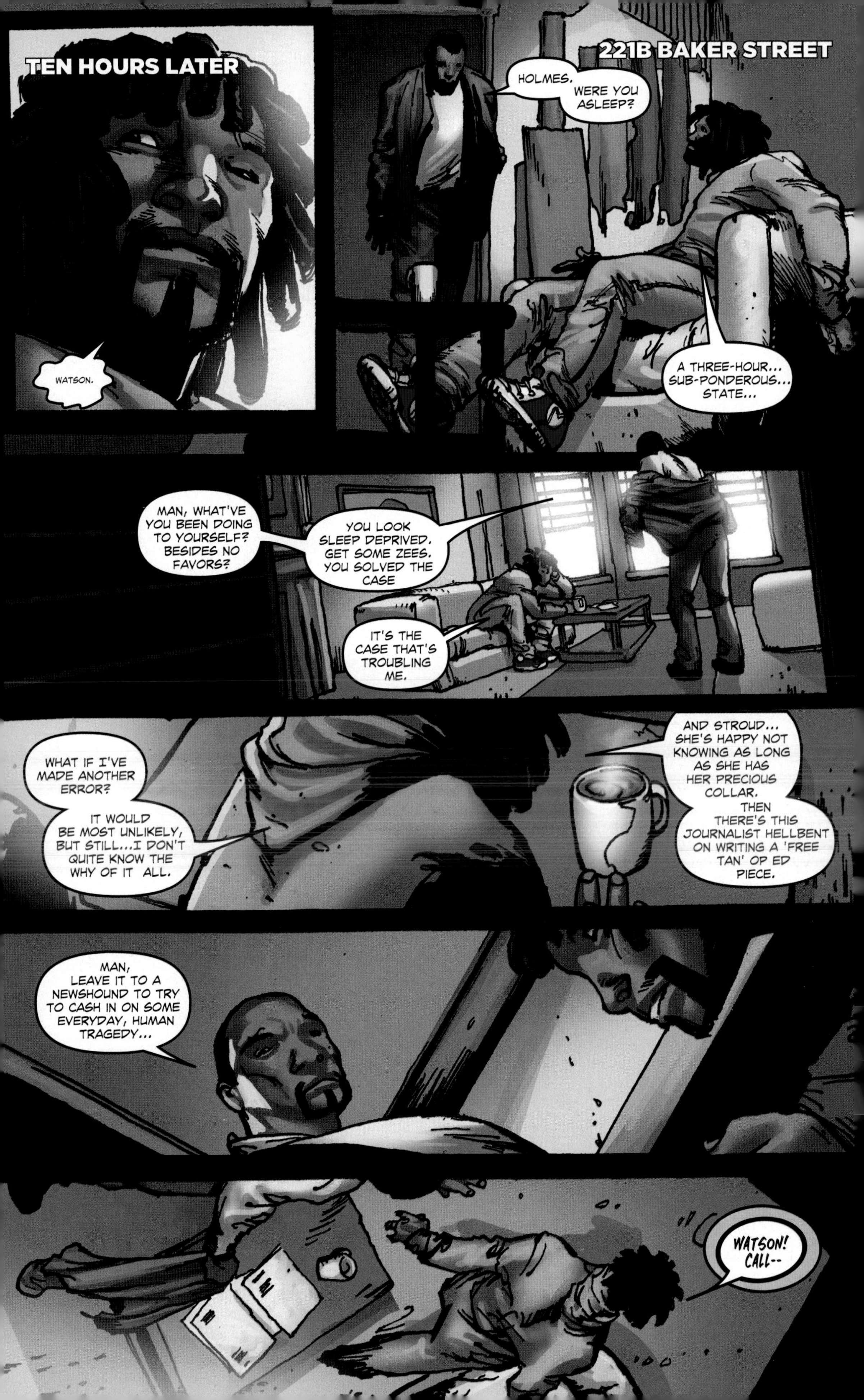
TEN HOURS LATER
WATSON.
221B BAKER STREET
HOLMES. WERE YOU ASLEEP?
A THREE-HOUR... SUB-PONDEROUS... STATE...
MAN, WHAT'VE YOU BEEN DOING TO YOURSELF? BESIDES NO FAVORS?
YOU LOOK SLEEP DEPRIVED. GET SOME ZEES. YOU SOLVED THE CASE
IT'S THE CASE THAT'S TROUBLING ME.
WHAT IF I'VE MADE ANOTHER ERROR?
IT WOULD BE MOST UNLIKELY, BUT STILL...I DON'T QUITE KNOW THE WHY OF IT ALL.
AND STROUD... SHE'S HAPPY NOT KNOWING AS LONG AS SHE HAS HER PRECIOUS COLLAR.
THEN THERE'S THIS JOURNALIST HELLBENT ON WRITING A 'FREE TAN' OP ED PIECE.
MAN, LEAVE IT TO A NEWSHOUND TO TRY TO CASH IN ON SOME EVERYDAY, HUMAN TRAGEDY...
WATSON! CALL--

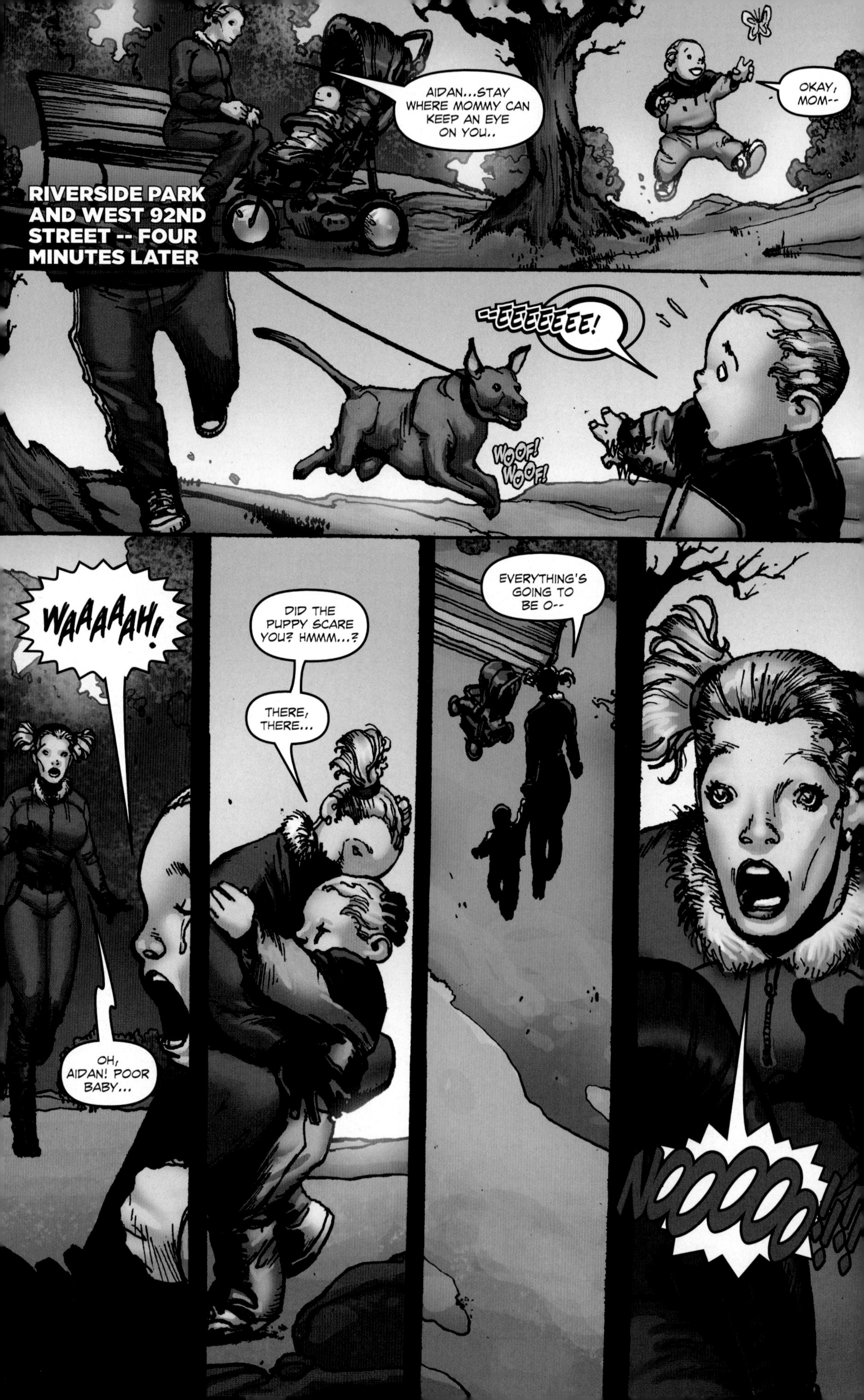
RIVERSIDE PARK AND WEST 92ND STREET -- FOUR MINUTES LATER
AIDAN...STAY WHERE MOMMY CAN KEEP AN EYE ON YOU..
OKAY, MOM--
--EEEEEEE!
WOOF! WOOF!
WAAAAAH!
OH, AIDAN! POOR BABY...
DID THE PUPPY SCARE YOU? HMMM...?
THERE, THERE...
EVERYTHING'S GOING TO BE O--
NOOOOO!!

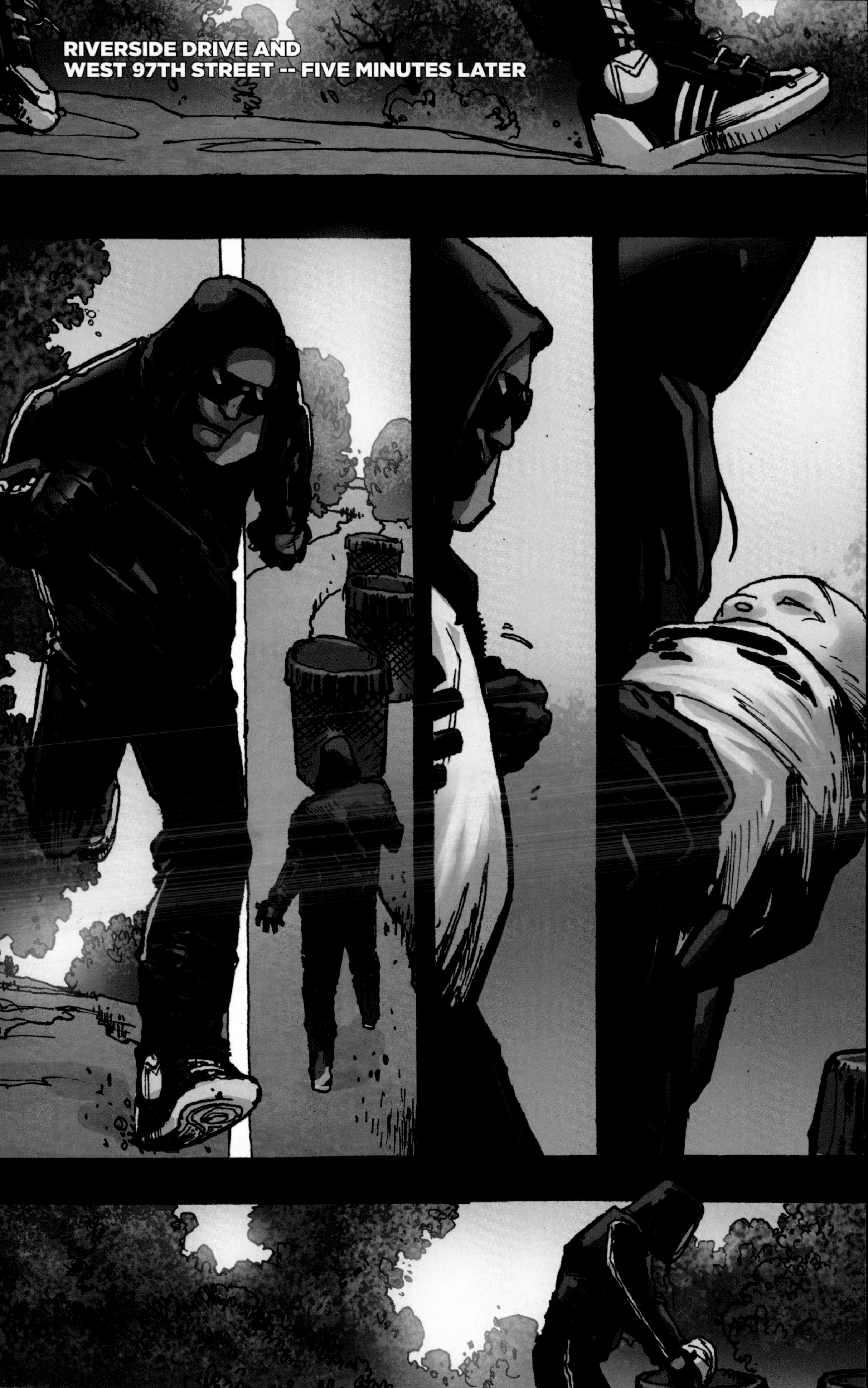
RIVERSIDE DRIVE AND
WEST 97TH STREET -- FIVE MINUTES LATER

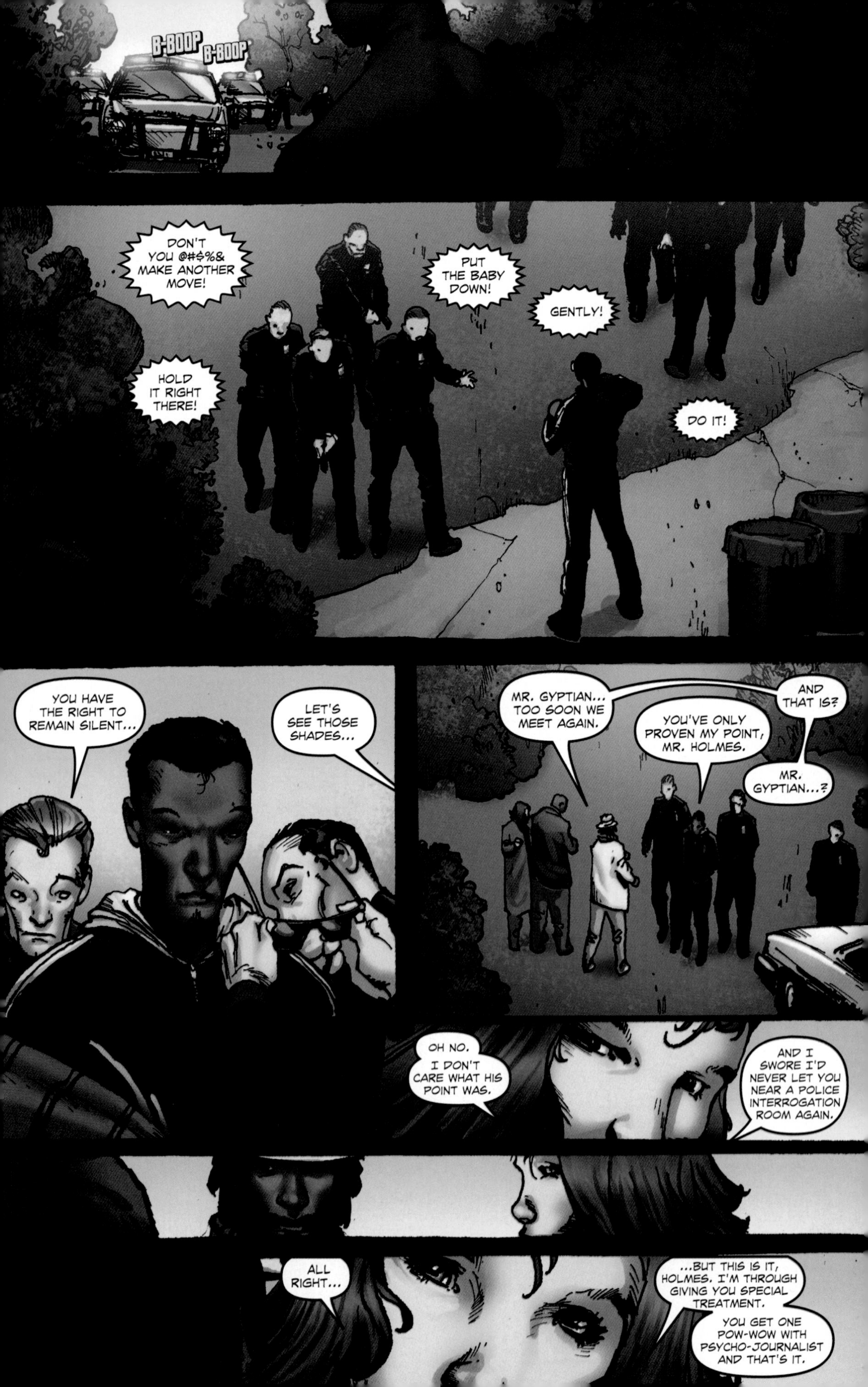
B-BOOP B-BOOP
DON'T YOU @#$%& MAKE ANOTHER MOVE!
HOLD IT RIGHT THERE!
PUT THE BABY DOWN!
GENTLY!
DO IT!
YOU HAVE THE RIGHT TO REMAIN SILENT...
LET'S SEE THOSE SHADES...
MR. GYPTIAN... TOO SOON WE MEET AGAIN.
YOU'VE ONLY PROVEN MY POINT, MR. HOLMES.
AND THAT IS?
MR. GYPTIAN...?
OH NO. I DON'T CARE WHAT HIS POINT WAS.
AND I SWORE I'D NEVER LET YOU NEAR A POLICE INTERROGATION ROOM AGAIN.
ALL RIGHT...
...BUT THIS IS IT, HOLMES. I'M THROUGH GIVING YOU SPECIAL TREATMENT.
YOU GET ONE POW-WOW WITH PSYCHO-JOURNALIST AND THAT'S IT.

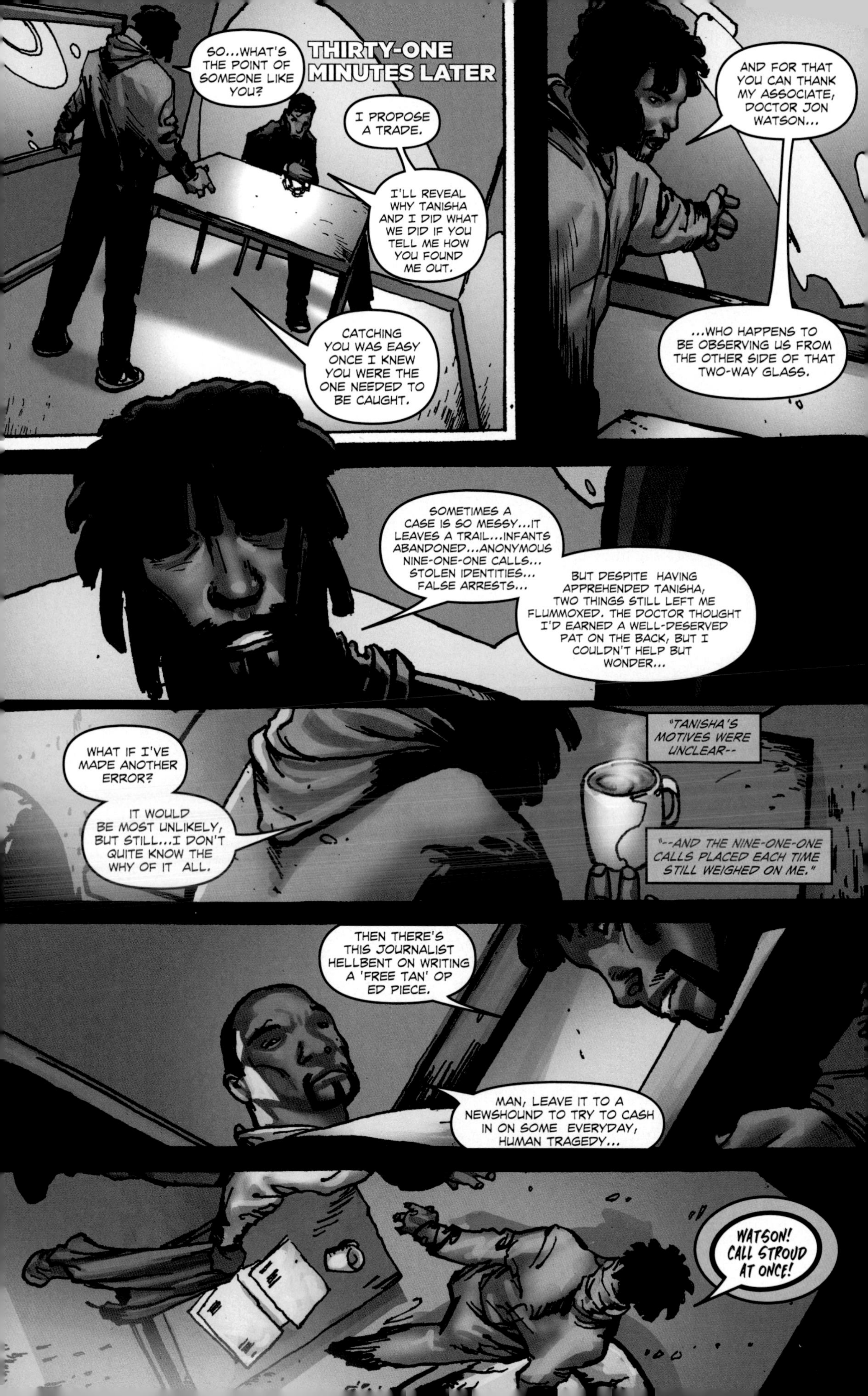
SO...WHAT'S THE POINT OF SOMEONE LIKE YOU?
THIRTY-ONE MINUTES LATER
I PROPOSE A TRADE.
I'LL REVEAL WHY TANISHA AND I DID WHAT WE DID IF YOU TELL ME HOW YOU FOUND ME OUT.
CATCHING YOU WAS EASY ONCE I KNEW YOU WERE THE ONE NEEDED TO BE CAUGHT.
AND FOR THAT YOU CAN THANK MY ASSOCIATE, DOCTOR JON WATSON...
...WHO HAPPENS TO BE OBSERVING US FROM THE OTHER SIDE OF THAT TWO-WAY GLASS.
SOMETIMES A CASE IS SO MESSY...IT LEAVES A TRAIL...INFANTS ABANDONED...ANONYMOUS NINE-ONE-ONE CALLS... STOLEN IDENTITIES... FALSE ARRESTS...
BUT DESPITE HAVING APPREHENDED TANISHA, TWO THINGS STILL LEFT ME FLUMMOXED. THE DOCTOR THOUGHT I'D EARNED A WELL-DESERVED PAT ON THE BACK, BUT I COULDN'T HELP BUT WONDER...
WHAT IF I'VE MADE ANOTHER ERROR?
IT WOULD BE MOST UNLIKELY, BUT STILL...I DON'T QUITE KNOW THE WHY OF IT ALL.
"TANISHA'S MOTIVES WERE UNCLEAR--
"--AND THE NINE-ONE-ONE CALLS PLACED EACH TIME STILL WEIGHED ON ME."
THEN THERE'S THIS JOURNALIST HELLBENT ON WRITING A 'FREE TAN' OP ED PIECE.
MAN, LEAVE IT TO A NEWSHOUND TO TRY TO CASH IN ON SOME EVERYDAY, HUMAN TRAGEDY...
WATSON! CALL STROUD AT ONCE!

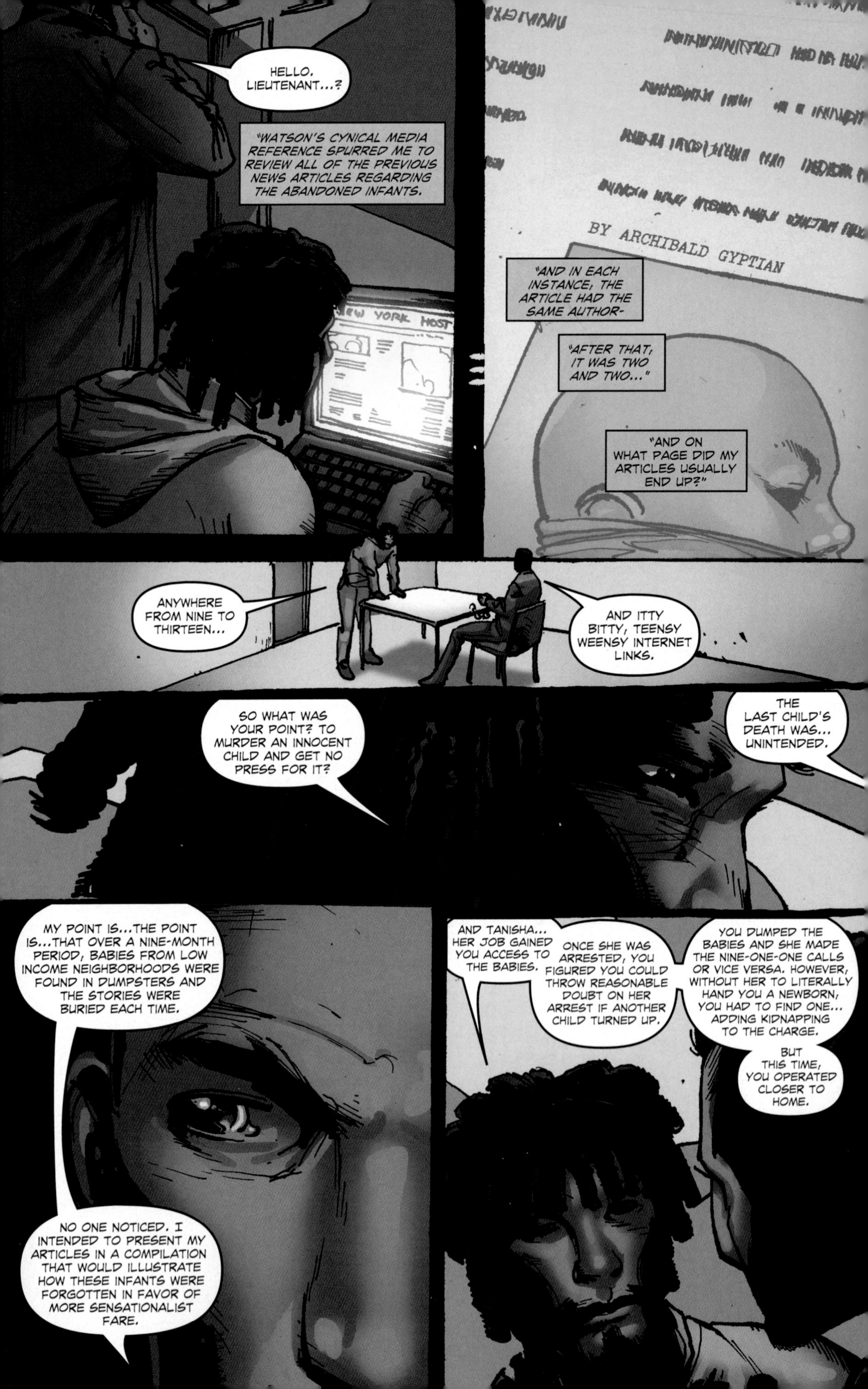
HELLO. LIEUTENANT...?
"WATSON'S CYNICAL MEDIA REFERENCE SPURRED ME TO REVIEW ALL OF THE PREVIOUS NEWS ARTICLES REGARDING THE ABANDONED INFANTS.
NEW YORK HOST
BY ARCHIBALD GYPTIAN
"AND IN EACH INSTANCE, THE ARTICLE HAD THE SAME AUTHOR-
"AFTER THAT, IT WAS TWO AND TWO..."
"AND ON WHAT PAGE DID MY ARTICLES USUALLY END UP?"
ANYWHERE FROM NINE TO THIRTEEN...
AND ITTY BITTY, TEENSY WEENSY INTERNET LINKS.
SO WHAT WAS YOUR POINT? TO MURDER AN INNOCENT CHILD AND GET NO PRESS FOR IT?
THE LAST CHILD'S DEATH WAS... UNINTENDED.
MY POINT IS...THE POINT IS...THAT OVER A NINE-MONTH PERIOD, BABIES FROM LOW INCOME NEIGHBORHOODS WERE FOUND IN DUMPSTERS AND THE STORIES WERE BURIED EACH TIME.
NO ONE NOTICED. I INTENDED TO PRESENT MY ARTICLES IN A COMPILATION THAT WOULD ILLUSTRATE HOW THESE INFANTS WERE FORGOTTEN IN FAVOR OF MORE SENSATIONALIST FARE.
AND TANISHA... HER JOB GAINED YOU ACCESS TO THE BABIES.
ONCE SHE WAS ARRESTED, YOU FIGURED YOU COULD THROW REASONABLE DOUBT ON HER ARREST IF ANOTHER CHILD TURNED UP.
YOU DUMPED THE BABIES AND SHE MADE THE NINE-ONE-ONE CALLS OR VICE VERSA. HOWEVER, WITHOUT HER TO LITERALLY HAND YOU A NEWBORN, YOU HAD TO FIND ONE... ADDING KIDNAPPING TO THE CHARGE.
BUT THIS TIME, YOU OPERATED CLOSER TO HOME.

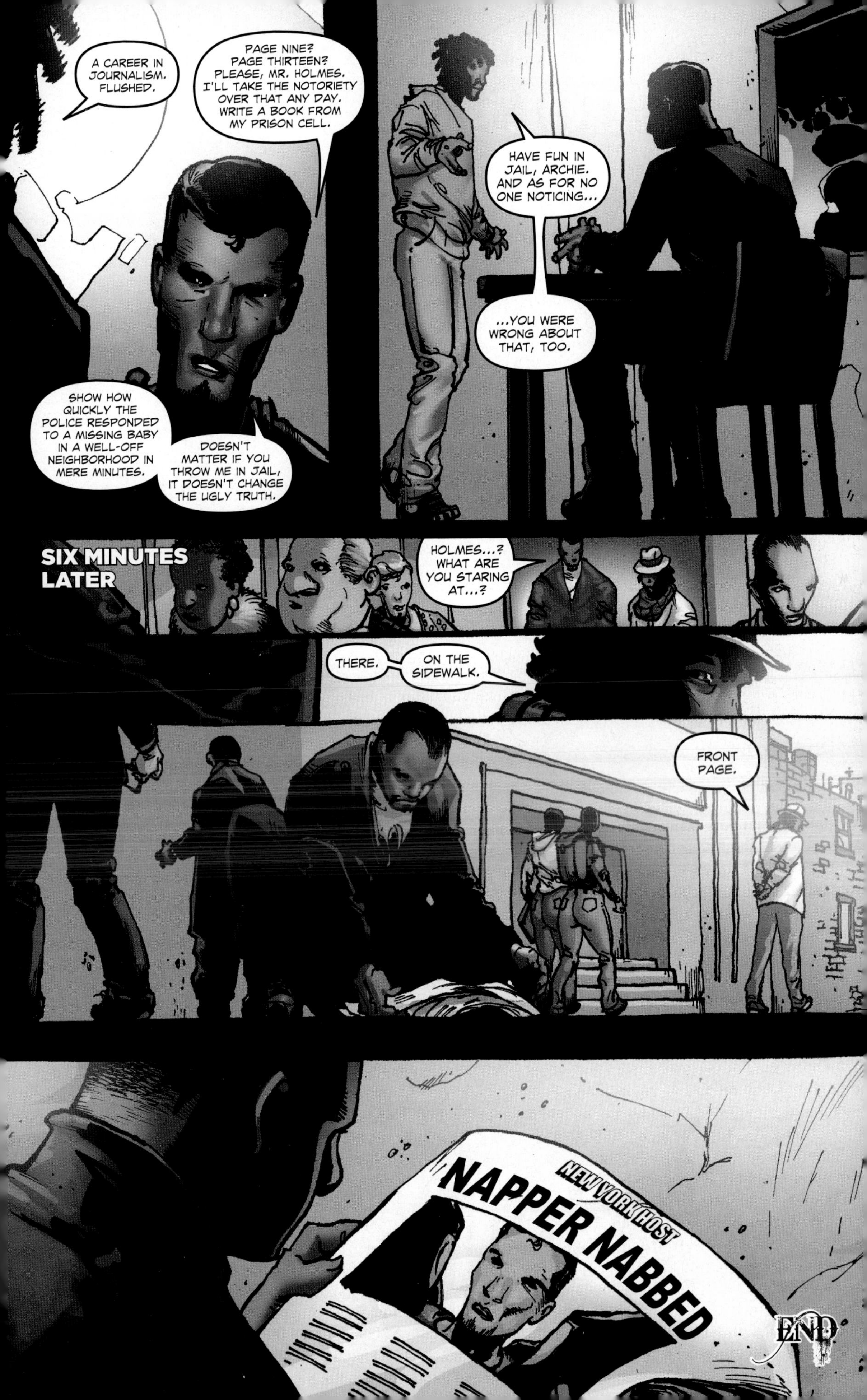
A CAREER IN JOURNALISM. FLUSHED.
PAGE NINE? PAGE THIRTEEN? PLEASE, MR. HOLMES. I'LL TAKE THE NOTORIETY OVER THAT ANY DAY. WRITE A BOOK FROM MY PRISON CELL.
SHOW HOW QUICKLY THE POLICE RESPONDED TO A MISSING BABY IN A WELL-OFF NEIGHBORHOOD IN MERE MINUTES.
DOESN'T MATTER IF YOU THROW ME IN JAIL, IT DOESN'T CHANGE THE UGLY TRUTH.
HAVE FUN IN JAIL, ARCHIE. AND AS FOR NO ONE NOTICING...
...YOU WERE WRONG ABOUT THAT, TOO.
SIX MINUTES LATER
HOLMES...? WHAT ARE YOU STARING AT...?
THERE.
ON THE SIDEWALK.
FRONT PAGE.
NEW YORK HOST
NAPPER NABBED
END

WATSON AND HOLMES #1KS

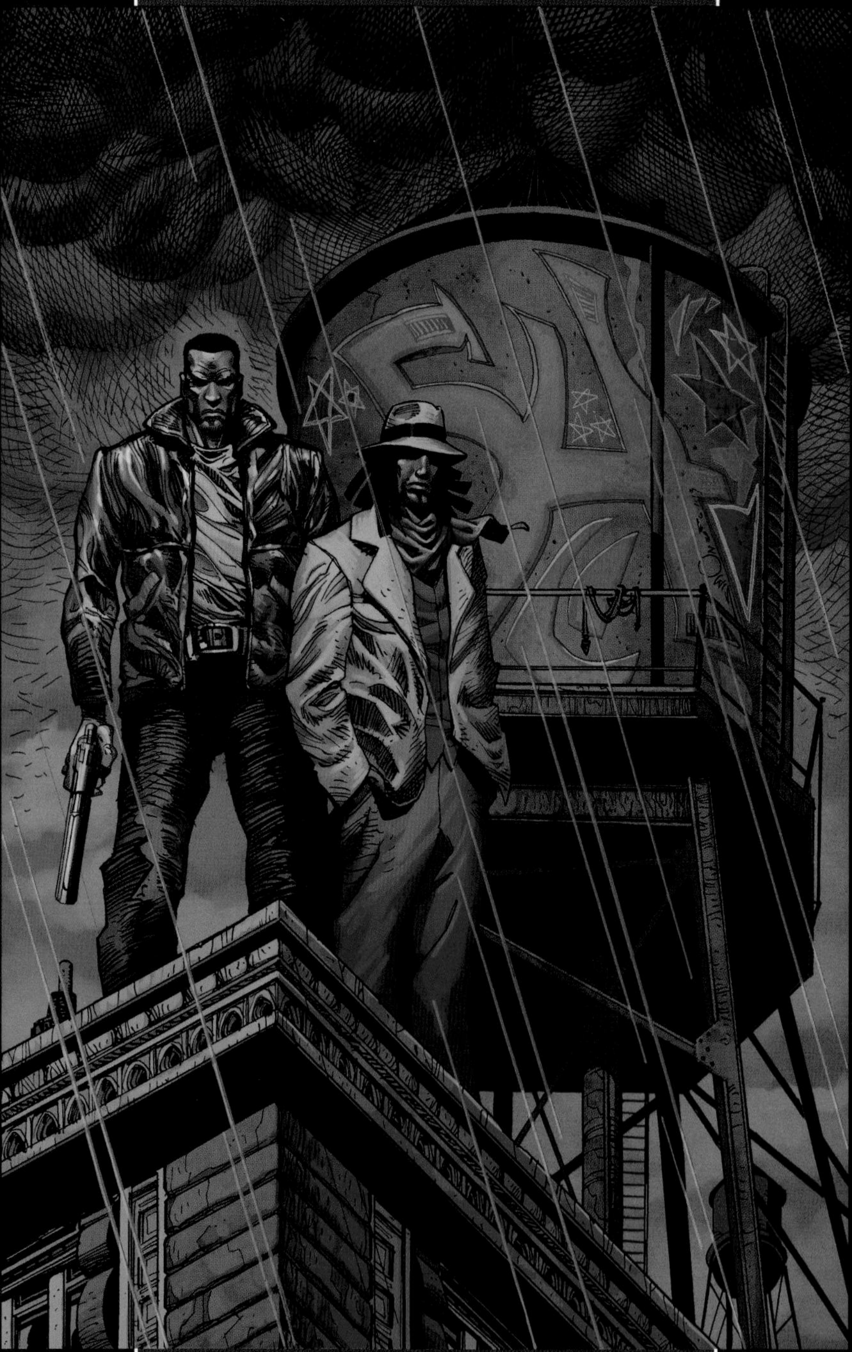

BY WALTER SIMONSON AND LAURA MARTIN

WATSON AND HOLMES #1A

BY RICK LEONARDI AND RYAN WARDLOW

WATSON AND HOLMES #1B

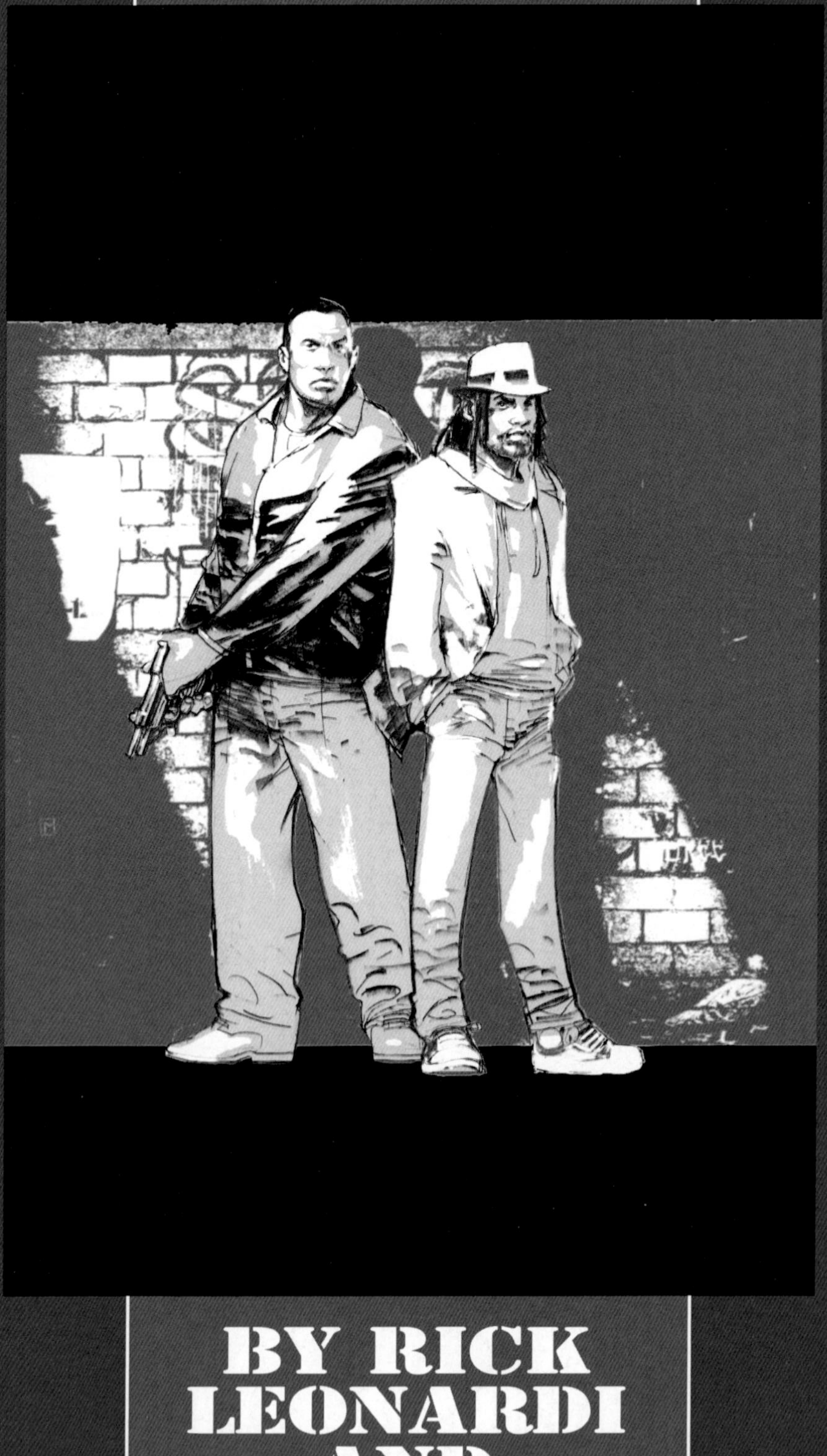

BY RICK LEONARDI AND BRANDON PERLOW

WATSON AND HOLMES #1c

BY LARRY STROMAN AND JAY DAVID RAMOS

WATSON AND HOLMES #2A

BY RICK LEONARDI AND RYAN WARDLOW

WATSON AND HOLMES #2b

BY RICK LEONARDI AND BRANDON PERLOW

WATSON AND HOLMES #2c

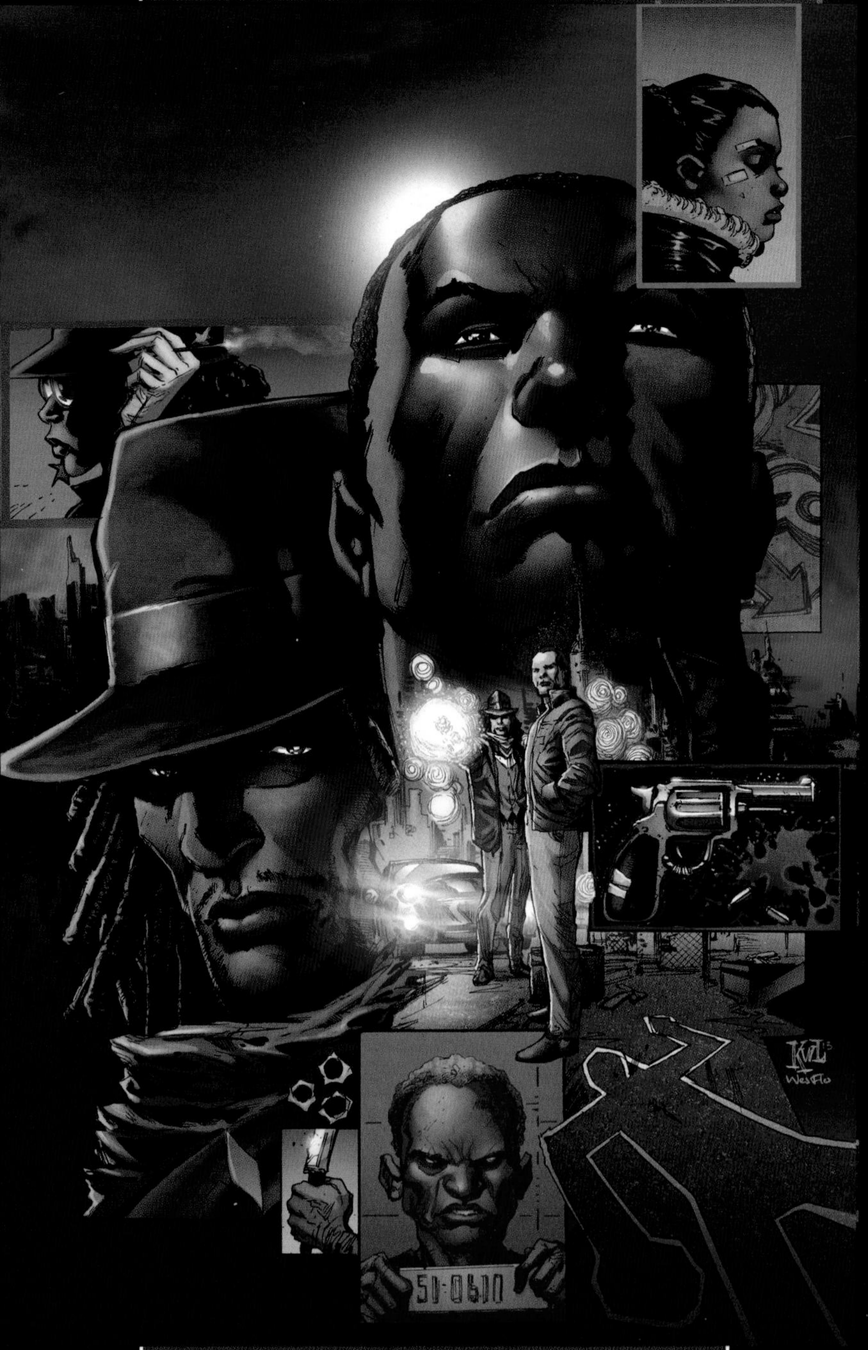

BY KEN LASHLEY AND GuruEFX

WATSON AND HOLMES #3A

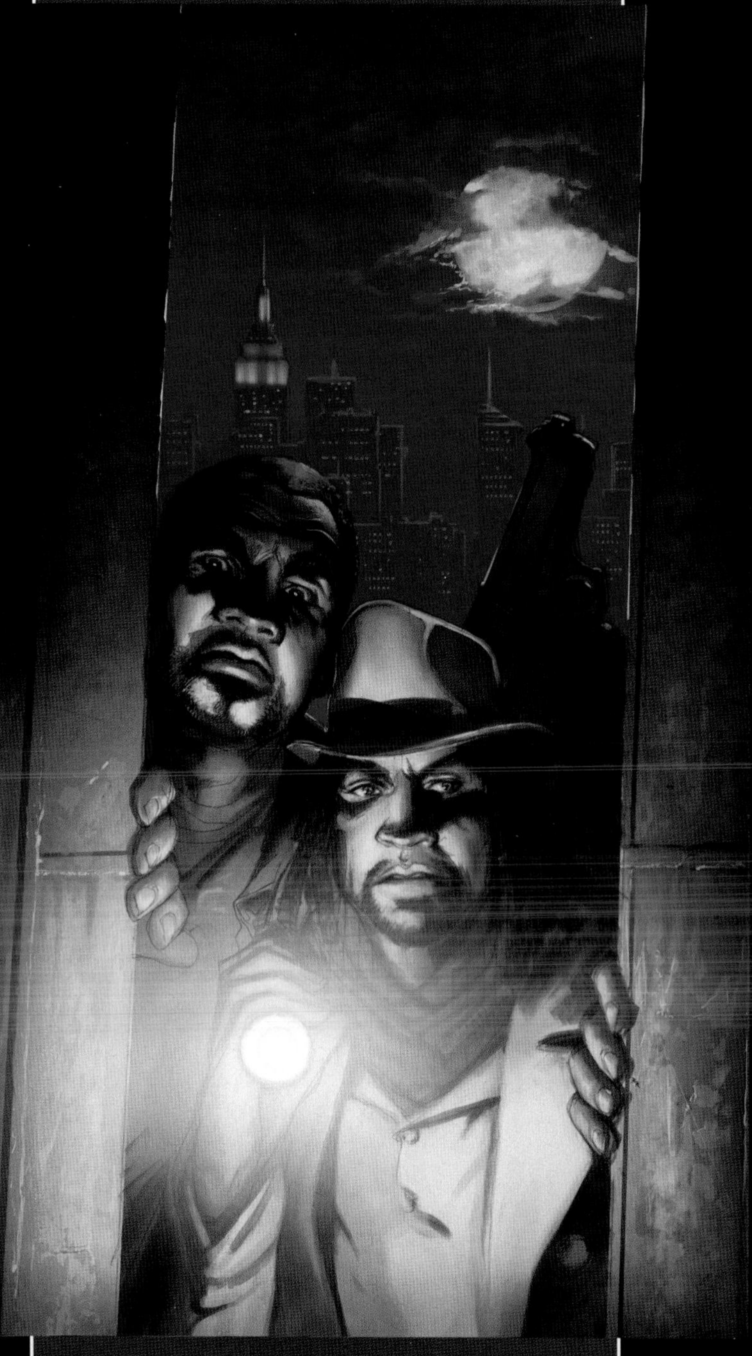

BY RICK LEONARDI AND RYAN WARDLOW

WATSON AND HOLMES #3b

BY RICK LEONARDI AND BRANDON PERLOW

WATSON AND HOLMES #3c

BY RYAN BENJAMIN

WATSON AND HOLMES #4A

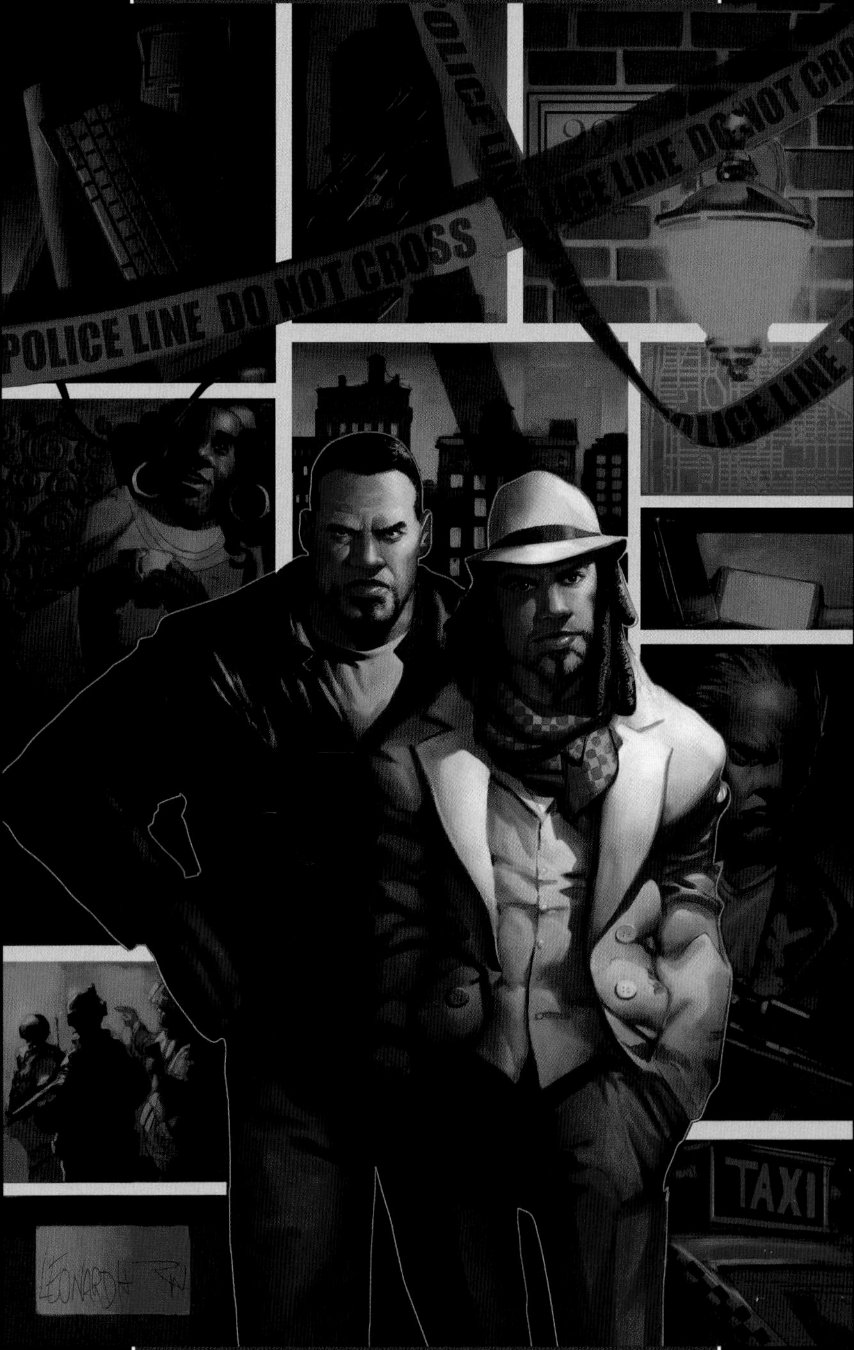
POLICE LINE DO NOT CROSS
TAXI

BY RICK LEONARDI AND RYAN WARDLOW

WATSON AND HOLMES #4B

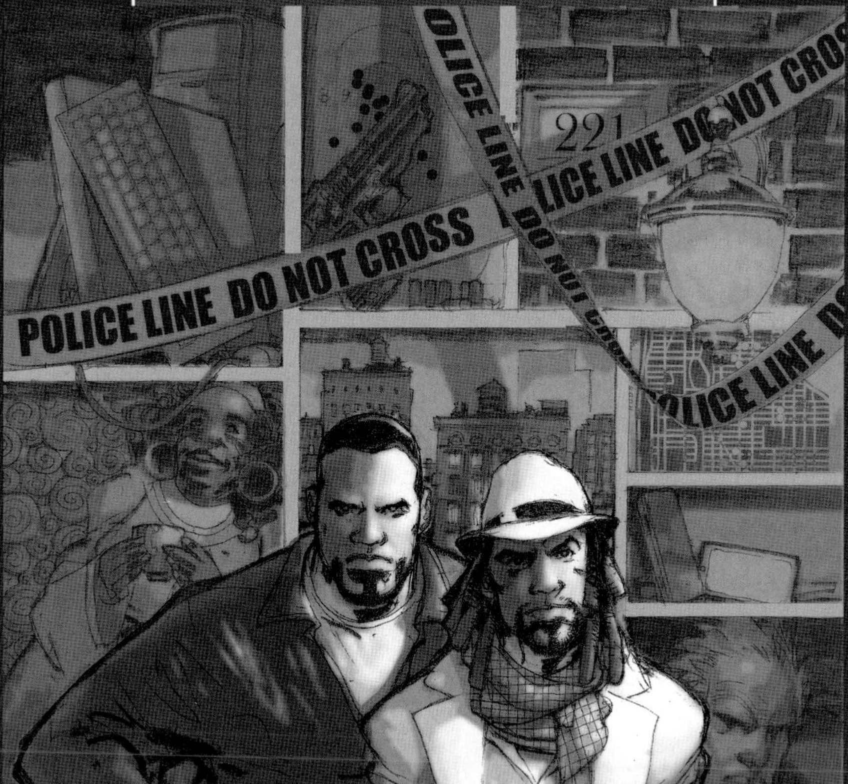
POLICE LINE DO NOT CROSS
POLICE LINE DO NOT CROSS
POLICE LINE DO
221
POLICE LINE
TAXI
LEONARDI

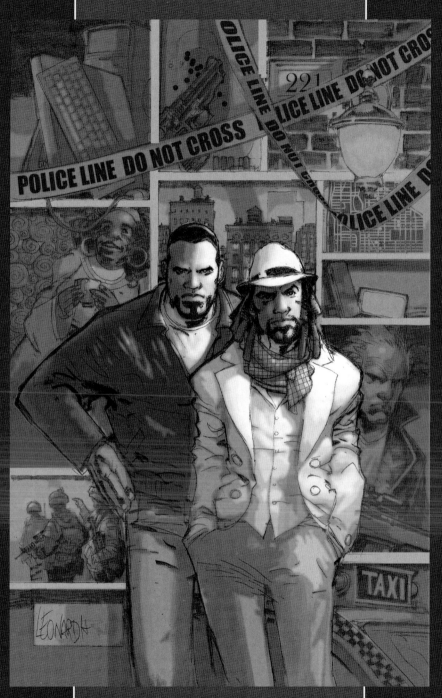

BY RICK LEONARDI AND BRANDON PERLOW

WATSON AND HOLMES #4c

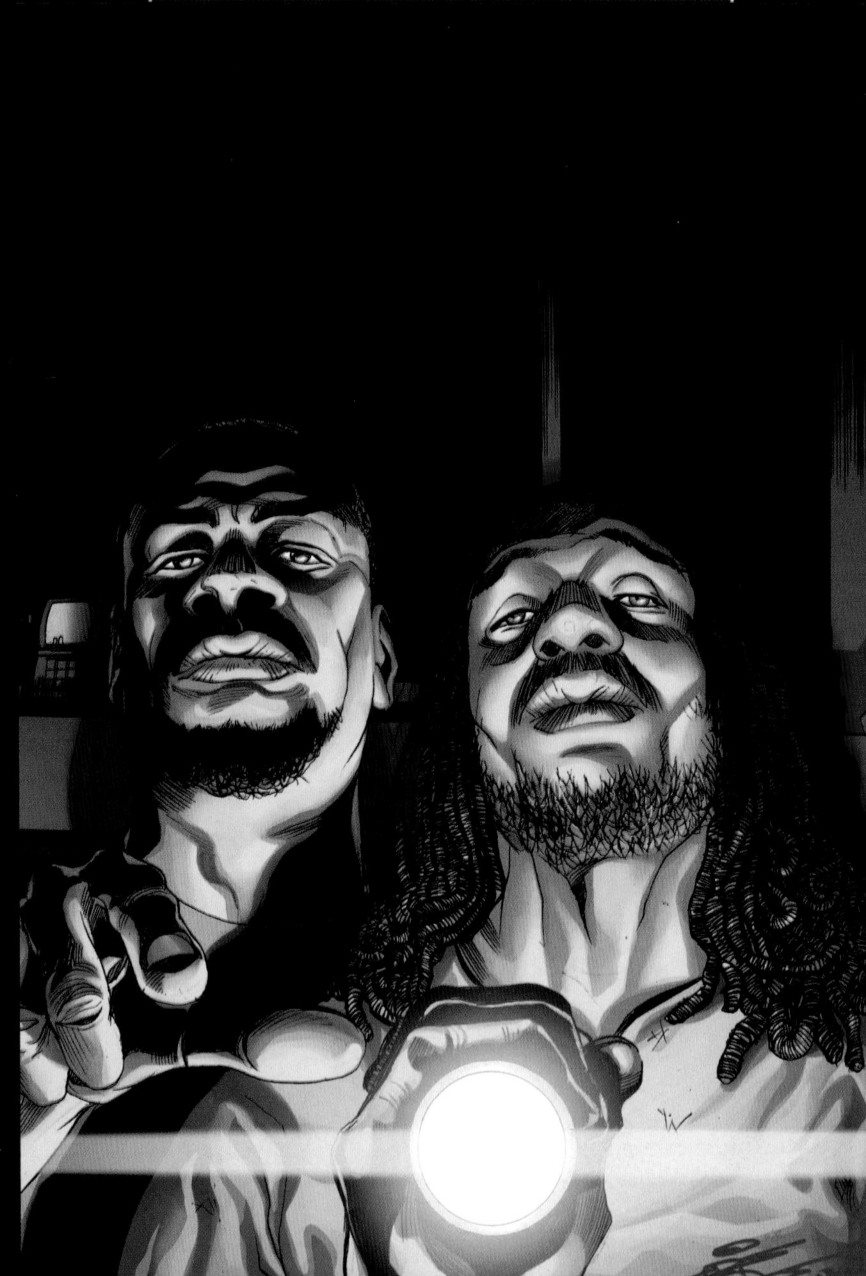

BY CHRIS CROSS AND JAY DAVID RAMOS

WATSON AND HOLMES #5a

BY LARRY STROMAN AND JAY DAVID RAMOS

WATSON AND HOLMES #5B

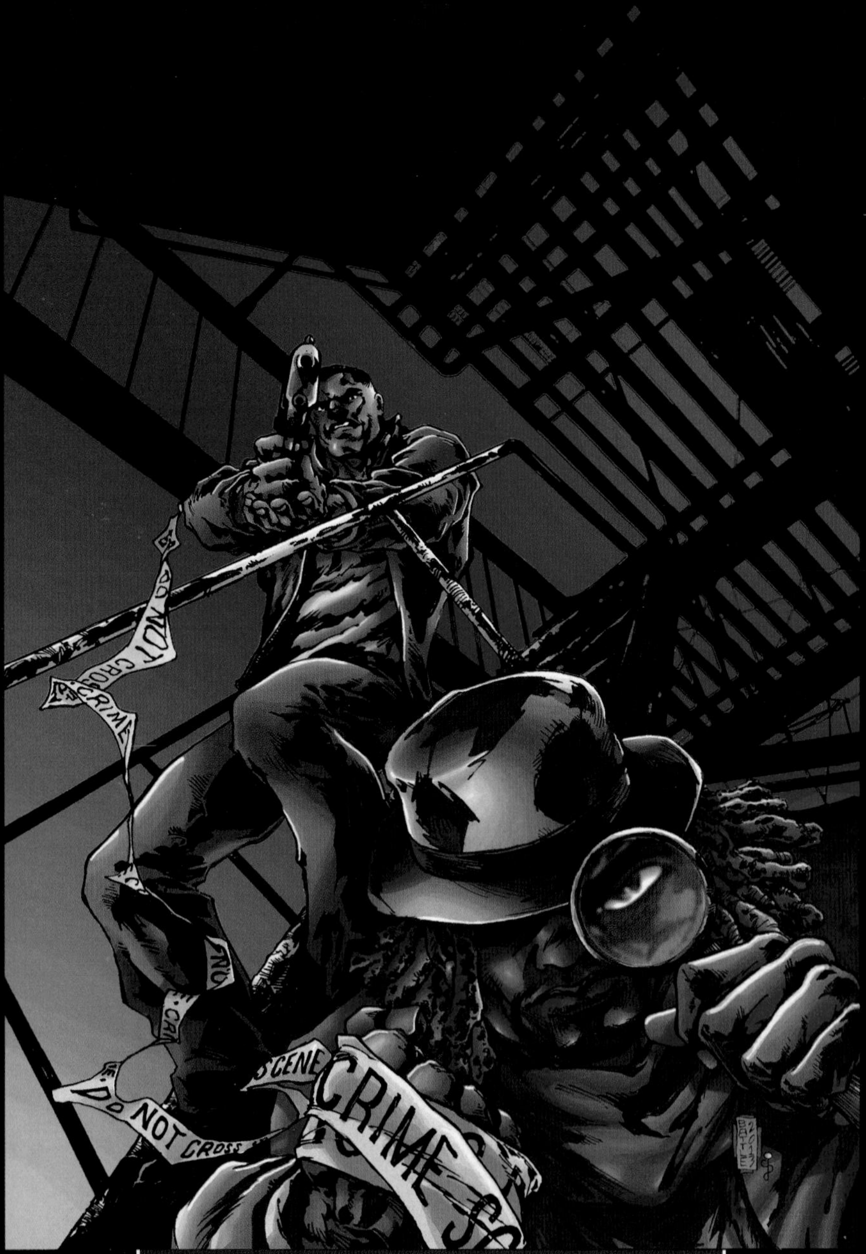
DO NOT CROSS
CRIME

BY ERIC BATTLE AND COREY BREEN